The Exp

"Rother gives rea[...]
able [...]
frigh[...]
—Ap[...]
Di[...]

"We'v[...]
write[...]
ing r[...]
—Gr[...]

"A na[...] nalis-
tic integrity . . . an in-depth account, perfectly executed,
of a true psychopath at work. Rother delivers a thrilling
account of murder and mayhem."
—**M. William Phelps**, author of *Cruel Death*

"One of the best true crime books I have read in years.
Rother's investigative journalist's tenacity and eye for
detail and her knack for telling a good detective story
that reads like a novel set this book above most."
—**Steve Jackson**, author of *Not Lost Forever*

"With this headline-grabbing case of multiple murder,
Caitlin Rother delves beyond the whodunnit to its cha-
meleonic center: a psychopathic con artist with a gift for
persuasion . . . A breathless tale of unthinkable events
that no true crime fan should miss."
—**Katherine Ramsland**, author of *The Human Predator*

"Impressively reported in a forthright narrative . . . a
pitch-perfect study of avarice, compulsion, and pure California illusion. Caitlin Rother at her best!"
—**Ron Franscell**, author of *The Darkest Night*

"Rother digs deep into the story of this horrible murder—
unearthing never-before-told details of the crime, the investigation, and the twisted mind of the man who set it all
into motion."
—**Susan Leibowitz**, producer of "The Last Voyage" for
Dateline

Also by Caitlin Rother

Body Parts

Poisoned Love

DEAD
RECKONING

CAITLIN
ROTHER

PINNACLE BOOKS
Kensington Publishing Corp.
http://www.kensingtonbooks.com

Some names have been changed to protect the privacy of individuals connected to this story.

PINNACLE BOOKS are published by

Kensington Publishing Corp.
119 West 40th Street
New York, NY 10018

All Kensington Titles, Imprints, and Distributed Lines are available at special quantity discounts for bulk purchases for sales promotions, premiums, fund-raising, and educational or institutional use. Special book excerpts or customized printings can also be created to fit specific needs. For details, write or phone the office of the Kensington special sales manager: Kensington Publishing Corp., 119 West 40th Street, New York, NY 10018, attn: Special Sales Department, Phone: 1-800-221-2647.

Pinnacle and the P logo Reg. U.S. Pat. & TM Off.

ISBN-13: 978-0-7860-2217-5
ISBN-10: 0-7860-2217-5

First printing: February 2011

10 9 8 7 6 5 4 3 2 1

Printed in the United States of America

DEAD
RECKONING

PROLOGUE

Alonso Machain was unemployed, with bills to pay, so he took up his friend Skylar Deleon's offer to help restore a family boat at the Cabrillo yard in Long Beach, California. As they were sanding the Hatteras together, Skylar boasted about his plans for fixing up his new toy, which he'd gotten from his grandfather. Then Skylar offered his twenty-one-year-old buddy a much more lucrative job.

"Well, how much are you talking about?" Alonso asked.

"A couple million dollars," Skylar said.

"Wow. How do you make a couple million dollars without it being illegal?"

"Well," Skylar said, "it's not really illegal, unless you get caught."

As Skylar's plan would evolve in the coming days of October 2004, the promised payoff for Alonso soon increased to "several million" dollars to help Skylar "take care" of some people who had done something bad and pissed somebody off. Skylar wasn't usually paid for these gigs, he said, but he got to keep the assets of the "targets," who were typically well-off. His first contract, for example, was a guy who'd been selling drugs in Huntington Beach schools and owed money to the wrong people.

Skylar said he'd split the proceeds of his next job with Alonso, but didn't give him much time to mull it over.

"So you want to do it or not?" Skylar asked a couple days later.

Alonso wasn't really sure what to think. Skylar was always talking about how rich he and his family were, and Alonso believed him. And although he knew Skylar liked to tell stories, Alonso never stopped to consider that the few times Skylar had thrown him a mere $20 for the boat restoration work, they'd had to drive to an ATM to get it. He decided to take the job.

Skylar went into more detail about the plan as he showed Alonso photos of a yacht called the *Well Deserved*, whose wealthy owners had put it up for sale. Alonso's role was to help Skylar get "in" with the owners, Tom and Jackie Hawks, then hold them down.

The fifty-five-foot trawler was moored in the upscale community of Newport Beach in Orange County, a sharp contrast to the sprawling mix of urban, industrial, and suburban areas of Long Beach, where Skylar lived with his wife, Jennifer, in neighboring Los Angeles County. Unlike the spacious homes in Newport, decorated in the mute beiges and sandstone of the wealthy, home for Skylar and Jennifer was a cramped converted garage behind her parents' duplex. Space was so tight, the Deleons had to stack their belongings on the floor and hang their clothing from a pole that ran between two dressers right next to the bed. It was a far cry from the opulent mansions featured on *The Real Housewives of Orange County* and *The O.C.*

Contrary to the story he'd told Alonso about the

$3 million a month he'd earned working with Ditech Funding, Skylar had been fired from his job as appraiser's assistant there, and looked at his wealthier neighbors in "the O.C." with envy. He coveted their waterfront homes, boats, and private planes that he couldn't afford, and he lied to persuade folks that he could. Although he wasn't anywhere near as smart or capable as Bernie Madoff in building a complex financial scheme, Skylar's scam was just as—if not more—deceitful. And when it came to lying and manipulating people, Skylar was pretty damn good at that, too.

The next time he and Alonso met, Skylar said he'd analyzed photos of the boat's interior for radios and weapons, such as spearguns, and had determined the best way to overcome the couple. Using stun guns and handcuffs, Alonso would grab Jackie in the galley, while Skylar took down Tom in the stateroom, where no one could hear him scream.

Skylar said he'd considered taking Tom scuba diving and finishing him off underwater, but he'd realized that would preclude the Hawkses from signing over the boat title and power-of-attorney documents Skylar was going to draw up.

"What I'll do is just take them out to sea and toss them overboard," he said.

They purchased two stun guns together, then Skylar sent Alonso, a former jail guard he'd befriended while serving time for armed burglary a year earlier, to buy a couple pairs of handcuffs.

The next day, November 6, Skylar said it was time to do the deed. By now, Alonso felt it was too late to extricate himself from the situation. If twenty-five-year-old Skylar really was a hit man, what would prevent him from harming Alonso?

As they drove to the dock, Skylar stopped a couple blocks away to scope out who was aboard, then called Tom to pick them up in his dinghy. The Hawkses were expecting them.

On board, Tom proudly gave them a tour of his home, but Alonso could see from Skylar's tone of voice and body language that he'd changed his mind. Skylar seemed far too relaxed to kill anyone as he chatted with Tom for forty-five minutes about possible modes of payment. Before they left, Skylar made sure that Tom and Jackie knew he was definitely interested in purchasing the vessel and would be back for a lesson on how to operate it.

Skylar told Alonso afterward that he'd changed his mind once he'd realized that Tom was too muscular for the two of them to handle this alone. They really needed a third man. Skylar also sensed some discomfort on the Hawkses' part, so he called Jennifer on his cell phone as soon as they got back to the car.

"Hey, you need to come down, take a look at the boat, to make these people feel a little more at ease," he told her.

So after sending Alonso on his way, Skylar and his pregnant wife went back on board, pushing their ten-month-old daughter, Haylie, in a stroller, to do just that.

PART I

SKYLAR
AND JENNIFER

1

Matt Hawks was probably the first one in the family to sense that something was wrong. His father and stepmother had been calling constantly to ask questions about their new grandson, Jace, and to listen to him make gurgling noises over the phone. It was driving Matt and his wife a little crazy.

But the calls from Tom and Jackie Hawks stopped completely after November 15, the day they'd taken a prospective buyer out for a sea trial. Skylar Deleon was only twenty-five, but he told the Hawkses he'd made enough to buy the boat from working as a child actor in commercials, starring in a kids' show called *Mighty Morphin Power Rangers,* and investing his earnings in real estate.

Don Trefren, one of Tom's oldest friends, was among the next to notice something amiss. He shared his concerns with Tom's older son, Ryan, a couple days after the sea trial.

"I've been trying to get ahold of your parents, and your dad's cell phone went straight to voice mail," he said. "It's not like your dad to stand me up."

Don had been trying to call Jackie's cell phone,

with the same result. He'd expected a call from Tom
by early evening on November 15, by which time Tom
was 90 percent sure they would have completed the
sale. Don had offered to load their belongings onto
his truck and transport them to a trailer in Prescott,
Arizona, where the Hawkses were going to stay until
they could buy a house and a smaller boat in the
resort town of San Carlos, Mexico.

Tom and Jackie had been married for fifteen years,
and were still very much in love. Jackie had been in a
wheelchair, recovering from the motorcycle accident
that had killed her first husband, when she met Tom
at a chili cook-off, near Prescott in August 1986.

Ryan was only ten that summer, but he would
always remember the first time he met her. She wore
these "crazy big sunglasses," and one of her shoes was
higher than the other. But she earned points by letting him feel the metal screws in her legs and horse
around on her crutches, which were bigger than
he was.

Once Tom and Jackie got to know each other
better, Tom nicknamed her "Patches" because she was
all patched up after the accident, which had rendered
her unable to have children. Nonetheless, she soon
grew so close with Tom's sons that they both called
her "Mom." She and Tom made sure to have the boys
participate in their Hawaiian-themed wedding ceremony three years later.

Now fifty-seven, Tom was a decade older than
Jackie, but they looked much closer in age. Both had
a vitality, a youthfulness, and a sense of adventure
about them. Quite a bit of mischief, too. They enjoyed working out together, and shared the dream
of retiring early to live on a yacht. The sailing life did
them both good. Their bodies were toned, their hair

was sun-bleached, and their tanned faces glowed with health.

The active couple considered Prescott to be their base, a scenic valley at the northern edge of the Bradshaw Mountains, about ninety miles from Phoenix. But they moored their yacht in Newport Harbor, because they loved watching the annual boat show and Christmas parade there. Newport allowed for an easy drive south to see Ryan and Jim, Tom's older brother, in San Diego County; it also allowed for a quick sail to Catalina Island. However, they'd spent most of the past two years cruising the waters around Mexico—down Baja California, around Cabo San Lucas, and north in the Sea of Cortez to San Carlos, scuba diving and swimming with whale sharks.

Life is just too short to put things off, and one cannot discover new oceans unless they have the courage to lose sight of the shore, Tom wrote in an article for *Latitudes & Attitudes* magazine in December 2003.

Tom had spent considerable time and effort fixing up the *Well Deserved,* which he'd purchased for $290,000 in November 2000. In addition to state-of-the-art GPS navigation equipment, Tom put in a beacon device to help the coast guard find them if they ever got stranded. "Captain Hawks," as he called himself, also made sure they could survive for a year with their salt- to freshwater converter and a boatload of food. Never at rest with his hands, Tom even insisted on restoring an old eleven-foot dinghy to near-perfect condition. He and Jackie took the same care of the boat's interior, polishing the hand-carved teak until it shined.

Things changed after Matt and his wife, Nicole, had Jace. Tom and Jackie wanted to watch their first grandchild grow up, but they were ready for a lifestyle change, anyway. Their fifty-five-footer was getting to be too much boat for the two of them. They'd come up with a way to use cameras and walkie-talkies to pull into the mooring, but the job really required three people. The plan to relocate to San Carlos, a few hours south of their grandson, would let them be close to family *and* maintain their cruising lifestyle.

If the Hawkses couldn't get the sale price they wanted this time around, they were going to take one last sail—to Alaska—before putting her back on the market.

Tom said it would take about $500,000 for him to break even after the refurbishments, but he would settle for $400,000. So he advertised independently on the Internet and in boating magazines to save $50,000 in brokerage fees. He also listed the yacht with two brokers for prices up to $480,000.

"He was kind of hoping it wouldn't sell," Jim said, so they could still do the Alaska trip, then lower the asking price to try again.

Skylar saw one of the ads and called Tom on November 1 to express interest in the trawler. After Skylar had paid several visits to the boat, Tom figured the sale was imminent. So he and Jackie invited Jim, Don, and two other longtime friends from Prescott to join them for a farewell cruise. Don and Jim sailed separately to meet them at Catalina Island on November 11, where they played Mexican train dominoes, toasted to all the good times on the *Well Deserved,* and Tom played one of his usual pranks, hiding Jim's dinghy and pretending it had floated away.

While they were celebrating, Skylar called to confirm their date for the sea trial.

"Tell the Hawks we want it," Jackie heard the buyer's

wife, Jennifer, saying in the background. "Tell the Hawks not to sell that boat."

Jackie told Jim that Jennifer was pregnant, and had come down to the yacht with her baby daughter, chatting with Jackie while Skylar talked with Tom.

Jim figured that Skylar would want a survey done before purchasing the boat, so he told Tom to be sure to have a cashier's check in hand before transferring the title.

"This guy isn't trying to negotiate the price?" Jim asked.

"No," Tom said. "He wants all my toys."

They all figured that Skylar was a rich guy, with money to burn.

On November 13, Jim and Tom sailed back to Oceanside and Newport, respectively. The brothers never really worried about each other, not after they'd both served in the military and had chosen somewhat risky careers—Tom as a firefighter turned probation officer, and Jim as a Vietnam helicopter pilot turned police officer.

But the weather was rough on the return trip, so Tom made a rare call to his brother to check on him.

"Hey, ugly," Tom said, issuing his usual brotherly greeting.

The call ended with an offer from Jim: "Let us know if you sell the boat, and we'll come up and help you move."

Jackie Hawks was usually conservative with her cell phone minutes, but she'd called her best friend, Patricia "Tricia" Schutz, an unprecedented three days in a row to update her on the negotiations with Skylar.

On Sunday, during their last conversation, Jackie

told Tricia the price for the boat and the mooring had risen to $450,000 because Skylar wanted them to leave all their bed linens, dishes, cooking utensils, scuba equipment, and kayaks on board. Jackie said she was going to leave just the basics in the kitchen, not her special spice rack and pressure cooker. She promised to call Tricia back later in the week to give her the latest.

Although it wasn't unusual for Tom and Jim to go five days without talking, Jim Hawks felt his brother surely would have called after selling the boat. But he was hoping—wishful thinking, perhaps—that Tom and Jackie had driven up to a Santa Barbara resort to celebrate, or were vacationing on a friend's yacht out of cell phone reach.

On Wednesday, November 17, Ryan talked to Tricia, who managed the couple's business affairs and paid their bills from Arizona while they were at sea. She was concerned because she'd set up a medical appointment for Tom at the VA Medical Center in Long Beach that Friday, but hadn't been able to reach him to confirm.

Ryan said he was trying to remain optimistic, thinking his parents could have gone straight to Mexico, found a good deal on a house, and were having so much fun they didn't realize they were unreachable by cell phone. Unwilling to accept Jim's argument that they wouldn't have driven through Carlsbad without stopping to say hello, Ryan and Matt called real estate agents and their parents' friends in San Carlos, including a scuba instructor who had certified them all to dive. Ryan tried e-mailing them, too, to no avail.

He was not encouraged after an Internet search

found no connection between Skylar Deleon and the *Mighty Morphin Power Rangers,* a show from the early 1990s about five teenage superheroes who fought evil forces with martial arts in the fictional town of Angel Grove, California.

After a week of exchanging concerns and possible scenarios, the Hawks family made a pact. If no one had heard from Tom or Jackie by Thanksgiving, Jim would file a missing persons report the next morning. Jim had wanted Ryan and Matt to do it in Prescott, where Tricia had the couple's financial information, but the boys wanted their uncle, who had recently retired as Carlsbad's police chief, to do it.

Back in Mentor-on-the-Lake, Ohio, Jackie's parents, Gayle and Jack O'Neill, were worried, too.

Jackie hadn't been home for more than three years. Soon after she and Tom began their life at sea, Jack had to have open-heart surgery, and Gayle came down with breast cancer. Jackie wrote her sister Beverly that she felt bad she couldn't be there, but that was part of the reason Jackie wanted to sell the boat—so she could be closer to *her* family as well.

Even though Jackie couldn't be with them in person, she always stayed in touch. She made sure to check in with her mom by e-mail as soon as they got into port, and after she and Tom bought a computer and a primitive satellite system for the boat, it was even easier to send e-mails about their latest adventures. As long as she could get cell phone service, she and Gayle spoke every Sunday.

Jackie never turned off her cell phone; she even answered it when she was busy or struggling to put on her wet suit.

"Mom, can I call you back?" she'd say.

That's why Gayle became concerned on Sunday, November 21, when Jackie's phone went straight to voice mail. When they'd talked the previous Sunday, Jackie hadn't mentioned going anywhere she couldn't be reached.

Gayle tried to tell herself they must have had some miscommunication. But, as Thanksgiving approached, and Jackie still hadn't gotten in touch, Gayle's worry escalated. Jackie never missed a holiday, birthday, or anniversary without calling. Then Tricia called.

"We're concerned—we can't find them," Tricia said, explaining that she'd been calling everyone she could think of and comparing notes.

Still, Gayle tried to remain optimistic, looking out the window with hope that Tom and Jackie would drive up and surprise her for Thanksgiving.

On November 23, Jim Hawks confided in Carlsbad police Sergeant Jay Eppel, whom he'd hired and supervised for many years. Well aware that his former boss typically hid his emotions, Eppel knew Jim's concerns about his brother's welfare had to be serious.

That same day, Jim and Don drove up to Newport to check around. They met up with Carter Ford, a fellow sailor who had last heard from Jackie in a voice mail message the afternoon of the sea trial.

"Hi, Carter, we're still at sea," she said. "I don't know anything. Talk with you later. Bye."

Jim and Don hopped aboard Carter's skiff at the Lido Isle Yacht Club and powered over to the *Well Deserved.* The yacht was in its usual mooring, however, Jim immediately sensed a change in stewardship. Tom had a tendency to be anal, yet the green canvas cover was askew and a towel hung sloppily out of a porthole. On closer inspection Jim saw that the combination lock on the cabin door had been replaced, and peering in, he noticed that Jackie's custom-made nautical quilt wasn't on the bed. The dinghy was tied up with a knot Tom never would have made, and its motor was submerged in the corrosive salt water. Tom always lifted it out.

All of this reinforced his hope that the boat had been sold, but Jim was puzzled, nonetheless. Jim's fishing gear was still on board, along with his sailboard and the surfboard that Don had had custom-made for Tom. Jim knew the couple wouldn't have abandoned these treasured items, so, careful not to touch anything in case the boat proved to be a crime scene, he left one of his old CITY OF CARLSBAD business cards on the cabin door. He wrote "retired" next to his former police chief title, and scrawled a note on the back with his home and cell numbers: *I'm trying to locate my brother Tom Hawks. Please call.*

Jim and Don drove around the parking lots and side streets surrounding the harbor, looking for the Hawkses' 1998 silver Honda CRV, but found no sign of it. Where could they have gone?

At this point, seventy-five-year-old Betty Jarvi knew nothing of Tom and Jackie Hawks's disappearance, unaware that her family was destined to become intertwined with theirs in a way she could never imagine. As she lay awake at night in Anaheim, about twenty miles north of Newport, she wondered only if she would ever learn who had murdered her son almost a year earlier in Ensenada, Mexico.

Jon Peter "JP" Jarvi had always been a headstrong boy—his first word was "no"—but he loved the ladies, and they loved him. At five feet eight inches, his athletic frame moved with confidence, his sandy brown hair smoothly combed back, and his Finnish father's bright blue eyes sparkling. He flashed that wide grin and chatted up just about anyone. Betty marveled that when the two of them dined out, the waitress was often sitting down with them by dessert.

JP was intelligent, but he had a short attention span, a daring drive for adventure, and a habit of choosing the wrong friends. He also had a taste for cocaine and, even worse, heroin. Nonetheless, he managed to graduate high school early, earned his pilot's license, and started flying rich people around in private planes. As he got involved with auto racing and the flying Team America, his world was all about speed.

He'd started using the hard drugs in high school, and as the result of several back and neck surgeries, he also got hooked on painkillers and lost his pilot's license. Although the drugs were hard to kick, he rebuffed his parents' attempts to do an intervention and refused to go into treatment.

"I don't want to be around all *those* people," he said.

JP got involved in making jewelry, and Betty thought he was getting his life back together. But after her husband, Norm, died in February 2002, JP got in with a bad crowd that introduced him to new illegal activities. That December, JP was arrested for counterfeiting.

"I've got to learn to be a better judge of people," he told Betty.

JP had served about six months at a federal facility in Los Angeles when he received his short sentence.

He was transferred to a jail in Seal Beach, where he shared a cell with Skylar Deleon for about two months.

After his release in October 2003, he and Betty went out for a meal several times a week. He was no longer friendly with his older brother, Jeff, who lived across the street from Betty, but she still enjoyed spending time with JP. He was so handy around the house, always fixing things for her, and a joy to be around.

Then, on December 27, 2003, the day after JP's forty-fifth birthday, Betty was cleaning up a mess in her kitchen when the doorbell rang, around 10:00 P.M. Flustered, she was surprised to see Jeff with a group of people standing behind him on her doorstep. Betty was as adventuresome as JP and thought nothing of standing in a field of black bears, but she knew something had to be wrong for such a contingent to be huddled there at that hour. Aware that JP's drug problems were serious, Betty had been bracing herself for the worst for some time now.

"Mom, I have to tell you something," Jeff said. "It's JP."

"How bad is it?" she asked.

"As bad as it can get."

Jeff and his wife, Jeanne, two Anaheim police officers, and Mark Logan, the assistant city attorney who lived next door, all filed into her living room. Jeanne's father, retired Anaheim police Lieutenant Lou Molina, also joined them.

As Betty sat in her favorite armchair, the officers briefly described what they knew: JP had been found with his throat cut on the side of a road in rural Ensenada, and two detectives were coming from Mexico to talk to her about it.

The next evening, the Mexican detectives, accompanied by an Interpol liaison officer from the Los

Angeles Police Department (LAPD), showed up at her house, so Molina and Logan came back to help out. The detectives handed her JP's driver's license, asking through the LAPD translator if it was her son's. They said they could tell it was a professional hit because of the killer's skill in slitting JP's throat.

In a bizarre move, one of the detectives took Jeanne aside and confided that JP's eyeballs had been displayed next to his body, with the empty frames of his dark sunglasses laid over them. The detective said the drug cartels often did this to indicate that a murder victim had "seen too much." Luckily, Jeanne didn't mention this to Betty until the trial, when she learned it wasn't true.

Later that evening, the Ensenada coroner's office e-mailed Betty some photos of JP's body so she could identify him. Molina and Logan made sure to preview them, and ultimately let her see only two. One showed a frontal view of JP's face, neck, and upper torso, his neck wound wrapped in a bandage. The other one showed his back, where she recognized his surgical scars.

"He looked very peaceful," Betty said.

Unfortunately, her two protectors forgot to delete the other photos, and Betty couldn't resist looking at them.

Betty spent the next year wondering what JP had been thinking in his last moments. Although she'd gotten the impression that the end had come quickly and painlessly, it would be several more years before she would learn that—sadly—this was not the case.

2

On the morning of November 17, 2004, Jennifer Deleon gave her father, Steve Henderson, $20 to pick up a few things at Target to help her and Skylar clean their new boat. Skylar was eager to take his father-in-law, Jennifer's brother Michael, and Steve's nephew Taylor on a fishing trip to San Clemente Island.

Bored and on vacation, Steve was excited to see Skylar's latest vessel, so he did as he was asked. Jennifer had directed him to get trash bags and disinfectant, so he bought a box of Hefty kitchen trash bags and two containers of Clorox Wipes, throwing in a bottle of TUMS Ultra for his indigestion. He then drove to the parking lot on the north side of Newport Harbor, where he'd arranged to meet the kids.

After Skylar went into the coast guard station to do some paperwork, they transferred the cleaning supplies into the couple's new red Toyota Highlander and drove to the 15th Street dock. Parking next to the American Legion hall, Skylar led them over to a dinghy that was tied up at the short wooden pier and would ferry them to the *Well Deserved*.

As they approached the mooring, Steve was amazed

to see that this "nice and big" boat the kids had described was actually a white fifty-five-foot yacht. Climbing aboard, the kids gave him a tour, showing off the control room, and knowing Steve liked to cook, steered him into the galley.

"Why don't you take care of the kitchen," Jennifer said. "Anything that looks old—just get rid of it."

Skylar and Jennifer said the boat had been owned by a nice couple, but cautioned that they'd used drugs, so there might still be some around. Steve went through the cabinets and refrigerator, tossing opened packages of bread and meat into trash bags. He wiped down the countertops and checked through the pots and pans, noting that the kitchen was well stocked, with a whole rack of spices from which to choose. He didn't find any drugs.

While he was busy in the galley, Jennifer and Skylar were down below in the stateroom, going through the former owners' clothing, which Jennifer separated into "keep" and "throw away" piles.

Steve told the kids he couldn't believe this boat was all theirs. But inside, he felt a little uncomfortable. He didn't quite understand how they could have come into possession of such a grand vessel, so he asked a few questions to try to understand their good fortune.

The kids told him that Skylar had gotten the boat as "payback" from some people in Mexico who had been involved in the burglary for which Skylar had gone to jail. However, they assured Steve that the $1 million transaction was entirely legal; they'd signed documents, with notary seals and fingerprints—the whole deal—to prove it.

"Don't worry, Dad," Jennifer kept saying. "Everything is fine."

After three hours of cleaning up, the sun was going down, and the three of them decided they'd done enough work for one day. So they piled eight Hefty bags of clothes and trash onto the dinghy and dropped them into the metal bins near the dock, leaving the same number of bags on board for the next trip.

The whole family came back the next day so Jennifer's mother, Lana, could see the boat, too. After showing her around, they threw away several more bags of trash and took home the clothing that Jennifer had marked "keep," some of which she ultimately gave to Goodwill.

As they piled into the Toyota, Skylar mentioned they'd also gotten another new car in the deal. Driving to another parking lot nearby, he pointed at a silver Honda CRV.

"That's the car," he said.

"Well, that's amazing," Steve said. "Why is it just sitting here? What's preventing us from taking this car home?"

"Well, nothing," Skylar said.

So Steve took the keys and got into the CRV with Lana. Steve poked around in the glove box and glanced at the registration, but didn't notice anything out of the ordinary. There was nothing much in the car but a few empty coffee cups. The kids had offered to let Steve and Lana buy the Honda to offset part of the sum Steve had loaned them, but Steve didn't want it.

As they were driving back to the Extended Stay America hotel, where they'd all been staying for the past month, Steve and Lana looked at one another with wonder. Skylar had said the car's owners were in some kind of trouble, so they'd fled the country and left it behind.

"Who would do this?" they asked each other.

The Hendersons and the Deleons had been staying in separate hotel rooms for the past month since Steve, Lana, and her mother had woken up in the middle of the night to find their living room on fire. Steve tried to put out the blaze, but the fire department had to be called. The insurance company kicked them out during renovations, and at the time, no one thought anything of the fact that Skylar was the only one who played around with the aquarium, which had apparently shorted out and started the fire.

Steve and Lana hadn't brought up their daughter to lie. She'd never been in trouble with the law. She'd done well in school, excelled in sports, and was involved with their church, even helping to build houses for the homeless in Mexico. They had no reason to disbelieve her, so Steve and Lana decided they would just have to have faith. It was easy for Lana. Unconditional love was the norm in her family, but Steve was still grappling with it.

The next evening, Steve and Skylar drove the CRV to a gas station, where each of them kicked in $300 for diesel and water for the fishing trip. They decided to leave that night, when the moon was full, calling Michael and Taylor to join them. Skylar said he liked to drive boats at night and gave Steve a quick lesson at the controls.

As they headed out to sea around 9:00 P.M., they looked through the binoculars the previous owners had left behind. They also tried to use the night vision goggles, but couldn't figure out how they worked. Because the wind was cold and the water was choppy, Steve stayed inside most of the night, alternating sleeping and keeping watch at the helm with Skylar as they cruised around San Clemente Island and trolled to the east of Catalina at a speed of five to seven knots. Although they fished for nearly twenty-four hours, they didn't catch a single bite.

A few days later, Steve was back to being bored, when he heard a knock at the hotel room door.

"How would you like to go to Arizona?" Skylar and Jennifer asked.

Steve was ecstatic at the prospect of new surroundings, so he jumped at the chance. The kids said they needed to get to Kingman before closing to file some paperwork for the boat, so they didn't have time to wait for Lana to get home from work before hopping into the Toyota with little Haylie.

It wasn't until they'd crossed the Arizona border and looked at their cell phones that they realized they'd lost an hour and weren't going to make it in time, so they changed plans and headed instead for Laughlin, because Skylar's cousin, Michael Lewis, lived nearby. They arranged to have dinner with him and his family at one of the new casinos, where they stuffed themselves at a buffet. Steve took care of the kids while the other adults talked at the other end of the table, but he didn't mind.

First thing the next morning, Steve dropped off the kids at a government building in Kingman, where Jennifer and Skylar took care of some paperwork—something about dotting the *i*'s and crossing the *t*'s on the boat purchase. When Steve came back from getting gas, Skylar and Jennifer said they needed to do some other business at Stockmen's Bank. They got there before it opened, so they were the first customers in line, where their attempted transactions were videotaped.

Skylar and Jennifer's attempt to access Tom and Jackie Hawks's bank account with a document giving Skylar a sweeping power of attorney over the Hawkses' financial affairs sent alerts up the management chain. A durable, binding power of attorney, which even survives a signatory party's death, is typically used in cases where family members suffer from dementia.

A teller called over Sheri Murphy, a customer service representative, who asked the couple to step over to her desk, where she checked Skylar's ID against the name on the documents, which had been signed by the Hawkses, notarized, and date-stamped that morning by the Mohave County Recorder's Office. When Skylar pulled the Hawkses' checkbook from his briefcase, she could tell that it was a Prescott account number, so she asked the teller to make a copy of the documents while she called that branch.

"Send it interoffice to me so I can review it," Prescott's assistant branch manager told Murphy, saying she would compare the documents with the Hawkses' signature cards to determine if the paperwork was valid.

Meanwhile, Skylar explained that they were taking care of the Hawkses' bills while they were in Mexico.

"How do I sign their checks?" Jennifer inquired.

Murphy said she should sign the Hawkses' name, then write "POA," or sign her own name with the same notation.

But Murphy ultimately told the Deleons, she couldn't release any of the Hawkses' money to them until the documents had been reviewed.

* * *

Back in the car Skylar and Jennifer told Steve they weren't able to get money out of the former boat owners' bank account because of some documentation issue. Curious, Steve asked them to explain more on the drive home. He thought it was strange that the boat owners would sign control of their bank accounts over to the Deleons and leave the country, but once again, the kids assured him everything was above board.

"Don't worry about it," Jennifer said.

The next day was Thanksgiving, which the Deleons and the Hendersons spent with Lana's family in Chino. Skylar captured the festivities with his new video camera, which the yacht owners had left on the boat.

Although the kids hadn't repaid much of the $30,000 they'd borrowed from Steve to reduce their credit card debt and to pay for Skylar's jail work-furlough program, Steve didn't even blink when they said they'd sold the CRV for $6,000. He didn't bother asking them to apply the proceeds to the loan, because, frankly, he never really expected to see his money again.

3

Two days before Thanksgiving, Tricia Schutz, whose name was on Tom and Jackie's account at Stockmen's Bank, had tried to check for any recent large deposits, but the bank's computer was down, and it stayed down for the next several days. Including the value of the boat and Jackie's settlement from the motorcycle crash, the Hawkses were worth at least $1.5 million. Although Tricia was frustrated by the computer glitch, she later wondered whether God had been "working in mysterious ways" to prevent the Deleons from accessing the Hawkses' money.

Once the computer came back up, a clerk called to tell Tricia that the Hawkses' account showed no financial activity for the past nineteen days—since the sea trial—so Tricia told her to flag it. That's when she stopped joking with her husband that she was "going to kick Jackie's ass" for not telling her where she went. She'd been calling the Hawkses' boating friends in San Carlos, to no avail, for the past few days, and now this.

After getting a call from the Prescott branch that Skylar had tried to access the Hawkses' account in

Kingman a couple days earlier, Tricia said, "It hit me that something was wrong, that they were in harm's way. *Majorly*."

As Thanksgiving came and went without a call from Jackie, Gayle O'Neill was flooded with fears as soon as her head hit the pillow. Had her fit, tanned, and attractive daughter been sold into slavery? Was she being held somewhere against her will, and were her captors starving or torturing her?

"I knew something was terribly wrong for her not to get in touch with us," Gayle said.

Word of Tom and Jackie's disappearance traveled fast. When Ryan Hawks attended his best friend's engagement party in Prescott the day after Thanksgiving, four guests asked about his missing parents. Ryan checked in with his uncle around 6:00 P.M., and Jim's voice sounded different, but he didn't want to get into details.

"I think you need to come home," said Jim, who hadn't been able to sleep any better than Gayle as his mind whirled with possibilities. "We need to talk."

Ryan had stopped by his parents' property in Prescott, hoping to find a sign of a recent visit, but after opening the barn door, he could tell from all the dust that no one had been there for more than a year.

So Ryan hit the road back to San Diego County, scanning the shoulders for any trace of his parents. Jim said that if they'd been in an accident or had been run off the road, they would have been found within two or three days, but Ryan couldn't lose hope.

Jim could see his nephew was struggling with the reality that Tom and Jackie could be gone for good, so he tried to soften the blow and told Ryan not to get angry when he said such things.

"I'm thinking like a cop," Jim said.

Ryan called his brother, Matt, from the road around midnight. The two of them discussed what their uncle had said to each of them—and, perhaps more important, what he hadn't said.

"What do you think happened?" Ryan asked.

There was a long, awkward pause before his brother answered.

"I think they're dead," Matt replied.

Ryan quickly hung up before he broke down, crying.

By the time Ryan reached Carlsbad, it was 3:00 A.M., and Jim was waiting up for him. He sat Ryan down at the kitchen table, which was stacked with materials from the family's search efforts, and laid out the depressing details he'd learned over the past few days.

"Here's what we know," he said.

Several days ago, Jim explained, the wife of the prospective buyer Tom had mentioned called at 7:00 P.M., and he'd scribbled down some notes as they talked.

"I got your note from a friend," she told him. Jim could hear phones ringing and other background noise. "I'm pregnant and I'm at work," she said, explaining that she and her husband had bought the *Well Deserved*. She was talking fast, and sounded nervous. Hesitant.

"I'm just trying to reach my brother," Jim told her.

"They talked about going to San Carlos," she offered.

Jim told her he thought it was odd that they'd left behind his sailboard and Tom's custom-made surfboard. But not wanting to make her more nervous, he backed off and tried to make casual chitchat.

"Well, it's a great boat, a fine boat. I hope you enjoy it," he said. "I heard that your husband was a Power Ranger."

Jennifer hesitated again. "Yes," she said.

Jim asked if she would talk to Skylar and call back if they came up with any information that would help locate Tom and Jackie.

Jennifer said she would. "I'm sorry. I'm tired and very busy," she said. "I've got to go."

As soon as he hung up, Jim turned to his wife. "She's lying," he said.

Since Jennifer's call, Jim told Ryan that he, Sergeant Eppel, Jim's daughters, Lee Anne, who was an Escondido police officer, and Lynn, who did preemployment backgrounds for a living, had been checking out the Deleons. Together they turned up some interesting information that would help the Newport Beach Police Department (NBPD) get a running start on the missing persons report he'd filed earlier that day.

Jim said Eppel had been taking the report at the house when Luann Kinney, the Stockmen's manager in Prescott, called to say that Skylar had just phoned from Mexico. Asking if his wire transfer into Tom and Jackie's account had been completed, Skylar said they'd authorized him to access their account through some power-of-attorney documents her branch should receive in interoffice mail that day from Kingman, where he'd delivered them a couple of days earlier.

At first, Kinney said, Skylar was evasive about his reasons for accessing the account, but he finally said he was trying to help the Hawkses buy property in San Carlos. Kinney, who'd already been alerted by Tricia that the couple was missing, told Skylar she needed to speak with Tom personally, and she asked if Tom could wait by a pay phone in the San Carlos marina for her call. Skylar stumbled over his words, saying he could only make outgoing calls on the phone he was using, and he didn't know exactly where Tom was. Skylar said he'd try to reach Tom and call back to confirm she'd received the documents, but he never did.

Eppel was still at Jim's house when Jennifer called again that afternoon, around four o'clock.

"Have you heard from your brother?" she asked.

Skylar had Mexican citizenship, she said, and had been looking into helping the Hawkses purchase property down there. She and Skylar also had been trying to reach the couple to arrange the boat-operating lessons they'd promised.

"I'm sorry I was so tired when we first talked," she said.

Jim subtly tried to get more information about the sale, and hoping to find a paper trail, he inquired whether they'd gone to a bank or had paid with a cashier's check. Jennifer hesitated once again, and Jim could hear someone talking in the background before she replied.

"They had the payment in hand when we left them," she said.

Jennifer said they'd done the transaction in the parking lot near the dock, so Jim asked if they'd used a marine document transfer agent.

"Yes, Mary Conlin or something," she said, adding that she didn't remember the company's exact name. "We told them to take their time getting their stuff off the boat," she said, explaining that they'd last seen the Hawkses driving away from the pier in their CRV. "We haven't seen them since."

Jim told her his family was very worried and was planning to file a missing persons report.

"Well, please call us or have them call if you hear from them, and we'll do the same," she said.

4

Skylar Deleon, born John Julius Jacobson, had always had a complicated love-hate relationship with his father. Sometimes, Skylar longed for his father's approval. Other times, Skylar wanted nothing to do with him, changing his identity to disentangle and disassociate himself from the controlling, abusive man with the same name. And sometimes, Skylar just tried not to feel anything at all.

Looking back years later, members of Skylar's fragmented family would try to blame his fatal flaws on his lack of parental role models. He'd seemed like such a sweet boy, but his mother and stepmother were drug addicts, and his father came from a lineage scarred by bizarre behaviors, suicide, and accusations of molestation and abuse.

"It's an absolutely screwed-up family," said Bryan Brah, a cousin who spent summers and holidays with the Jacobsons growing up.

Skylar's grandmother Marlene had Skylar's father with her first husband. Her second husband, Julius "Jake" Jacobson, adopted her four-year-old son, John, then they had two children of their own, Jerry and

Colleen. Depression plagued Jerry, who came home from college one Christmas break and shot himself in the chest with a shotgun. Colleen married Michael Lewis and had two boys, Michael and Russell, who became Skylar's childhood friends. Colleen later married Dean Francisco.

Marlene, who died in 2008, had a volatile personality and a reputation for being physically and emotionally abusive. Even when her son John was an adult, Marlene periodically disowned him, prohibiting visits until he'd worked his way back into her good graces.

An extremely strict disciplinarian, Marlene was "a total domineering woman in her own right. She was really crazy. I mean, barely-functional-in-society psychotic," said Bryan, who said John modeled his parenting methods after hers.

Bryan saw these firsthand when he was a strong-willed, ten-year-old. After sassing Marlene, she promptly grabbed him by the neck, shoved a bar of soap into his mouth, and rubbed it against his teeth, sending the slimy shavings down his throat.

"You little son of a bitch," she said. "You're not going to talk that way to me."

Marlene drove little Bryan to tears by telling him he would get crabs and parasites after sitting on a toilet seat at an Indian restaurant. She also had terrorized his then-five-year-old aunt by locking her in a closet and saying spiders were crawling all over her.

Years after Jerry's death, Bryan shocked his relatives by confessing that during summers at Marlene and Jake's house, Jerry had sexually molested him as a child. Sexual molestation and physical abuse are typically part of a cycle that starts when an abuser is molested or physically harmed as a child; often he or she will inflict similar methods on other children later on.

"Marlene called me a goddamned liar," Bryan recalled.

Bryan was seven when his mother called the military police to pick up Marlene's son John at their house in San Diego after he'd gone AWOL from the U.S. Marine Corps. John got a dishonorable discharge after serving two and a half years as a private gunner, with eight unauthorized absences and an arrest for robbing a man in a 7-Eleven parking lot, using a crowbar.

"I think it's pretty ironic that his son followed in his footsteps," Bryan said.

Skylar's mother, born Lynette Birchett in St. Louis, Missouri, also had a history of being abused. So it was no surprise that she ended up with John Jacobson, a five-foot-five-inch man nicknamed "Big John," who beat her and threatened to kill her more than once, and whose own son accused him of molestation.

Lynette was only thirteen when she left her divorced mother's house to live with her sister. Lynette was eager to leave again, two years later, after friends of her sister's husband molested her while he took pictures. She was sixteen when a girlfriend invited her to a block party in Van Nuys, California, where she met the handsome twenty-one-year-old John. They started dating and she willingly moved into his apartment.

John was in athletic shape from erecting chain-link fences, when he started selling marijuana to help pay the rent. He soon realized that cocaine paid better money, and Lynette quickly evolved from a troubled teenager to a drug addict, using PCP and cannabinol, and freebasing cocaine.

In November 1977, police searched their apartment and found three bags of pot, two of them laced with PCP, and a shotgun. But police never found their second apartment, where they stored their other guns and drug supply, so John and Lynette got off easy.

Lynette continued to use drugs, even after she discovered at eighteen that she was pregnant. Planning to abort the fetus, she kept mum, and was in a hospital gown, waiting to have the procedure at a clinic, when John burst in.

"You are not going to get rid of my baby," he said. "I will kill you first."

John always carried a gun and had a volatile temper, so Lynette was too scared to disobey him. She simply got dressed and left the clinic.

"I want to get an amniocentesis," she said when they got home, explaining that the baby might not even be his. They often had people over to do drugs, and John forced her to engage in threesomes and foursomes with their guests.

That's when the Jacobson hammer came down. Marlene called Lynette, saying, "It doesn't matter. It is John's baby, no matter what."

Lynette felt she had no choice but to stay in the relationship, so she married John in Las Vegas on December 4, 1978.

Once she'd committed to having the baby, she stopped doing drugs and was determined to stay clean until she gave birth. John Julius Jacobson was born on August 12, 1979, weighing seven pounds eleven ounces. She loved that boy, whom they called "John John," "Little John," or "Johnny." She breastfed him until she started doing coke again.

Hers was an all-day, everyday habit as she scooped the white powder with a long fingernail and inhaled a blast before making Johnny breakfast. Another blast before she played with him and got him dressed, and another while she and her friends partied by the pool. At night, John's friends would come over, and they would party some more.

"We were quiet enough, but sometimes [Little] John would wake up," Lynette said.

Eating was not a priority for Lynette, who ultimately got so skinny that, at eighty-nine pounds, she had to buy her clothes from the little girls' department. She thought about leaving Big John, but he had hooked up with some serious drug dealers who drove around in vans with guns, threatening people who crossed them.

"It was getting to the point that if I stayed, I was going to die because I was so skinny. And . . . if I left with John, I would've been dead, too."

Big John was "a mean man," Lynette said. "If everything didn't go his way, he was going to take it out on you. If dinner wasn't cooked right, you are going to have it in your face. . . . Everything was controlling and manipulating."

Instead of going to the hospital to treat her cuts and bruises, she'd go to her mother's house down the street. But Lynette wasn't the only target of John's abuse. He would swat the baby's diapered bottom so hard with a wooden spoon that he often broke the implement.

"You're hitting him too hard," Lynette would say. "He's only a baby."

"He can't feel it," John would retort. He claimed the diapers were cushioning the blow, but Lynette would see red marks when she changed the infant.

John also slapped and choked his son as he grew into a toddler. "That was his favorite thing," Lynette recalled. "Backhanding him and grabbing him by the neck as hard as he could."

John's bad behavior escalated as he got involved in the dangerous manufacturing of methamphetamine, which meant the armed men who came to the house grew more dangerous, too. Lynette was petrified of the biker gangs and Colombian drug dealers, but she couldn't call the police because her own garage was piled high with meth.

Their life did have its occasional normal moments, though, such as when she and John opened their own restaurant, Backyard Barbecue, in the San Fernando Valley. She also played Tinkertoys with her son, and took him to Disneyland with her sisters and his cousins.

"He was smart," she recalled. "I mean, he was bottle-broke at one, potty-trained at two."

But she didn't watch Little John all that carefully. As a baby, he fell through the bars in his crib, and had to be rushed to the hospital. And, when he was eighteen months old, he drove his Big Wheel into the pool. Lynette had gone into the house to get a drink when she saw the cycle in the water, so she ran out and jumped in to rescue him. Lynette laid Little John on the cement and followed the 911 dispatcher's directions to turn him on his side, where he coughed and sputtered as she pushed the water out of his lungs.

Tiring of Big John's abuse, she started fighting back and decided she wanted a divorce. She was in the process of obtaining a restraining order when John started choking her on November 7, 1980. She broke loose and ran out of the house; he grabbed a large kitchen knife, chased her into the street, and dragged her back inside. There, he choked her again, jabbed a knife at her stomach, raised it over his head, and threatened to kill her. Lynette kicked him in the groin, grabbed Little John, and tore down the street, with her husband still in pursuit with the knife.

"Somebody, please help me!" Lynette screamed. "He's going to kill us!" She kept running until she reached a friend's house and begged him to call the police. John was arrested, but he quickly bailed out.

"He was going to kill both of us," she recalled. "[If] he couldn't have John, nobody could."

Still, Lynette was determined to find a way out. She didn't want to leave Johnny behind, but she didn't want Big John to kill her for trying to take him, either. She felt she had to save herself, so she finally left and moved in with a friend. But that didn't last long. She missed her son too much, so she tried to come back.

"Okay, fine, I just want John," she told her husband, who was sitting with his friend Dave and a rifle, with Johnny nearby. After Big John hit Lynette and threw her against the fireplace, Dave started fighting him, which allowed her time to jump over the couch and run out the door.

Big John fought her for legal custody of Johnny and won. Lynette got visitation rights, but John refused to comply with the court order, and she was too scared to battle him in court.

"I was supposed to get him, like, every weekend or every other weekend. And every single time that I would go . . . to pick him up, or he would go to drop him off, he would start a huge fight," she said. "John controlled this child. He was like a pawn to him."

Without Lynette to intervene, Big John continued to abuse their son. If Johnny didn't say exactly what his father wanted to hear, he'd get a wallop. If the child tried to defend himself, that only made his father more angry.

"He would get really mad and say he was going to beat him over the head with a baseball bat if he tried that again, so he would just start hitting [Johnny, who would] . . . cower down," she said.

Big John was obsessed, for example, with Johnny's nail-biting habit, so he'd shove toothpicks under the tissue in his nail bed and leave them there. This punishment continued while Johnny was a teenager, when Big John would bite his son's fingers as hard as he could, chomping on each nail that the boy had bitten. Johnny would try to withstand the pain as long as he could, because if he showed any weakness, his father would inflict the pain for even longer.

"I didn't see my brother cry very often," Johnny's half sister Stephanie said later. "Maybe a tear here and there. But never did I see him break down."

Lynette got to see Johnny only when it was convenient for his father. She later testified that this often corresponded with a weekend when he wanted to run off with women like Sharon*, a stripper, with whom he moved to Redding with Johnny to live. That meant Lynette saw Johnny only when Big John was passing through town on a drug run, or when she made an occasional visit to Redding. Sharon confided to Lynette that Big John had forced her to watch him having sex with men, something Lynette had seen for herself.

John was twenty-nine in 1984 when he met Lisa Wildin, a twenty-year-old recovering cocaine addict who had withered to eighty-five pounds before she asked her mother to help her get clean.

She was fine, until one of her girlfriends asked her to go out with John, who was being possessive with another friend. Lisa, married at sixteen and divorced two years later, wasn't looking for a relationship, so she agreed to break his heart and move on. But things didn't go as anticipated.

John, who told her he was a car salesman, would pick her up in a limousine and take her to a fancy restaurant and a night on the town.

"He could sell an Eskimo ice cubes is what I used to say," Lisa recalled.

The next day, he would show up with a picnic basket and take her horseback riding.

"It was like he was the man of everything," she said. "He swept me off my feet. I fell in love."

When he stayed the night with her, he would lay out lines of cocaine on her dresser. She begged him not to, but he didn't listen.

"Well, just in case you change your mind," he'd say, knowing full well that an addict couldn't resist for long.

He was right. Lisa was soon back on the blow. Within six months, she'd moved into his apartment in Encino with him and his son. Like Lynette before her, he provided her with plenty of cocaine during the day, and quaaludes and marijuana at night. Other drug dealers would come over and spread kilos of coke over the coffee table when John wasn't home.

Although John repeatedly moved them from house to house, concerned that the police were watching them, they were living the high life. Limos picked them up for meals, and John bought Lisa a whole new wardrobe of sexy outfits, including a mink stole, insisting that she throw her old clothes away. Still, he was never satisfied with her appearance, often driving her to tears as she tried to please him.

But John was just as dissatisfied with his own son, whom he treated like a possession. He got upset when Johnny wet the bed and beat him when he got a blemish, accusing him of not washing his face properly.

"Poor Little Johnny," Lisa recalled. "If he didn't have his hair combed quite right, or if his shirt wasn't tucked in right, then he would usually get smacked or punched around. We always had to look perfect."

When Johnny was six, he told his mother, Lynette, that his father had been molesting him and made him sleep in the same bed, naked. Lynette called Big John and tried to get to the bottom of it.

"Well, you know I don't wear clothes to bed," he said. "He's my fucking son."

Lynette told him that wasn't right, Little John should have his own room. Apparently, he did have his own room. However, it was so full of junk, he couldn't sleep in it. Big John denied, however, that he was molesting their son.

Nonetheless, Johnny didn't want to go back to live with his father, so Lynette tried to keep him when his grandfather Jake came to collect him.

"I'm not giving him back to you," she said, relaying the molestation allegation.

"Nah, John wouldn't do that," Jake said.

"Well, I talked to John, and John said that he sleeps with him, naked," she said. "I know for a fact that John is gay. I mean I know it. I've seen it."

Lynette was also concerned because Johnny had been walking with his head down, wearing mascara, and dressing up like a girl.

"What are you doing?" Lynette asked her son. "You

are a boy. You don't wear mascara, and you don't act like that."

Johnny explained that a neighbor had been making him pose, put on eye makeup, and "do things."

"Did you tell your dad?" she asked.

"Yes, but he didn't do anything," Johnny said. "I don't know why I'm alive."

When Lynette asked Big John what was going on, he told her he'd "take care of it."

Around the same time, Johnny raised Lisa's concerns when she saw him pretending to stab his teddy bear.

"What are you doing?" Lisa asked, worried.

"I'm getting rid of the bad guys," he said.

Johnny described how he'd been molested by a neighbor, so Lisa told John they should file a police report. But John told her the same thing he'd told Lynette—he'd "take care of it."

"I wasn't married yet to John. . . . I had no recourse," Lisa said later. "John told me what to do, and so I just took care of Skylar. Looking back, yeah, I should've gone down and immediately filed the report."

Lisa loved Johnny as if he were her own son, so she tried to provide him with the care and love his father withheld. When he came down with chicken pox, she soothed his itchy blisters with calamine lotion, Benadryl, and soaks in the bathtub.

She didn't really cook, but she made a deal with Big John. If he made it home for dinner at least twice a week, she would cook them real meals all week long. But he didn't hold up his end of the bargain, which meant they often ate takeout, cereal, or pizza.

Lisa tried to protect Johnny—and herself—from Big John. When he took Johnny to drug deals or to friends' houses where they drew lines of coke on the table, she grabbed the boy and took him outside.

"Do you think that Little Johnny should be here?" she asked.

"He's my son. He'll be fine," Big John replied. "He knows what to do. He knows to keep his mouth shut."

If Johnny disobeyed his father, he had to stand in the corner, holding his leg up without letting his shoulders touch the wall, or withstand another beating. So Johnny learned to be stoic through the punishments.

"If he cried, it got worse," Lisa said. "When he knew he was going to be seriously hurt, he learned to smile and do a nervous little giggle, because then his father wouldn't hurt him as badly."

Despite all of this, Lisa said, Johnny managed to maintain a very sweet nature.

"He wanted to make everybody happy," Lisa said. One day Big John was pulling his usual verbal abuse on Lisa at a gas station. After his father went into the market, Johnny looked up at her and said, "Don't worry, Mom, because one day I will be eighteen, and then I will marry you, and then Dad won't ever be able to be mean to you again."

At one point, Johnny wanted to go live with Lynette, but Big John told him she didn't love him.

"I won't have anything to do with you if you go there," Big John threatened. "You won't have a dad, and your mom doesn't love you, anyway, and then nobody will love you."

When Johnny started crying, Lisa tried to console him. "No," she said, hugging him. "Your mom does love you."

But Johnny wasn't sure what to think. Maybe his father had a point. If Lynette loved him, why wasn't he living with her?

"John just had a way of just brainwashing and making you think what he said was so," Lisa said.

In the mid-1980s, Lynette started dating Eddie Fisher, a guy from the neighborhood who helped her get off drugs.

Lynette and Eddie never had any problems with Johnny during his visits, or later when he lived with them for a period that encompassed two Christmases. Eddie told Johnny that he would buy him a toy gun if he kept up his grades, cleaned up his room, and kept the chicken coops clean, which he did. Johnny knew how to follow the rules.

"He was never mean," Lynette said. "He wasn't like that. I have never heard [Little] John raise his voice or anything in my life. It just wasn't in his character."

Johnny had fallen behind in school from all the moving around, so they got him a tutor. He seemed happy and his health was fine—except for the grand mal epileptic seizures, which started when he was six. Lynette attributed them to the cocaine and methamphetamine floating around Big John's house.

The doctors put the boy on phenobarbital, but Big John never gave it to her when he handed Johnny over for a visit. After reading a news article that said the drug could actually cause seizures, she and Eddie weaned Little John off it by giving him progressively lower doses, and the seizures eventually stopped.

Despite Big John's threats to kill Eddie and Lynette, Eddie saw Big John as a big coward. "He wasn't man enough to stand [up to] a man, but a female he would," he said. "I always say that he had a Napoleon complex. He was a short, little guy, but everybody owed him in the world. . . . He would say stuff like, you know, he did this, did this, did this, but ninety percent of it . . . was just a bullsh** story. He always had to be the big guy. . . . He put the fear in people. The guy could talk, and you would actually believe him."

Meanwhile, Little John was watching all of this very closely. And learning.

5

In April 1987, Johnny Jacobson was seven when his father got caught running drugs through Oklahoma and was arrested in a motel room with a woman and a suitcase filled with 138 grams of rock cocaine. John Senior was charged with distribution of cocaine, conspiracy to manufacture methamphetamine, interstate travel, and aid of racketeering. He paid his $30,000 bail and returned to California. Through a plea bargain, all charges but the coke distribution were dropped.

John and Lisa, about to have their first baby, got married right after the arrest. When Lisa first learned she was pregnant, she'd been doing an eight-ball of coke a day—an eighth of an ounce, or 3.5 grams. Under a doctor's care, she weaned herself off the drugs until she was clean.

Big John was free on bail—and apparently still dealing drugs—when their daughter, Stephanie, was born in May. By the time she was only six months old, John had her posing for a photo, surrounded by $100,000 in drug money he'd set on the kitchen counter where she'd just finished eating lunch.

That November, John was sentenced to three years, with four years' probation, but was allowed to delay reporting to the high-security federal prison near Lompoc, about an hour north of Santa Barbara, until January 25, 1988. The night before Lisa drove him there, he got her pregnant again.

John had arranged for his friend Richard to take care of Lisa and the kids while he was away. Richard was friends with a known child molester, who wasn't allowed anywhere near the house, so Lisa was horrified to find the molester there with Stephanie and Johnny when she got back from the prison. She told the man to leave and called Richard to complain, but he brushed her off.

"It doesn't matter what John says, because he is not here," he replied.

Crying and upset, Lisa tried the other emergency number that John had left her—for one of his Colombian drug friends.

"Don't worry, baby, I take care of you," the Colombian tried to reassure her. Within half an hour, he showed up with six other Colombians, all carrying guns, and ordered Richard and his friends to get out.

"I take care of you, baby, it's all good," the Colombian told Lisa.

Lisa was happy to get rid of Richard and his molester friend, but she also knew, *No, this is not good at all.*

Lisa regularly drove the kids to Lompoc to visit John, only to be yelled at for Johnny's wrinkled clothes and Stephanie's puffy eyes.

"It's a four-hour drive. She is two, and, yes, she is just waking up," Lisa would retort.

So Lisa packed up and moved them to Lompoc

where they could visit John four times a week without any grief. Stephanie took her first steps at the prison, and celebrated her first birthday there. Their son Justin was born in October 1988, while Big John was still inside.

Lisa offered him a deal when she picked him up to drive him to his mother's house in Westminster upon his release in August 1989.

"If you can, just for four hours, don't call me a stupid bitch, I'll be fine. I will stay with you forever," Lisa said.

But John couldn't even make it out of the prison gates. She'd forgotten a phone number, which triggered a rant. Lisa just looked at him and smiled.

"Thank you for my ticket out," she said. "I'm dropping you off at your mom's, and I'm done."

When they arrived at Marlene's, John wouldn't let Lisa take Johnny with her. So she just took Justin and Stephanie, and filed for divorce. This drove John nuts, so he called her continuously, moaning that he wanted to see "his babies."

"You come here, I will have you arrested," she told him.

But he kept calling, first saying how much he loved Lisa and the kids, then threatening to kill her and her boyfriend.

On September 24, he told his parole officer he had a gun and was heading north to "take care" of his wife. "The cops are going to have to shoot me," he said, sounding despondent and confused.

Like his half brother Jerry, Big John had a dark side, and experienced bouts of depression. He'd told Lynette that he wanted to commit suicide after borrowing money from Jake and gambling it away.

He'd done the same thing with Lisa over the years, often cutting across his wrists when she threatened to leave him.

"He probably had ten or twelve scars going across," Lisa said later, running her finger across her own wrist. "Each time I would go back, because I didn't want to be responsible for him doing it, until I finally smartened up and told him to cut up and down instead of side to side."

The parole officer called the police in her area. They, in turn, advised her to go to a women's shelter. But refusing to give in to his antics any longer, she said she wouldn't be intimidated into leaving her own home. She had a gun, too.

Ultimately, they persuaded her to have John meet her at a park by promising to hand over Stephanie and Justin. Police arrested him when he arrived there several hours later, and sent him back to prison on a parole violation for making terrorist threats.

Lisa couldn't afford to keep Little John this time, so he went to live with Lynette and Eddie. With Big John safely behind bars once again, Lisa moved to Oklahoma, Tennessee, and finally Kansas.

As soon as Big John got out of prison in June 1990, he demanded that Lynette give his son back. In the meantime, he'd come up with a new idea of using his boys to make money.

Johnny and Justin were going to be action-movie actors, he decided, so he enrolled them in acting and jujitsu classes, and had Johnny working out with weights. During the Jacobson clan holiday get-togethers, the family couldn't believe how muscular the boy looked.

According to Skylar, as a child he did no more than ten commercials, including spots for Nintendo, Hyundai, Buick, and "some camera thing." But he had no idea how much money he made, because his father kept it all.

"I didn't see it," Skylar said, giggling, in 2009, "so I don't know."

Skylar's manager didn't want to be interviewed for this book, so there was no way to confirm which, or how many, commercials he did.

Skylar said he was unaware that one of his acting jobs had actually been for a public service announcement until he saw himself on TV, playing a child with cancer.

"He was told to go and play basketball . . . and when it actually aired, it was like, 'Hi, I'm Billy, and I have leukemia. . . . I'm with Make-A-Wish Foundation,'" Jennifer said later.

Johnny auditioned for *Mighty Morphin Power Rangers,* and got a couple small parts in the 1993 to 1994 season. For the next decade, he told people he had a starring role, or let them assume that he did. He later acknowledged that he had a "guest lead" role in one episode, which involved teaching kids to do karate, "then I got zapped away or whatever." In a second episode, he said, his character didn't even have a name in the script. Neither role was a speaking part.

He never liked acting, he said, because "I couldn't remember my lines, and my dad made it hell because I couldn't remember. . . . I wasn't this or I wasn't that. Something wasn't right, so I hated it."

Big John got so furious one day he got kicked off the set for repeatedly yelling at Johnny.

"He really didn't want to be [an actor]. It was his dad pushing him into it," said Lynette, who was on the set that day. "And it was more what his dad wanted than what he wanted. . . . Me and John fought over it, because he would keep him out of school and stuff all the time."

Johnny began using aliases while he was acting, including Jon Liberty.

At the time he and his father were living in Orange County, where Johnny went to Huntington Beach High School, less than two miles from the beach. He surfed every day, even when the water was really cold, later telling people he'd been on the surf team, which wasn't true.

"That kid never did anything for us but give us a rash," said Greg Crook, the school's assistant principal.

Stephanie Jacobson came out to stay with her father and brother for four summers, mostly so she could spend time with Johnny, who took her to the beach with their cousin, Michael Lewis, and gave her surfing lessons.

She remembered their father constantly belittling Johnny, saying he was worthless and would never come to anything. He'd call her names, too, but Johnny "got the wrath of it all. . . . He would get all these daily checks of things that he was not supposed to do, and if he did it, he would get punishments for them."

Big John would pull Johnny's hair, she said, "hit him so hard in the stomach, it would knock his breath out," make him sit in the corner on his knees or in the bedroom for hours with no food. If he missed a meal, he'd have to go without.

Stephanie fell off the front of Justin's bike one day, landing nose first on the cement. Johnny brought her home, covered with scrapes; he cleaned up her wounds and propped her up with pillows on the couch.

"My dad comes home and freaks out," she recalled. "Johnny is worthless once again; he can't be responsible for anything, and him and my dad get in a huge fight."

As Johnny worked toward his black belt, he learned how to control his father's physical abuse and emotional rants by taking him to the ground in a hold until he calmed down. During one such rampage, Stephanie and Justin were crying so loud, the neighbors called Child Protective Services (CPS).

From February 1993 to May 1995, Lynette received a series of calls from CPS social workers, relaying reports of John abusing their son. However, Lynette denied that any abuse was going on, so the reports were all deemed unsubstantiated. Years later, Lynette testified that she was too scared of repercussions from Big John to tell the truth.

The reports echoed Stephanie's observations: Big John bit his son's fingers, punched him in the ribs for getting D's, grabbed him by the neck, dragged him up and threw him down the stairs; Johnny had black eyes from his father punching him, slamming him into the wall, and pulling his hair, only to keep him out of school the next day and order him to lie about his injuries; Johnny's father was constantly berating him, which left him "a nervous wreck."

During the CPS interviews, Johnny acted withdrawn, contending that his father had been in jail for "organized crime" related to "selling/manufacturing drugs," but he wasn't allowed to discuss whether drug sales or use were still occurring. When he was interviewed with his father present, one social worker reported seeing a bond between them, and said they offered a reasonable explanation for his injuries: Johnny, a child actor, had been bruised in his advanced karate program and he'd only been grounded for bad grades. Big John denied all the abuse allegations, ultimately demanding a formal written apology from CPS.

Still, relatives could see the boy's obvious fear of his father. "Skylar was very deferential to his dad, even to the point of if you'd talk to him, he'd look to his dad to see if it was okay to talk or interact," his cousin Bryan said later. "He was just this little kid, this quiet kid," especially in comparison to his cousins, Michael and Russell. "I thought Skylar was the good kid and those kids were the bad kids. They just seemed out of control."

In December 1997, partway through Johnny's senior year, John Senior decided they were moving to Marion, Kansas, a town with about two thousand people and no stoplights, so he could get Lisa back. She told him not to, but he insisted on coming.

"My daughter needs me now," he said.

So he bought a house there with the settlement he'd won after falling forty feet off a ladder while working in Anaheim Stadium. He would take off for weeks or months, selling bumper stickers in his truck, and leave Johnny alone to fend for himself. Sometimes he would pull Johnny out of school to come along for the ride.

Big John still had custody of Stephanie and Justin in the summertime, and when he was in town, he constantly fought with Lisa over them. He continued his threats to kill her, one of which came attached to a rock that he threw at her window: *Next time it will be a bomb.*

Although he repeatedly reported her to police and CPS for being a bad mother, Big John's intimidation tactics fell flat in Marion. The only way he knew to fight back was to paint defamatory messages aimed at responding police officers such as *Officer Keyes, you don't deserve the title,* on the side of his truck, and drive around town.

By then, Big John had come to depend on Johnny being there for him.

"He couldn't do anything without [Skylar]," Stephanie recalled. "He also had to have control over Skylar . . . and Skylar could have no life. He had no friends, because my dad would not allow that. Because he had to be by my dad's side all the time."

Johnny put up with his father's temper tantrums, even though he could have exerted his karate skills to quell them. "Skylar always tried to keep the peace," Stephanie said. "And it was a very hard task to do with my dad."

Curiously, Big John bought his son lots of things during this period: surfboards, bikes, Nintendo games, and wet suits. He didn't have time, but he had money, which he used to try to buy his son's love. Even so, if he got mad, he took the gifts right back.

Johnny was happy to spend time with Lisa again, coming over to fix her front porch, or whatever else needed doing around her house.

One day Lisa got a call from his high-school guidance counselor, saying he was going to fail all his classes if he didn't get back to campus. Johnny had flunked English during his junior or sophomore year, he said, because he "couldn't concentrate." He had problems reading books because his thoughts drifted after only a few paragraphs.

Lisa told him what he needed to do to graduate, and her mother took him to a learning center a couple times a week until he got caught up enough to earn his diploma in May 1998.

That November, Johnny enlisted in the U.S. Marine Corps, partly because his father didn't want him to.

"John had been in the marines, but got a dishonorable discharge, and he had always said how the marines suck and you don't ever go there," Lisa recalled.

Later, Skylar acknowledged that he'd "joined for the wrong reasons." But in addition to rebelling against his father, he said, he was trying to shift his mind-set away from his growing desire to have a sex change operation. "I was thinking, 'This is wrong, and maybe I can change my head.'"

Just like the other grunts in boot camp, Johnny learned how to kill an enemy soldier with the bayonet at the end of his rifle, and to slice someone's throat with a hunting knife. But he did not get sent to battle. With the rank of rifleman, he worked as a clerk at Camp Lejeune in North Carolina, starting in January 1999. He didn't last long, however.

He went AWOL twice, first for a week that September, then in January 2000 for almost ten months. He headed down to the beachfront community of San Miguel in Ensenada, Mexico, where he spent some time with his father, and surfed the good right-breaking waves. He was declared a deserter and avoided a trial by court-martial by accepting an "other than honorable" discharge in January 2001.

While he was in Ensenada, he grew close to a girl

named Marisol Valenzuela-Medrano, the sister of his friends Jose and Luis, and the daughter of Diodoro Valenzuela-Salido apparently nicknamed "Yoyo," the Mexican man he later claimed had raised him, whose son Jose had the same nickname.

Ultimately, Skylar left Mexico and stayed for a while with his grandparents in Orange County, who had no idea that he had gone AWOL. He then returned to Kansas to move in with Lisa and also with his dad. At some point he tried to get back into the marines.

In two letters that wove a telling tapestry of lies and half-truths, he first asked to be readmitted, then requested an honorable discharge. He claimed he'd had some of his best times ever in the marines, fulfilling his dreams by learning, meeting challenges, and finding his destiny.

He wrote that he'd had a "fairly normal" childhood, raised by a father whom he appreciated for teaching him "how to act and how not to act, be respectful, and always take my problems and solve them myself." He said his fiancée, who lived in Mexico, was studying to be a doctor, but they had no children because he wasn't ready for that responsibility. He also claimed to have headed his high-school surf team, competed in international surfing and martial arts competitions, and paid his way to college at the Universidad Autónoma de Baja California in Ensenada. Eventually, he said, he hoped to get a job with the federal Immigration and Naturalization Service.

He contended that he'd left the marines "under extreme duress" to help his father recover from a ladder fall. He regretted his decision every day, he said, describing it as his worst one ever. All he wanted was a second chance to fix it: "I understand that what

I did was not only wrong, but also degrading and [showed] a lack of character."

The U.S. Marine Corps rejected his pleas, noting that he'd already been "counseled concerning poor judgment." Nonetheless, Johnny subsequently spun legends about his brief time in the service, exaggerating it in every way he could. He had a convincing *Force Recon* emblem tattooed on his left shoulder blade, he pulled out photos to prove that he'd shot his way through Afghanistan as a sniper, and he even produced discharge papers that said he was a sergeant and sniper with training in counterintelligence and desert warfare. He also claimed to have an NSA "secured identity" as well as twenty-eight confirmed, and seven unconfirmed, kills in the elite Yankee 2FR Recon unit.

By the time Johnny returned to Southern California and met his bride-to-be, Jennifer Henderson, he was going by the name of Skylar Deleon.

On March 12, 2002, he petitioned to make the change permanent with the Orange County Probate Court. *Current name has been used fraudulently by father with same name,* he wrote. It was reason enough for Pro Tem Judge Richard Frazee to grant the change two months later.

Eventually, Skylar brought his new wife to meet his side of the family. His aunt Colleen hadn't seen Johnny for some time, but she was surprised when he introduced himself as "Skylar." When Colleen or Skylar's grandmother called him "Johnny," Jennifer corrected them, stressing the importance of using his new name as they blended their two families. She didn't want them making the same mistake in front of the Hendersons.

6

Jennifer Lynn Henderson wasn't too shy or too scared to go after what she wanted. A little risk didn't seem to pose a problem, either.

She had come a long way since she was a baby, with big brown eyes, even bigger ears, and fuzz for hair. She'd made it through the typical awkward adolescent years as a somewhat homely and plain-looking girl, an introvert posing for photos with no smile and a blank expression, the chin-length bob and bangs, and the striped T-shirts you'd never see in a fashion magazine.

By the time she'd matured into a high-school senior, her hair had grown longer and blonder, she'd begun tweezing her eyebrows and applying makeup, and she'd also started smiling—with self-confidence, and maybe even a bit of hope for the future. It was then, perhaps, that she started dreaming about the what-ifs and the Prince Charming who would come along and take her away to a better life. College was never really in the picture.

Despite—and perhaps even in rebellion to—her restrictive upbringing in an Evangelical Christian family,

Jennifer didn't seem to be attracted to the straitlaced guys. Sami, her best buddy at Millikan High School, crafted a free-associative run down memory lane for the 1999 yearbook, titled "Remember when," in which Sami detailed a long list of their typical teen activities in Long Beach. These included some of Jennifer's romantic misadventures and would-be suitors, such as the dog lover who trailed obsessively after her at the mall and the coworker whose friends went to her church. Jennifer didn't date all that much, but when she did, she seemed to be drawn to the more troubled souls, including those with gender confusion.

Make him put his lipstick away, Sami wrote. *Why do you have to pick the ones with all the problems?*

Under the homage to the now-attractive Jennifer, the Hendersons printed an angelic picture of their daughter, whom they saw as a cherished gift from above: *God has given you many gifts. Use them, don't take them for granted.*

By the time she was twenty, Jennifer was trolling through the Internet chat rooms for cute boys, against her mother's wishes. In early 2002, she was about to give up on Internet dating when she sent out four last messages, including one to a twenty-two-year-old whose Web name was "bajaskylar." He was the only one to respond.

Skylar, who was working at Ditech Funding at the time, was new to Internet dating, but he wasn't taking it seriously. Whatever happened happened, so he asked Jennifer to send him a photo. He liked what he saw, so they e-mailed back and forth, moved on to phone calls, and decided to meet at a mall for dinner. Jennifer brought a friend for a ride home, in case Skylar turned out to be creepy or, worse, a complete dud. Once Jennifer was comfortable that he was neither, the friend left them alone to get to know each other.

"On that day her life literally got ruined," Michael Molfetta, her attorney, said later.

Jennifer and Skylar soon sought her family's approval at Lana Henderson's sister Terry's house in Cypress, claiming that he was a loan officer. What he didn't tell them, however, was that although he'd been hired as one, the Ditech trainers realized immediately that he lacked the proper job skills and demoted him to an appraiser's assistant, who did clerical work and ran real estate comps for the loan officers.

Lana could tell he was very nervous that day, as was she. But she decided that she liked the young man, who seemed very polite and nice. "He had a motorcycle, and I thought, 'Aah,' and it was one of those fast ones," Lana recalled.

One thing surprised her, though. When Jennifer had talked about the perfect guy, she'd always said she wanted someone tall. So Lana was surprised to see that Skylar stood only five feet nine inches, about the same height as Jennifer's father.

"I thought, 'Oh, my God, he's short,'" she said.

When Lana was Jennifer's age, she'd already married Steve, who was four years her senior. The couple had met in church during high school and got married in March 1981. Jennifer was born five months later in Dallas, Texas, and their son, Michael, came in March 1984.

To her friends, Jennifer was a sweet, loving, caring, and religious homebody, who, when she wasn't at the mall with her girlfriends, was at church, at Bible study club, or on the athletic fields.

Jennifer played shortstop and center field on both the high school and Bobby Sox softball teams. "Her coaches kept pestering her, 'You're going to throw your shoulder out,'" Lana recalled.

Jennifer also managed the boys' varsity and junior varsity football teams, making sure they had their equipment, medical supplies, and plenty of water.

"She was a good girl. She never was in trouble," Lana said. "She was a good student."

The summer after graduation, Jennifer and her father checked out the Career Academy of Beauty on the spur of the moment. She promptly signed up for the full-time beautician's program, which lasted nine months, and Lana became her model.

While Jennifer was working toward her license, she got a job as a cashier and greeter at Polly's Restaurant in Long Beach. As her experience as a stylist grew, she progressed from one salon to the next, until she rented her first chair at Running with Shears.

"She just really liked foo-fooing people and she's good at it. She's really good with color, which is her moneymaker, of course," Lana said. "She's good with people. She's got an excellent personality. She's sweet, she's genuinely sweet, and that's not just her mommy talking."

While Jennifer was first dating Skylar, she shared an apartment with Erin Dworzan, a high-school friend, in a low-end Long Beach neighborhood. During their courtship, Skylar brought Jennifer roses, called her frequently, and took her out to dinner. Erin thought things were moving pretty fast. Jennifer thought so, too, apparently, because she began to pull away, unsure whether she wanted to keep dating him.

Jennifer's friends could see that Skylar would say or do anything to keep her happy. When he sensed her withdrawing, he knew he had to do something.

Skylar borrowed a friend's motorcycle and said he got hit by someone running a red light. He called Jennifer's friend Molly, claiming that he was in intensive care at a hospital six hours north, in Berkeley, and asked her not to tell Jennifer, knowing she would. When Jennifer called, he exaggerated his injuries and claimed he was ready to sign his will. Skylar was nowhere near death, however, the accident did permanently damage his bladder, so he had to wear an adult diaper.

The ploy worked. Jennifer felt sorry for him, moved into an apartment with him to help his recuperation, and their bond grew tighter than ever.

In Erin's view Jennifer was smart, but she could also be naïve, especially when it came to men who told her what she wanted to hear.

"In general, with guys and stuff, like, she tended to trust what they would say, even if maybe they were playing her," Erin said. She didn't always stand up for herself, "because I think she liked to believe that they were treating her the way she wanted them to treat her, even if maybe they weren't."

The couple didn't spend too much time with other people, but by all accounts Skylar and Jennifer seemed to fill each other's needs: she'd found someone to need and pay attention to her, and he'd found someone to nurture him, with a loving family that accepted him. Although neither one showed much overt emotion in front of others, they were obviously very much in love. In private the two were ensconced in their own little bubble world, constantly talking on the phone in gooey-sweet voices and declaring, "I love you."

Asked in 2009 what had made him fall in love with Jennifer, Skylar furrowed his brow and couldn't come up with anything specific. "We just got along really good," he said.

Jennifer's parents had the same impression. "I've never seen them argue," Lana said in 2006. "He's a good kid. They've heard us argue, my husband and I, but they don't do that. And I know that sounds weird, but they don't."

Jennifer's friends thought Skylar seemed childlike, immature, and somewhat irresponsible, but he was always very sweet to Jennifer. The nice personal-injury settlement he'd gotten after the accident didn't hurt, and the next thing everyone knew, the two were engaged.

The small wedding party made its way down a twisty, narrow road and some cement stairs to Little Corona del Mar, a secluded cove cloistered by low cliffs and jagged rocks at the southern tip of Newport Beach, California. There, in front of the bride's parents and two friends, Skylar and Jennifer exchanged vows that Sunday afternoon in September 2002 after dating for just six months.

Dress was barefoot and casual, even though Jennifer's $10,000 engagement ring, a beautiful princess-cut diamond set in platinum, was not. Twenty-three-year-old Skylar wore a white shirt and khaki shorts, and twenty-one-year-old Jennifer had on a white sundress. With the seagulls calling and the tide gently lapping at the shore, the young couple promised to love and cherish each other for the rest of their lives.

It was a quick but intimate marriage ceremony, thrown together after Skylar said he'd been recalled for duty by the marines. As it turned out, though, he didn't have to report, after all. The marines wouldn't take him back after his less-than-honorable discharge, a fact he never mentioned to Jennifer's parents, who were very proud of their son Michael's service with the marines in Iraq.

Steve said Skylar had asked for Jennifer's hand, but Skylar later insisted that it was Steve who pushed them to get married "because we were living together, [saying], 'Blah, blah, blah, this isn't right.'"

Skylar had no criminal record when he met Jennifer. But by way of some twisted synchronicity, the two of them forged a greater malevolent force together than they were apart.

"If there's such a thing as evil in the world, then Skylar and Jennifer are it," Orange County prosecutor Matt Murphy said. "She's an evil, greedy, sociopathic devil. Nothing bad ever happened to that chick in her entire life. Some people are just frigging bad people."

Not so, said Jennifer's attorney, Michael Molfetta, who believed that she would have led an entirely different life without Skylar.

"No question in my mind," he said. "She never meets Skylar Deleon, she never commits a misdemeanor."

So what happened?

"Skylar Deleon happened," Molfetta said. Whether he brought this "evil" out of her or woke it up is unclear, but no one saw any signs of it in her before. She was never cruel to anyone, nor was there any "synergistic combustion" when they got together. "She can just look in the mirror and say, 'I wish I'd never sent that e-mail.'"

Gary Pohlson, Skylar's attorney, and some of Skylar's family argued that it was the other way around—that Jennifer was the one who ignited the flame that fueled his acts of thievery and murder through a contagious case of greed.

"I think Jennifer made him want money and put a lot of pressure on him to get money," Pohlson said. "And he didn't know how to get money, so he came up with these schemes." Skylar never offered that explanation himself, but told Pohlson that "he'd never have done this without Jennifer."

In Pohlson's view, "Jennifer was really turning him into a different person, and the money was a big part of it for her, while it was not for him. At least there was no sign that he'd been that way before."

But according to Skylar's cousin, Michael Lewis, the fires of evil and greed were already burning back in high school, when Skylar asked him to "watch his back" by sitting in a truck outside a drug dealer's apartment in Huntington Beach while Skylar and his jujitsu friends committed a "home invasion." The plan was to force the dealer to the ground, then steal and sell his drugs. Skylar and his buddies got angry at Michael for not stopping a gray-haired woman from entering the apartment and catching them in the act.

Whatever the cause, those criminal urges resurfaced three months after Skylar married Jennifer.

Neither Skylar nor Jennifer made much money, but that didn't stop them from racking up $18,000 in credit card debt. When they asked Steve Henderson to borrow money to pay their bills, he promptly withdrew the sum from his retirement account and handed it over. Quick as it was, the marriage made Skylar family forever, so Steve and Lana were determined to do whatever they could to help the struggling young couple. The Hendersons could see how much their daughter adored Skylar, and they liked him, too. He seemed to be a good, polite kid—a little timid, but so very charming.

But even after borrowing the $18,000 from Jennifer's father, the couple still didn't change their spending habits. So Skylar relied on his own father's teachings to come up with a quick-money scheme.

Skylar was earning $14 an hour at Ditech, where he befriended Ted Wangsangutr, a mortgage loan processor who shared his affection for motorcycles.

Skylar told Ted that his motorcycle and wallet had been stolen, so he couldn't access his bank account to pay for an upcoming vacation. Ted graciously took him to an American Express office, paid for the vacation, then drove Skylar back to his house in Anaheim, where Jennifer picked him up.

Ted also loaned Skylar his motorcycle, which Skylar was riding when he got a speeding ticket for going 120 miles per hour, then crashed a couple weeks later. Skylar claimed he'd been hit by an ExxonMobil executive in a brand-new Mercedes, so that's what Ted told his insurance company. As he learned later, that was not the case.

Skylar made occasional payments to Ted, but Ted decided to forgive the debt after leaving for a new job at E*TRADE. When Ted came back to Ditech, Skylar insisted he wanted to pay the balance, suggesting they meet at Ted's house on Friday, December 6, 2002. But Ted forgot and went on a diving trip.

When Ted returned Saturday, around midnight, he saw he'd missed fourteen calls from Skylar. He also found that someone had locked his front door's dead bolt, which he never used; he didn't even have a key for it. So he went around back, saw that his sliding glass door was broken, and that some of his things inside had been moved or were missing, including an extra set of keys to his Lexus and motorcycle. He called friends and family to see if anyone had come over, but they all said no. He didn't put two and two together until he got the last phone call from Skylar. But when Ted confronted him, Skylar denied any wrongdoing, and still wanted to come by to repay the loan.

The next night Ted came home to find the dead bolt locked again. This time he knew something was up, so he went back to his car and was calling his uncle when he saw several men run out his front door. The men took off in their respective cars, so Ted chased after the one wearing a hood, who turned out to be Skylar. After police arrested him and brought Ted in for questioning, they asked Ted if he'd ever bought or sold drugs. Apparently, Skylar had tried selling the police a story that Ted was a drug dealer who'd been "flaunting" his money, the same tale he would later tell Newport Beach police.

Ted Wangsangutr was not the only victim of Skylar's criminal manipulation. Wade Lohn, who worked at Ditech.com, was pulled into the scam as well. Like Skylar, Lohn was an appraisal assistant, and the two of them went to the gym together. Wade had been in the marines for eight years, so he felt a kinship with Skylar,

who said he wanted to get back into the Special Forces
or find a job in law enforcement.

Skylar told Wade that a guy owed him money, but
he was intimidated by him and his friends. Claiming
he wanted to approach the guy calmly and work it out
in a civil fashion, Skylar asked Wade to act as backup.

"No problem," Wade replied.

Skylar gave him Ted's address, and when Wade
knocked on the door, Skylar opened it up, wearing
dark clothing. Another friend of Skylar's, David
Ramos, was inside, and Skylar said they were just waiting for Ted to return from dance class.

Sure enough, Ted rolled into the driveway, and put
his key in the door. But after encountering the dead
bolt, he went back to his car.

"Why don't you open the door for him?" Wade
asked.

"It's not him," Skylar said, taking a .45-caliber semi-
automatic handgun out of his backpack, in which he
also had walkie-talkies and a pair of the same plastic
flex ties that police use to apprehend suspects.

Wade was shocked. *Holy crap!* he thought. What
kind of mess had he gotten himself into? When he
told Skylar the gun wasn't necessary, Skylar said it was
"just to scare him, in case anything happened."

Then Skylar said, "We're leaving," grabbed his
backpack and ran for the front door.

"Why?" Wade asked, confused.

Wade followed him out, then watched, dumbfounded, as Skylar took off in his car, with Ted in close
pursuit. David Ramos took off in a separate car, so
Wade didn't know what to do other than head home.

When all three were arrested and charged in the
break-in, Jennifer's family was shocked.

"But he admitted what he did," Lana said in 2006.

"He was accountable, and that showed me a lot of character for the boy, and I love him dearly. He's a good boy. He's a good father. He's a kid, still, but he's a good kid."

Even with Skylar's pending burglary trial, Jennifer decided she wanted to have a fancy and more formal wedding, where she could wear a proper white dress in front of her family and friends from church. So Lana, a receptionist for an orthopedic physical therapist, and her husband, Steve, an instrument and electrical technician for BP, agreed to spend $10,000 to hold a catered affair on the *Spirit of Newport*. Skylar really had a thing for boats.

He'd told the Hendersons that he was an orphan with no blood family, and had been adopted by a rich Mexican named Yoyo who lived in Ensenada. So Steve and Lana were surprised when Skylar's mother, Lynette, showed up with his half siblings, Denny and Cassie, to attend his wedding. But because the Hendersons were forgiving Christians, they put their questions aside and let Skylar's relatives stay at their house for the weekend. They were family now, too.

On the morning of March 8, 2003, Skylar went with the Hendersons to the Hope Chapel, where Steve was praying at the altar about his daughter's wedding later that day. As soft music played, Steve's heart filled with joy as Skylar asked to join him, and accepted Jesus Christ as his personal savior. Faith was important to Steve, who had met Lana at church, so he was very pleased to be part of his son-in-law's special moment.

That evening, more than one hundred friends and family members came to the ceremony on the two-level yacht as it cruised around Newport Harbor.

Jennifer was just glowing, wearing her now brown hair up with ringlets that gently kissed the nape of her neck. Her simple ankle-length white gown dipped to show off her ample bust as she posed for photos with Skylar and her beaming parents. Skylar looked dapper in his black tuxedo and white rose bouton-niere as he stood next to Jennifer, who held a bou-quet of white roses and calla lilies to her chest. They seemed so happy and so much in love, even with Skylar's future hanging in the balance.

Jennifer announced she was pregnant so soon af-terward that Lana wondered if their daughter, Haylie Jewelian, had been conceived that very night. But Lana would never dream that the darling little girl would be used as a pawn in her parents' unthinkable crimes.

Two months later, Skylar pleaded guilty to armed burglary, and admitted in his plea agreement with the Los Angeles District Attorney's Office that he had "willfully and unlawfully entered the dwelling house of Ted Wangsangutr with the intent to commit theft" with a firearm. He was sentenced to a year in jail, with seven years left on his sentence if he violated his three years' probation. He promised to stay away from Ted, and was forbidden to own, use, or possess "any type of dangerous or deadly weapon." Skylar's attorney per-suaded the judge to let him into the work-furlough program, which was housed in the Seal Beach Police Department's (SBPD) jail.

According to Orange County prosecutor Matt Murphy, the fact that Skylar had brought a gun and a pair of handcuffs to rob a coworker's house—tools of the trade he would use again in his later crimes—only proved that Skylar had been prepared to kill someone, even then.

It's unclear whether Jennifer knew anything about the burglary, but she stuck by her husband, nonetheless—even after he claimed to be a hermaphrodite who needed a sex change operation to remove a uterus that posed a cancer hazard. As long as he promised to wait until after they had a baby or two, Jennifer said she could handle it. She supported her man, regardless of his sexuality issues.

They were in love.

After Skylar was sentenced to a year in jail, he and Jennifer convinced her parents that he would be killed in the county lockup by his father's enemies in biker gangs and the Mafia from his drug-trafficking days. So Steve agreed to pay $2,100 a month so Skylar could participate in the work-furlough program, which the couple promised, once again, to repay. That way, Skylar was free to leave the jail to work and had to spend only his weekday nights and Sundays at the privately-run thirty-bed facility. Steve figured Skylar would spend his days working at Total Western Inc. (TWI), where he'd helped get Skylar a job as an electrician's apprentice.

But Skylar only worked at TWI for five months that year and three months in 2004. Mostly, he stayed at home with Haylie, while Jennifer worked as a stylist at the hair salon. The Deleons had agreed to pay off their $30,000 debt to Steve in $150 monthly chunks, but they only gave him a hundred dollars here and there, and they didn't seem to curtail their spending all that much. In fact, Skylar somehow found the money to buy Jennifer a diamond-studded wedding band and a "repower" for a Sea Ray boat.

Jennifer liked diamonds as much as the next girl, but what she really wanted was to move her growing family out of the garage and into a nice house. Skylar was like a kid with all his toys—the souped-up truck, the scuba equipment, the motorcycles, and the boats—but his wife was the one thing he prized the most.

"I definitely loved her to the point that there was nothing I wouldn't do for her," he said.

And he would do anything not to lose her.

The newlyweds moved into the Hendersons' garage, which had been divided by drywall so it could still house a car. The other half, which was fifteen by twenty feet, had been converted into a "rumpus room." It had no bathroom, however, so the Deleons had to walk the path to Lana and Steve's unit in the back. The Hendersons rented out the front unit.

Jennifer's friend Meghan Leathem moved into a condo next door, so she and Jennifer often sat on the wall separating their buildings to chat. Skylar would also hang out at Meghan's during the day or in the early evening while Jennifer was at work, helping Meghan hang drapes, move her refrigerator, or make salsa.

Meghan thought it strange that a husband and ex-pectant father like Skylar had only random jobs and no steady work. But then, Skylar was a little odd, with his stories about killing people in the Force Recon. Meghan, who had earned her degree at Cal State Long Beach, listened earnestly and believed his war stories. She also believed his claim that he had medical reasons for needing a sex change operation, so it made sense when he wanted to try on her dresses.

He told her "that he needed to become a woman so he wouldn't get cancer and die," she said. "He said the only way to convince the therapist . . . that he needed to become a woman was if he could dress up and look like one. . . . Even though he told me he didn't want to be [a woman], it is just that he needed to convince them of that so he could have the surgery."

Meghan said Jennifer was very uncomfortable and embarrassed to discuss this topic, acknowledging that "it was very odd and weird, but if it was something for her husband . . . to live, then, absolutely, she would want [him] to go through with that."

Sometimes, Jennifer seemed to hide her feelings, wanting to appear happy and even-keeled, but from time to time, the mounting financial burden under which she and Skylar lived caused her calm veneer to crack.

At one point Skylar suggested they declare bankruptcy, move to Mexico for a fresh start, and come back in ten years after they'd recovered financially. But that idea fell by the wayside when he announced that his military recruiting officer was going to give him a non-FDA approved pill that would stop his uterus from expanding, keep him from dying, and allow him to reenter the service.

Meghan was upset by that prospect, which would take him away from his wife, with the baby coming, but Jennifer seemed happy to hear the news.

"Jenn was excited because it meant a steady income from Skylar and possibly living on base somewhere, where they would have their own home and have a fresh start and a family," Meghan said. "Skylar was excited, too."

But that plan never came to fruition, either.

While Jennifer was pregnant with Haylie, she applied for a job as an independent contractor at Little John's Family Hairstyling in Long Beach. Owner John Chmielinski found it curious that she brought her brother and her parents, and that *they* started asking *him* all kinds of questions. He wondered who was interviewing whom.

"My basic feeling was, this is a good Christian family," with a brother who had just come back from Iraq, he said. "Seemed like she had all her ducks in a row. . . . It worked out really well. You couldn't ask for a better person working there."

Chmielinski gave her a two-week trial run, then hired her once he saw how good she was.

"She was like an artist," he said. "She wasn't run-of-the-mill. She could have done really well. . . . To be a cosmetologist you have to be on the artsy side."

He also found her pleasant and likeable, as did her customers. "She was very cordial to people who came in. She was always here for them."

In fact, her clients liked her so much, they'd bring her gifts. "She had it made," he said. "If she hadn't been with that dumb ass, she would've ended up doing really well for herself."

After Haylie was born in January 2004, Skylar would bring her in and tell Jennifer about his day. Sometimes he'd ask Chmielinski to cut his hair—U.S. Marine Corps style, "high and tight," as if someone put a jar on his head and "scraped off the sides." While he was in the chair, he'd talk about his time in the Special Forces. When Chmielinski asked about the scar on his lip, Skylar said his drill sergeant at boot camp beat him up.

"He was clean-cut, regular. He looked like he was just out of the service . . . very honest and sincere-looking," Chmielinski recalled. "Boy, that was a good cover, wasn't it?"

But at the time he saw the Deleons in a purely positive light: "As a couple they were very young, the American dream. Two kids, him needing work, wanting to go forward with life."

The Deleons continued to struggle financially, and things got even harder that spring, when Jennifer came to work with some news.

"I can't believe I'm pregnant again," she said.

Jennifer had worked until two weeks before Haylie was born, and Chmielinski didn't charge her for rent at the salon during the weeks she took off to recover and take care of the baby. He was surprised and not altogether pleased that she'd decided to have another baby so soon.

7

Skylar started serving his jail term on June 13, 2003, and did everything he could to bend the furlough program rules. Within a month, he had finagled his way into "working" at home. In a letter to the judge he wrote that he'd finished his electrician's job in El Segundo, and his new job site, the THUMS offshore oil island, *would have required me to work too many inconsistent hours, which does not comply with the regulations of the Seal Beach Detention Facility. Due to these changes, my only other employment opportunity would be to work from my home.*

The judge granted his request, ordering him to return to jail every evening at five-thirty, Monday through Saturday.

The fact that Skylar used a gun during the burglary should have kept him out of the program at the jail, which was staffed by a private corporation, Correctional Systems Inc. (CSI), and was overseen by the Seal Beach Police Department. The SBPD didn't accept inmates who had committed violent crimes, but Sergeant Bob Mullins said the judge's order in Skylar's file simply stated that he'd been sentenced for burglary—not *armed* burglary—so it was unclear where in the system the glitch had occurred.

"I couldn't fathom a guess—could have been at court, could have been CSI, could have been something we missed."

The other irony is that Skylar served a little more than half his sentence, which is common for prisoners who exhibit good behavior. In this case, however, he'd committed all kinds of *bad* behavior. It's just that no one knew about it.

Skylar had been there for two months when counterfeiter JP Jarvi showed up in early August. JP was only there until October 14, but he and Skylar had plenty of nights over those nine and a half weeks to forge a moneymaking plan in the four-man cell they shared.

Skylar made things even easier for himself in jail by befriending one of the guards in the privately run facility. At nineteen, Alonso Machain was young and unsophisticated. Born in Mexico, Alonso had been a C-plus high-school student in the largely Latino community of Pico Rivera. With a slight build of five feet nine inches, he weighed only 135 pounds, and was anything but physically threatening.

Alonso was working the graveyard shift for $9.50 an hour, a pittance compared to the unionized state correctional officers, especially when dealing with inmates with AIDS, or who were HIV-positive. But hoping to apply to the Los Angeles County Sheriff's Department someday, he saw the job as a stepping-stone.

Alonso didn't have much to do, up all night by himself, so he enjoyed listening to Skylar's stories. At first, he didn't believe that Skylar had a major role on

Mighty Morphin Power Rangers, but he was convinced after Skylar brought in photos of himself on the set. Skylar also showed off his souped-up truck, saying he'd spent $67,000 to install a special engine, tires, and other accessories.

He told Alonso that he, too, was a Mexican citizen. His dad still lived down there, he said, and was very wealthy. His burglary charge was just a misunderstanding—he and his buddies had broken into a house to play a prank on a friend, dressing up like criminals with weapons, but then the "victim" called the cops and they didn't believe it was a joke, either. He'd been facing more than fifteen years in prison, but after throwing money and good lawyers at the case, he'd gotten his sentence dropped to one year.

As the months went on, Alonso was also taken in by Skylar's promises to help him get a better paying job at Total Western, where Skylar worked as an electrician's assistant. Skylar claimed it was just a hobby for him; his real money—ranging from $100,000 to $4 million a month—came from appraisals he did on his home computer for big lenders such as Washington Mutual, Greenlight, and Ditech, where his mother was a vice president.

Skylar called one day to ask Alonso to retrieve an ATM receipt from his cell, saying he didn't want anyone else to find it. Alonso was duly impressed when he found a receipt for an $80,000 transfer from one account to another, wondering who had $80,000 just sitting in a bank somewhere.

They'd sit and talk at two or three in the morning, or play games on Alonso's PlayStation, while the other prisoners were locked down. Skylar always seemed to know what was going on in the jail, and

Alonso figured he wouldn't do anything to screw up his situation when his parents were paying so much to keep him there.

The furlough inmates were allowed to be out for twelve hours during the day, and had to sign a log-book on their return. Sometimes Skylar would be late getting back—like the time he showed up with a badly sunburned back after flying someplace in his family's private jet—but he would usually call Alonso to warn him in advance. Alonso didn't let any of the other inmates get away with this stuff, but Skylar was different. Besides, Alonso's supervisors never verified the inmates' whereabouts.

On December 27, 2003, for example, Skylar left at 8:00 A.M., called the jail and Alonso's cell phone around 9:00 P.M. to tell him he was running late, but he didn't arrive until ten. Alonso marked it in the log, then just let it go.

Their friendship grew to the point where Alonso regularly took these sort of chances with Skylar, even when they got him a weeklong suspension. One day, Skylar took him to the marina on Alonso's work time to see his yacht—only Skylar said he couldn't open the gate to the mooring area without a key, so he had to point it out from afar.

"It's that one," he said. "See that one?"

Alonso was interested in making more money, and with Skylar's encouragement he was leaning toward the real estate business. Skylar said he had land in Mexico, where he wanted to build a water park, like Raging Waters in San Dimas. He also said he'd purchased a bunch of homes in Signal Hill, which he planned to resell for a profit.

"Get your real estate license," Skylar said. "I'll help you out."

Skylar loved to talk about his investments, even to other inmates. Skylar confided to Alonso that JP Jarvi had persuaded him to help launder some counterfeit money—made with actual money presses so it looked legitimate—by renting Skylar's jet for $50,000, then putting the cash into one of Skylar's Mexican bank accounts. He said he and Jarvi actually had proven the bills were good by changing them for real money at a bank.

The next thing Alonso knew, Jarvi was out of jail and Skylar had another story about him.

"Remember Jarvi?" Skylar asked.

"Yeah, what happened?"

"He's gone."

"What do you mean 'he's gone'?" Alonso asked.

"He's dead," Skylar said with a knowing smile.

Skylar said he'd talked to his dad in Mexico, where Jarvi had pissed off some people. Alonso figured Skylar knew more than he was saying, but he didn't press for details because he didn't really want to know.

8

JP Jarvi was smart and quick witted, but he grew bored easily.

"His IQ was high, but he didn't do all that well in school because he was goofing around," his mother, Betty, recalled.

When JP and his brother, Jeff, were kids, a family with five sons moved in next door on the cul-de-sac. The two older sons got into drugs, and JP fell in with them, too. His parents had no idea at first, and once they did, they didn't know how to handle it. Growing up in Wisconsin, they'd never come into contact with cocaine, let alone heroin.

JP had a problem getting along with his teachers at Katella High School, especially the ones he thought were "overbearing," so he transferred to an accelerated night program during his junior year. Motivated to start his adult life, he came home with a diploma in February 1977, four months before he would have otherwise graduated.

At eighteen, he moved out of his parents' house, even before Jeff, who was two years older, and immediately developed an interest in dentistry equipment.

Because JP was good with his hands—and enjoyed flirting with the dental assistants—he started his own business repairing dental equipment. But that didn't last long.

Next came flying lessons, as aviation became the new bright light that drew his attention. JP gave away his repair business and bought a twin-engine Cessna so he could earn money taxiing businesspeople around. For a time his primary client was a contractor who was building homes in Las Vegas. JP enrolled in pilot-training school for one of the major airlines, but he quit before he even got started.

"He just didn't like the routine of constantly flying," Betty said. "That was not fun."

JP enjoyed being around rich people with fancy cars, boats, planes, and nice clothes, so he moved to Newport Beach. "He liked to run with a rich crowd—that's what got him into trouble," Jeff said.

In his early twenties JP worked with the Indianapolis 500 and was excited to be an announcer for Team America air shows, ferrying around World War II–era planes, and narrating the pilots' daring maneuvers for the crowd.

"He was so proud of that," Betty said as she turned page after page of snapshots of her son posing with his fellow pilots, eight or nine of whom died in flying accidents.

JP ran into some trouble when his alternator went out on a flight home from Florida. The wheels wouldn't come down, so he had to crash-land the plane on its belly. He came out of it okay, but he didn't follow through on the paperwork with the National Transportation Safety Board, so he lost his license. At least that's what he told his family. Around this time, JP started saying things that didn't make any sense to Jeff, who was angry about his brother's irresponsible activities.

JP had hurt his back in a motocross accident at sixteen, and tried to ignore the lingering back pain that came with it. Years later, a doctor for the Blue Angels suggested that he get X-rays, which showed that his back and neck had been broken for some time. Over the next decade, he had several surgeries to insert, remove, and reinsert metal plates in his back and neck, which made him rigid from the waist up.

"I could run my hand over his back and could feel the screws," Betty said, gesturing on her own back. "They were really hurting."

So JP added painkillers to his drug regime.

Before she became a mother, Betty taught elementary school and high-school geometry and science, but even after her sons were born, she remained "a rock hound," collecting turquoise and other gemstones.

Once Jeff started working as a machinist, Betty decided to enroll in silversmithing school with her husband, Norm, who knew more about torches and welding than she did. Before long, Betty and her enterprising family had found a niche in the jewelry industry by manufacturing ring mandrels—the tapered metal rods used to form rings, which, to Betty's surprise, were in high demand. The business expanded, and soon they were selling gem-cutting and jewelers' tools internationally.

JP, who floated in and out of the business, took an interest in refining gold, which can be done with heat or deadly chemicals. JP used table salt, turning the powder by-product into fourteen- and eighteen-karat pure gold. He also earned a fairly decent living by installing equipment in local jewelry shops and by making his own pieces.

The handsome JP was fastidious about his appearance. His love life had its ups and downs, but he usually had at least one girlfriend on the hook. Not one but two women from Canada, one a former Miss Canada and one a TV anchor, sent flowers to his funeral.

"So he got around," Betty said. "He lived more life in his short life than most people do in ten lifetimes."

He never had a relationship that lasted longer than a few months, until his late thirties, when he met a nice woman named Tina. Heroin is remarkably difficult to kick, but he'd apparently managed to stay clean during their two-year relationship.

"She was that type of girl he wanted to hold on to," said Jeanne, Jeff's wife.

JP and Tina had gotten engaged and were living together when he relapsed with cocaine. Although she knew about his drug history, she got scared and moved out. She'd already bought her wedding dress, but she told JP he needed "to clean up his act" before she would move back in with him. His addiction ran so deep, however, that he couldn't do it.

"She made the right call," Betty said. "I was in agreement with her. He needed to deal with that himself and he went from bad to worse."

The breakup hit him hard. Jeanne had been friends with JP since elementary school, even before he'd introduced her to his brother, and she could see that life without Tina had left the typically charming and jovial guy feeling sad and empty.

"He was very funny," she said. "He made me laugh,

but I could tell when he was high. . . . I could tell when he was depressed, too."

Around 2000, JP impulsively married Melanie, a woman ten years his senior, who was just out of a bad marriage. JP waited until after the wedding to introduce her to his parents. Betty believed the marriage was annulled after only a year, but there is no record of this in Orange County. The relationship imploded, Betty said, because Melanie behaved so erratically.

After Melanie, JP started hanging out with a woman in her midthirties who reportedly had been in prison for being an accessory to murder. She was another bad influence. While his parents were traveling, JP took Betty's jewelry from her house and pawned it. Jeff and Jeanne believed the woman, whom Jeff confronted twice in Betty's yard, was using JP so she, too, could steal from his mother. The whole situation caused angry rifts in the family, especially because Norm continued to pay JP a salary long after he'd quit the family business.

"At least he's not homeless," Norm told Jeff.

After Norm died in 2002, JP's "paychecks" stopped, so he had to look for other sources of income. Cocaine was expensive.

"He went downhill real quick," Jeff said.

That December, Betty came over to have lunch with JP to find a slew of Secret Service cars parked outside his condo. Inside, she could see the officers at JP's computer, which they were carrying when they took him away.

He was arrested for possession of digital or electronic images for counterfeiting obligations of the United States, and for possession of counterfeit currency with intent to defraud, a charge that ultimately was dismissed. Essentially, Betty said, JP had been bleaching five-dollar bills to make them look like fifties.

"They weren't very good, or so I hear," she said. "The kitchen sink was a mess. It was all green."

Initially, JP was taken to the Metropolitan Detention Center in Los Angeles. He posted bail in early February 2003, but was back in custody later that month. Then in June, he called his mother and said, "Sell my condo. I'm going to be in here for at least ten years."

Betty started getting the condo in shape to put on the market, installing new carpet, a new sink, stove, and tile. If JP was going to be in prison for the foreseeable future, she thought it best to sell or rent the condo, which they had co-owned since Norm died.

That July, JP was sentenced to only eight months, with four years of supervised probation, and was transferred to the Seal Beach jail in early August to finish his term. The condo sold after he was released in October, but the escrow was too long for JP to wait for the money, so he decided to borrow against it, reportedly for a lucrative investment opportunity.

"A very rich businessman told me he has inside information on an oil deal," he told Betty, "but the man himself can't invest because it's insider [trading]."

He needed $50,000, he said, and because the condo was half his, Betty felt she had no power to stop him.

"He seemed desperate for money," she said, explaining that he'd already made the loan arrangements with a friend from high school, so she agreed to cosign the paperwork because he would have the money once escrow closed, anyway.

Betty believed JP's story because he seemed to meet wealthy people as a matter of course. Right after high school he'd bought himself a fake designer watch, got a job delivering Rolls-Royces, and met a man who invited him to accompany his daughter to a yacht party. Lately he'd been talking about investing in a gold mine in Alaska, where he was thinking of moving. He also mentioned going in on a boat with a partner.

"It never occurred to me it was someone he met in jail," Betty said, noting that he'd never even told her he'd been housed in Seal Beach.

She didn't remember him referring to Skylar Deleon, although she did recall him making an oblique reference to "the movie star." She also remembered him coming over one day covered in sawdust.

"What on earth have you been doing?" she asked.

"I've been working on a boat," he replied.

JP and his mother cosigned a note and deed of trust, borrowing $50,000 against the sale of their condo, on the morning of JP's forty-fifth birthday, December 26, 2003.

After Betty left the escrow office in Newport Beach, JP said he wanted to turn the loan into cash at the Wells Fargo nearby. So they issued him a $50,000 cashier's check.

It sounded easy enough, but because it was the day after Christmas, that particular branch had only $25,000 in cash available. So operations manager Shirley Cantu cashed JP's check, paid him $25,000 in hundred-dollar bills, and issued a cashier's check for the balance, around 10:30 A.M. An hour later, JP cashed that check at the Laguna Beach branch, and handed the $50,000 in cash over to Skylar.

Twice that night, and once the next morning, JP made three short calls to the Detection and Treatment Resources hotline for alcohol and drug rehabilitation services. Its website offers a warning against "heroin rapid detox," a more formal name for "going cold turkey," and lists services for short- and long-term rehab. His family knew nothing of the calls, but it's possible that JP had been inspired to get clean with the promised proceeds of Skylar's moneymaking venture.

Skylar's cousin, Michael Lewis, was coming to town to visit relatives for the holidays, so he and Skylar made plans to hang out. Skylar told Michael that his Sea Ray, *Dr. Crunch,* was in the shop, so they couldn't go scuba diving. Instead, they decided to go surfing and spearfishing in San Miguel, a beach town just north of Ensenada, which they'd visited half a dozen times before. Skylar had some friends there.

On December 26, Skylar picked up his cousin in his white Ford Expedition and they went to Mo Beck's boatyard, where Skylar pulled $17,000, in hundred-dollar bills, out of a white business envelope to pay for the repairs. Michael had never seen Skylar with so much cash before, but he didn't think much of it because Skylar said he'd started a couple of businesses in which people wanted to invest, and he'd also been busy working as an electrician.

Later that afternoon, Skylar said he needed to go to Robbins Brothers in Fullerton. "I got to stop and pay Jennifer's ring off," he told Michael, who watched Skylar pull out another handful of hundreds to pay for the $1,995 platinum wedding band, which was set with five diamonds in a row, weighing a half-carat in total, and matched Jennifer's engagement ring. Skylar told the salesman he could pay for it in cash because of the work he did.

"[He] kind of made it sound like he was maybe military of some type, maybe Special Forces, or maybe something of even a bounty hunter," said salesman Ronald Jackson.

From there, Skylar took his cousin to a car repair shop to explore souping up his F250 truck engine, then dropped him off at Michael's mother's house. They planned to meet at Skylar's first thing the next morning, right after he left jail for "work." Skylar said a friend would be joining them.

Before he met up with Skylar that morning, JP Jarvi went over to his mother's, around nine o'clock, to pick up his birthday gift. He and his brother hadn't talked much in years, but Jeff grudgingly wished him a happy birthday in Betty's front yard.

Inside, Betty gave JP four 100-dollar bills and two $50s. He seemed excited, saying he was going to Mexico with a friend.

"He went out the front door and I walked out to his van and stuck my head through the window," she said. "I said good-bye and take care and happy birthday, and that . . . was the last time I saw him."

When Skylar met up with his cousin at the house, a little after 8:00 A.M., he handed Michael the keys to his truck, saying it was acting up, and asked if Michael would drive it to determine the problem. Michael agreed and transferred his wet suit into the truck, while Skylar piled several surfboards into the Expedition. Skylar gave Michael $120 to cover gas, tolls, and food, and loaned him a cell phone so they could talk without Michael having to pay for international calls on his Arizona-based phone.

After stopping for a breakfast burrito, they headed over to a boatyard, where they waited for Skylar's friend to arrive. JP showed up in a red van, got into Skylar's Expedition, and they were on their way.

They stopped again to get some food at an ampm in Doheny State Beach, then headed down to the border, stopping one more time in San Ysidro to top off their gas tanks. As they were driving past Rosarito Beach, about twenty minutes south of the border, Michael started getting calls from Skylar.

At first, it seemed like Skylar just wanted to shoot the breeze, but then his voice changed and got unusually serious. First, he said he was going to drop off JP with some friends in Mexico for a few days, but ten minutes later, Skylar called again to say that the friends were going to pick up JP. Then it was something else JP was going to do. Michael couldn't put his finger on it, but something didn't seem right.

They stopped at a surf spot to check out the waves, but rather than grab the boards and hit the water, Skylar said he had to deposit some money in the bank. This change of plans wasn't all that unusual. Skylar and his father often pretended to want to spend time with you when they actually had something else in mind, then disappeared for an hour or two.

So Michael and Skylar headed into downtown Ensenada and parked near the Banamex bank, where Skylar went off on his own for about fifteen minutes.

Michael and JP stayed in their respective cars, until JP came over to shoot the bull. JP said he'd had back surgery some years ago, and he was excited that Skylar was going to teach him how to surf. He also mentioned that they were going to be staying at Skylar's house.

"Huh," Michael said, adding that would be nice to see. He had no idea that Skylar had a house in Mexico. While they were down there, JP said, they'd go to some bars; he even offered to pay for a hooker for Skylar and his cousin.

When Skylar returned, he and JP got back into the Expedition. Then, leaving the motor running, he came back over to tell Michael that JP had been in jail with him for money laundering, and *he* was the reason Skylar had gotten busted in the first place. And *now*, Skylar said disdainfully, JP was talking about getting them underage prostitutes.

"Follow me and watch my back," Skylar said.

Skylar led Michael north and inland along the coastal toll road to a back way out of Ensenada for about fifteen minutes, then he turned around, went back to a Y in the road, and took the other fork. Along the way Skylar called Michael again, talking about the house they were taking JP to.

Michael was used to Skylar calling the shots and wanting to do things his way. But Michael was hungry, so he asked several times when they could stop to eat.

"In a little bit," Skylar kept saying.

When Michael asked what house he was talking about, and where they were going, Skylar said, "Don't worry about it. Just follow me." They were going to be dropping JP off somewhere soon. "Not that much farther."

They came to a military checkpoint, where the guards waved Skylar ahead, leaving Michael stopped behind another car. By the time Michael caught up, Skylar had parked at the side of the road in a soft dirt turnout. They were in the middle of nowhere, a deserted rural area surrounded by hills.

Michael turned his truck around, stopped on the other side, and looked over his shoulder. He watched his cousin help JP out of the passenger side, leaving the door open as he led JP away from the road, with one hand on JP's head and one on his back. JP had a T-shirt or sweatshirt wrapped around his face so he couldn't see where he was going.

Michael wondered if JP had to go to the bathroom, but he was getting a bad feeling about this. A few weeks earlier, Skylar had said something about how easy it would be for someone to disappear in Mexico. Was this what he had in mind for JP? If that was the case, Michael thought, he never would have gone down there with him.

JP was in no way restrained. In fact, he looked totally trusting of Skylar, "almost like a father escorting a kid into a room to show him a big surprise at Christmastime," Michael testified later.

As Michael watched them head down a gully, he could see a black object poking four to six inches out of Skylar's back pocket, which he later realized must have been a knife handle. He figured Skylar had seen him, yet Skylar didn't try to communicate with him. Was this a drug deal? He didn't see any other cars, but were other people waiting down below?

"I didn't know what he [Skylar] was going to do," Michael said. "Rob the guy, leave him on the side of the road, you know, beat the crud out of him, or what.

I had no idea, so I just didn't want to be a part of any of that."

Michael knew he needed to get out of there, and fast. Right before he drove off, Michael saw a white vehicle that looked like it might be stopping, but he didn't wait to find out. Skylar had already said they should meet up in San Miguel if anything happened, so that's where he headed. He'd just passed the checkpoint when Skylar called. He was right behind Michael.

"What's going on?" Skylar asked. "Why'd you leave?"

"I don't know what you're doing," Michael said.

Skylar hung up, and as he drove past Michael, he made a gesture like he was snapping someone's neck, an act with which he'd always had a fascination. After watching the movie *The Long Kiss Goodnight,* or sometimes just out of the blue, he'd remark how easy it would be to do. Michael feared that his cousin finally had succeeded.

When they stopped in San Miguel, JP wasn't in the truck, and Skylar had changed out of his long-sleeved surfer shirt into a short-sleeved one. Michael figured the other shirt was still with JP.

"Let's go down to Puerto Nuevo to have lobster," Skylar suggested, and took off for the restaurant.

They parked nearby and walked over, but retreated once they saw the long line. There was sure to be a wait at the border as well, and Skylar was worried he wouldn't make it back to jail in time.

"Hey, let me drive the truck," Skylar said.

"No," Michael said. He didn't know what had just happened and he didn't want to.

Skylar somehow managed to get ahead of him by cutting the lines of cars at the border. Michael didn't catch up to him until northern San Diego County, where they decided to grab a bite at T.G.I. Friday's in Carlsbad. But there was a long line there, too, so they arranged to meet at California Pizza Kitchen in Long Beach.

Finally sitting down to dinner, Skylar said something that would always stick with Michael.

"Welcome to our side," Skylar said, smirking and giggling, which only made the moment more surreal for Michael, who had recently become a good Christian. "You're working for the Devil now."

Later, Michael would tell detectives he knew then that Skylar had killed JP, but on the witness stand he downplayed his own culpability.

"It was kind of the rubbing your nose into something," he testified. "Like, you know, he knows you did something wrong. That he knows even if you did want to say something, you couldn't, because you would be included in that. It was a 'you are suckered into this' kind of smirk."

As they parted ways, Skylar headed back to jail for the night, and Michael drove to Skylar's house to drop off his truck.

"Did you have a good time?" Jennifer asked as Michael handed her the keys.

"Yeah, right, sure," he said.

Skylar became an enemy at that point. Scared his own cousin would hurt him or his family, Michael vowed to avoid Skylar in the future.

When Skylar called in October 2004 to invite him on a diving trip, where "somebody wasn't going to come back up," Michael declined.

"I am not hanging out with you one-on-one anymore," Michael told him. "If you want to hang out, we will hang out with family."

* * *

Back at the jail, Alonso Machain let Skylar use the computer, which he used to buy a $923 anal-sex machine from a gay website—kentwistedmind—with his credit card.

The device, which could be set at different speeds, consisted of a rectangular box that housed piston-driven machinery that drove a dildo attached to a long metal pipe, all of which was mounted on a stand. The pipe with the dildo moved forward and backward in a thrusting motion that simulated sex.

Betty Jarvi told the Mexican detectives who came to talk to her a couple days later that she recognized the surgical scars in the photos of JP's body, but apparently, that wasn't enough. They needed two people to identify him in person.

"Bring cash," the detectives advised her. "Bring a lot of cash."

That comment spooked her, so it took two weeks before she was emotionally ready to drive down to Ensenada to collect her son's remains.

Jeff, who was skeptical that JP was really dead and was scared this was a trap, didn't want to go with her. He hadn't trusted his brother for as long as he could remember, and the police had no idea who did this or why it happened. So Jeff's father-in-law, Lou Molina, the retired police lieutenant, agreed to go with Betty. They left Anaheim at 9:00 A.M. and arrived at the mortuary around noon.

"They had frozen JP, turned his lips all black," Betty recalled.

Even though JP's neck was wrapped in a bandage, she could still see the knife wound. The autopsy showed that he'd been skillfully cut from front to back, left to right, and slightly downward, the markings of a trained right-handed killer.

From there, she and Molina went on a nightmarish roundabout from one place to the next, signing legal documents until it grew dark. Somewhere along the way, someone handed her the money that was left in JP's wallet—the $500 she'd given him for his birthday.

"Skylar missed the boat on that one," said Betty, who has typically used humor to cope with difficult situations.

After visiting the crime scene and stopping for lobster at Puerto Nuevo, they made it back to Anaheim around midnight. Molina had to do grand jury service the next morning, but Betty's work in Mexico wasn't done. After grabbing two hours of sleep, she got up at 3:00 A.M. and drove all the way back to Ensenada.

She was still waiting outside the mortuary in her car that evening when she fell asleep with the lights on, killing the battery. She finally collected JP's ashes around 7:00 P.M., and after getting a jump, she started the drive home. Exhausted, she went off the road and got a flat tire in a patch of evil weeds, then drove for ten miles on the rim, lost in an unlit industrial area, before she could get her tire changed at a gas station. After another wrong turn, she crossed the border at Tecate, nearly forty miles east of where she'd intended, and arrived home well after midnight.

Betty put JP's ashes in the storage area out back, then hit the pillow with a thud.

* * *

On January 28, 2004, Skylar called his cousin and told him the police were asking questions about Jarvi.

"Why?" Michael asked. "Why are you being questioned?"

"His van was at my house. That's why," Skylar said. "They had a LoJack on his van or something."

Later that night, Jennifer Deleon left Michael a message on his voice mail at work.

"Mike, you need to get ahold of me," she said. "We need to talk about the trip to Mexico when we got the ice cream."

When he called her back, she said, "The police are looking at your cousin for someone that got killed."

Jennifer explained that they needed to tell police that she and Michael, not he and Skylar, had gone to Tijuana together that day so she could go shopping and satisfy her craving for banana ice cream.

"That ice cream in Mexico sure was good," she said.

Skylar called again in a couple weeks, saying that he was a suspect in Jarvi's murder, and two weeks after that, he said he'd been cleared.

"Then at the end, he just said that bad things could happen if anyone found out that we were down there—or if he was down there," Michael said. "I took it personally as a threat."

But even Michael would be surprised at how far his cousin would go to keep Michael quiet.

Once Skylar was released from jail on January 12, 2004, he requested that he be allowed to travel and work outside the United States. The court granted the allowance, and in April the court also allowed him to transfer his probation case from Orange County, where he'd committed the burglary, to Los Angeles County, where he lived.

Tired of working for slave wages, Alonso quit his guard job at the jail and let Skylar get him a better gig at TWI. This job paid Alonso a whopping $1,000 a week, but he was also working twelve-hour days, seven days a week. After two months of this, he decided the money wasn't worth it, so he returned to his old security job at Lakewood Mall, which paid even less than the jail.

But things weren't all bad. Skylar started calling more often, inviting Alonso to go fishing near Catalina or San Clemente Island in his Sea Ray, which was equipped with wet suits, scuba tanks, weight belts, GPS equipment, and a depth gauge. They caught a bunch of fish on one trip, but lost all but two to the waves that washed them overboard on the way back. Skylar really seemed to know his way around the ocean, where to find the best fishing spots, and where the water got really deep.

He invited Alonso over to his house once, explaining that he and his wife were living in the back while it was being remodeled. It was a duplex, clearly not the house of a millionaire, but that didn't quite sink in for Alonso, who had no idea he was being groomed for a much bigger job.

Alonso worked about six months at the mall before he started yearning for a bigger paycheck once again, so Skylar got him another job at TWI. Alonso wasn't sure he wanted to work around the clock again, but he agreed, nonetheless, and joined Skylar in Wilmington, at the BP plant in October. Skylar pointed out Jennifer's father, but told him not to say anything, because Steve was a big shot in charge of their contract.

Meanwhile, Skylar was talking about buying another boat, circling the ones he liked in magazines—ranging from $400,000 into the millions—and showing them to Alonso. The *Well Deserved* was at the lower end, which Skylar thought was "pretty cheap." If he didn't like it, he said, he could sell it.

But Alonso soon lost this job, too. When he called in October 14 to spend the day with his family, he didn't realize that two other workers had just been laid off, and his supervisor didn't appreciate his attitude. So Alonso was right back in the hole again, needing money to pay his bills and looking to his wealthy buddy for a new opportunity. And this time Skylar came through with a doozy.

PART II

THE BIG PAYOFF

9

After Jennifer, the ocean was Skylar's big love. Because he liked riding the waves, fishing, and boating so much, Jennifer teased him about being a fish. In early 2004, Skylar decided to explore the depths of the sea and signed up for diving classes with Adam Rohrig at Pacific Sporting Goods Scuba Center in Long Beach.

Adam had entered the navy, aiming to become a SEAL, but he never made it past the grueling morning-exercise regimen under the Special Forces guys, so he decided to finish college, instead. On top of teaching diving and taking classes at Cal State Long Beach, Adam also worked as a bartender.

Skylar took to diving immediately. Set on becoming an instructor, he bought an $1,800 training package and became Adam's assistant, known as a dive master. Steve Henderson helped pay for Skylar's scuba equipment as a birthday gift, hoping he would use it to earn money working at Club Med or in the boat-chartering business he'd been talking about launching.

Skylar soon became more involved with the shop and enjoyed helping Adam with the other students.

"He seemed relatively competent in the water and comfortable with himself," Adam said.

He often went above and beyond his dive master duties, pushing for more responsibility and asking all kinds of questions. "Most dive masters, you have to kick them out of bed to get them to come with you, because it is a pretty early thing, and he would show up, like the day before. He would be there the day after," Adam recalled.

However, Skylar's enthusiasm, which Adam described as "puppy dog syndrome," was so over-the-top, it became annoying. Adam never programmed Skylar's number into his cell phone, but he knew it by heart because Skylar called so often. Adam tried to back him off a bit without being mean.

"It's not like you really want to smack someone in the face who is helping you for free and say, 'No, you're not ready to do that.' You kind of want to feather it a little bit," he said.

The two of them had a few hours to talk several times a week while Skylar was helping with the fifty-hour open-water course, much of which Skylar spent trying to impress him somehow. Skylar told their coworkers that he'd been on a TV show, and that his grandfather had owned and sold Ditech. He also bragged to Adam that he'd been a sniper in the marines' elite forces in Afghanistan and showed off his discharge papers reflecting the thirty-five kills, a logbook of six hundred dive hours, and his Special Forces tattoo. Adam found all of this boasting inconsistent with his experience with the strong, silent types he'd trained under.

"You can talk your mouth off and look at them and try to get them to talk to you in a conversation, and they won't. They probably won't even look at you.

They have a definite air of confidence, and I didn't get that from him."

Skylar not only mentioned that he'd been in a minimum-security jail, he also delved into some extremely bizarre personal matters. He confessed, for example, that he was a hermaphrodite and produced a picture of a man's genital area after a sex change operation, claiming it was his post-op photo. Adam had spent enough time changing swim trunks with him to know that wasn't true. Besides, the caption read *Figure 2*, just like in a textbook.

"He was also married and had a kid, so that . . . really doesn't jibe with being a hermaphrodite," Adam said.

One day Skylar pulled up in a jacked-up truck with a "crazy-ass suspension." The next time he came by in a Dodge Viper with a nerdy-looking guy, like two kids on a joyride.

Skylar showed Adam his Sea Ray, saying he'd had the engine rebuilt and installed a new navigational system, but Adam said it was too small for Skylar's would-be charter and diving business.

"We can't use this boat, it's not appropriate," Adam told him, wondering why Skylar had installed such sophisticated equipment when it clearly exceeded the boat's abilities.

Later, Skylar showed him a photo of the Hatteras, which looked about thirty years old. Given its age, Adam thought Skylar's plans to repower the boat were naïve.

"I figured maybe he didn't know any better," he said.

Then, in October, Skylar started asking Adam some strange questions. They were standing outside the dive shop when Skylar casually asked if Adam would be interested in earning a whole lot of money for driving a boat and helping him "make someone disappear."

"You are insane," Adam replied, amazed that Skylar would pose such a question no differently than "What are you doing after work?" But he shrugged it off, thinking Skylar was just trying to sound important. By this point he was well acquainted with Skylar's relish for embellishment, and he didn't want Skylar to think he was at all impressed.

Skylar brought up the idea again a few days later. "Remember that thing we were talking about? You think you want to do that?"

"No, I don't want to do that," Adam said. But curious, he pressed for a few details. "How do you think that you are just going to get away with getting rid of two people?"

"We take him deep, and we put him deep," Skylar replied. "No body, no crime."

"You're crazy," Adam said. "I don't think it works that way."

But Skylar wouldn't drop it. "How much weight would it take to sink someone who was wearing a BC?" he asked, referring to a buoyancy compensator, an inflatable lifesaving vest that keeps divers afloat between dives, and can also be used to offset the added weight of scuba gear.

"The same amount of weight it would take to sink you if you were diving," Adam retorted, wondering why Skylar would put a flotation device on someone he wanted to sink.

Still thinking Skylar was talking smack, Adam tried to poke holes in the idea and prove it was ludicrous. But Skylar said he wouldn't give up any more details if Adam wasn't "in."

"Well, I don't want to know any more, then," Adam replied.

A few days later, Skylar gave Adam one last chance. "Are you sure you don't want to help?" he asked.

Adam said his answer was still no, and when Skylar asked if he would take a hit from his new stun gun for $100, he refused that offer as well.

In November, Adam told Skylar he wanted to get a notary license so he could earn some more money, move out of his mother's house, and live on his own.

"Can you notarize something?" Skylar asked.

"I can't notarize, I'm not a notary," Adam said.

"I have some documents I need notarized, and I'd be willing to pay a lot of money."

"How much?"

Skylar said he would pay $4,000 or $5,000 for a "blank notary," which Adam took to mean a blank piece of paper notarized fraudulently. Skylar explained that he had some money in Mexico that he needed to launder, or couldn't declare. Adam realized this was illegal, but he didn't associate this apparently "victimless crime" with the boat deal Skylar had mentioned. Despite all of Skylar's talk, Adam didn't think Skylar seemed capable of doing anything like what he'd described.

"Well, I know some notaries I can ask," Adam replied, thinking this would be some easy money for his best friend, Kathleen Harris, whom he'd known for nearly a decade.

But he never imagined what he was getting them both into.

10

At the same time Skylar was grooming Alonso Machain and Adam Rohrig to join in his scheme, he was also trying to recruit a coworker at Total Western.

One day Skylar was bragging to Myron Gardner, supervisor of the electricians' group, that he'd been in jail and was out on probation.

"That's no big deal," said Myron, who said he'd gone straight after being sent to the California Youth Authority (CYA) as a teenager, and later serving time for manslaughter, robbery, and drug possession. He didn't like to talk about the domestic violence, although he'd gotten in trouble for that, too. Myron was trying to live right now that he had a fiancée and two children, Krystle and Myron Junior.

"I'd let him know how my life had benefited and been redeemed," Myron recalled later.

Skylar also boasted about his moneymaking and money-laundering activities, running cocaine and marijuana down to Mexico, where he had a house, and "washing" $300,000 or $400,000 at a time. He even brought his boat to work, a twenty- or thirty-footer, pulled behind his Ford truck.

Skylar approached Myron several times about helping him with one of his drug deals, offering him a couple thousand dollars to watch his back, saying he didn't trust the people in Mexico. Myron declined his offers several times, never quite sure whether Skylar was telling the truth.

When a couple police officers came to talk to Skylar in early 2004, Myron told him he should handle that sort of thing *after* work, not at the job site. Skylar said it was something to do with a guy who'd gone missing.

"They won't find the guy," Skylar told him. "That's what happens when guys try to rip me off. I take care of it."

Knowing Skylar was one to exaggerate, Myron thought nothing of his comment.

In October 2004, Skylar tried again to recruit Myron, this time for a major deal involving a boat, but Myron still wasn't interested. Skylar was so persistent, though, that Myron agreed to try to help him find someone else.

"If I run across someone, I'll let you know," he told Skylar.

Based on their earlier conversations, Myron assumed this deal also involved drugs in Mexico, at least that's what he later told police and testified in court. He also claimed that he turned down Skylar's offer to pay for Myron's recruiting help.

"Basically, I just wanted to get him out of my hair," he said.

After agreeing to help find someone to watch Skylar's back, Myron told police, he went down to Whistler Liquor in Long Beach. A guy he knew as "C-Dog" had asked him for some money a couple nights earlier, and Myron figured he'd find him hanging around the neighborhood.

So Myron approached C-Dog, said he knew a guy who would pay good money for a job in Mexico, and arranged a November 14 meeting with Skylar at the liquor store. C-Dog backed out, but he told his friend Orlando Clement about it.

"Man, I'll do it," Orlando told Myron. "Why didn't you tell me?"

Myron called Skylar to set up the meeting with Orlando, then called again later to check in. "Did you meet with the guy?"

"Yeah. In fact, the guy's here with me now," Skylar said. "I'm going to take him and buy him some clothes. I want him to look presentable."

Everything was supposedly all set until Skylar called the next morning to say that Orlando never showed up. Myron had just given Skylar the bad news that Orlando had changed his mind, when "Crazy John" Kennedy, known as "CJ," called, following up on a tip from Orlando.

"Why didn't you tell me this guy was looking for somebody to go to Mexico to make some money?" CJ asked.

Myron said he wasn't sure if Skylar had already left, but CJ could try to reach him.

"I don't know the guy," CJ said. "Why do I call him? You're the one that know him. He work for you. You call him and let me know."

So Myron arranged a meeting, then fielded calls from them both, asking how well Myron knew the other one. He purposely never learned any more details of what the deal would entail.

Myron called Skylar once more in the early afternoon of November 15 to make sure it had gone through this time. "Did you meet up with Kennedy?" he asked.

"Yeah," Skylar said. "We're together right now. He said he wants to go home and change clothes."

As they were driving through the Newport Harbor area to meet Tom Hawks, a friend of CJ's called from Inglewood. Although CJ would later claim he'd never set foot in Newport, the signal for his phone pinged off a cell tower on a bank building on Westcliff Drive, right near the *Well Deserved* mooring, at 1:50 P.M.

CJ called Myron when he got home that night, none too pleased. It was 1:30 A.M. and Myron could hear the anger in CJ's voice.

"Man, that guy lied," CJ said.

"What are you talking about?"

"I don't want to talk about it, man, but that guy lied. Man, he ain't no good. We didn't go to Mexico."

"You didn't go to Mexico?"

"No, we didn't go to no Mexico, man. I told him to call you and let you know when he got my money," CJ said.

CJ didn't want to go into details on the phone, so Myron said they should talk in the morning. Then he called Skylar.

"Skylar, what happened, man?"

"Everything's cool," Skylar replied calmly. "No problem."

"No, man," Myron said. "You got the guy pissed off. He don't want to talk to you. He's the one that asked me to tell you to give him his money."

"I told the guy, don't worry about it. I'm going to take care of him."

"What happened to going to Mexico?"

"We had a little change in plans, but everything's cool," Skylar said.

The next morning, Skylar called Myron again. "Everything is going to be all right. I'll take care of him," he said, explaining that he had to do some paperwork to get the boat cleared and free up some money before he could pay CJ.

Besides, Skylar said, "He got a couple thousand dollars out of the deal. That will hold him for right now."

When CJ showed up in front of Myron's house a couple days later, Myron tried to reassure him. "He's going to pay you, man," he said.

But CJ was still furious. He blamed Myron for getting him into an ugly mess, and he wanted to get paid for it.

"What happened, man?" Myron asked again.

They went out to sea on some boat, CJ said, and "there was a couple peoples on that boat, too, besides just me and him."

"What you mean?"

A man and a woman, he said. "We took care of them, man. We got rid of them." CJ's voice was getting angrier and more threatening as he tried to get the message across that this was some *serious* business. "That guy still owes me a lot of money. I want my money. Man, you introduced me to this guy. You're going to call him and get my money, or somebody will be in trouble."

Myron was worried. The Crips were powerful. Not so much the original gangsters (OGs), who were his age, but the younger ones, who were just coming up, needed to pay their dues and had something to prove. They looked up to CJ, who had a reputation for being dangerous. Myron was well aware that despite CJ's recent years studying to be a minister, he was still known as a shot caller around the neighborhood. And if CJ didn't get his money, Myron's life was in danger.

But things would get worse before they got better.

11

Even though Skylar was able to land the occasional job, Jennifer's friend Meghan Leathem could see that the Deleons never had enough money to catch up. With Haylie to take care of, and a baby on the way, Jennifer seemed to grow increasingly down, spending less time on her appearance. Her face showed more signs of stress than ever before.

Meghan tried to help out the couple financially, and ease their anxiety, so Skylar could have the sex change surgery, but Jennifer didn't want her charity.

"I would buy, like, Haylie, you know, toys, and Jenn a Christmas present, and stuff like that. I could tell that she felt uncomfortable accepting it," Meghan said of the maternity sweat suit she'd bought Jennifer.

But in early November 2004, everything seemed to turn around for the Deleons. It seemed that Skylar and Jennifer were finally going to achieve their dream.

As one of Jennifer's regular clients, realtor Terry Rogers was well aware that her stylist didn't make much, so she was surprised when Jennifer called on

November 2, saying she and Skylar were interested in buying a waterfront home, selling for $1 million to $2 million, with a docking area at least fifty-five feet long—big enough for two boats. Jennifer said they were interested in the Huntington Harbor area, Belmont Shores, or Naples, an exclusive community of canals like its Italian namesake, where residents docked their yachts behind their harbor-view homes.

The couple seemed to be in a hurry, because they showed up later that day. Jennifer said they were coming into a new boat and some money from Skylar's family in Mexico. Asked if she knew any potential buyers for one of their two boats, Rogers gave them a contact.

As the two women talked, Skylar looked at properties on the computer, like a kid in a candy store. "Skylar was really excited. He just wanted to look at homes right away," Rogers said.

Initially, Jennifer did most of the talking, but Skylar soon jumped in, directing his comments at Jennifer, who then spoke to Rogers for both of them.

Rogers asked them to fill out some financial forms, on which Jennifer listed each of their gross annual salaries as $48,000. She said they could make a down payment of $200,000, and wanted to keep their house payments to $3,000 to $5,000 a month. Her loan pre-qualification application set the time frame at six to twelve months.

After looking over the paperwork, Rogers could tell they didn't have enough money to pay taxes on a $1 million house, let alone $2 million, so she suggested they buy investment property, instead.

"I had advised her that it might not be the wisest to make a large purchase," Rogers testified later.

Jennifer said she'd talk to her accountant, then get back in touch.

"Jenn told me it may go or it may not go," Rogers said. "And she kept saying she never wanted to waste my time. They were working on the deal, and if it did [go], then she would be able to do this deal."

That same morning Jennifer left a message for her tax accountants, Jo Ann and Dave Zahn, who also were investment consultants.

Urgent. Need to come in and talk to you, the secretary wrote in the message. *Please give her a call.*

Skylar and Jennifer came right over to meet with them.

"So how can we help?" Dave Zahn asked.

"We are coming into a large amount of money and a boat," Jennifer said, adding that she and Skylar wanted to purchase a new house.

The Zahns had been working with Jennifer since 2000, so they knew her annual salary had been growing along with her hair business, but only averaged around $21,000. They also knew that Skylar's income had been intermittent and was unreliable at best.

"Where is this money coming from?" Dave asked.

"I moved a motorcycle full of dope," Skylar said, explaining that the money and yacht were payment for committing a crime and going to jail for a man who was now fleeing the country and leaving Skylar all his assets. The Deleons' plan was to sell the man's yacht and buy a smaller boat.

Dave Zahn was surprised and uncomfortable. As he delved deeper, Skylar's story continued to build, and the Zahns' mutual discomfort escalated.

Skylar seemed more interested in buying a very

large, expensive house, while Jennifer seemed more concerned about getting one that would be best for their family. She also wanted to handle the income properly for tax purposes. Unlike some other clients, she'd always been reliable and conscientious.

But once Jo Ann heard where the money was coming from, she pulled back and chatted with Jennifer about Haylie, her parents, and her upcoming due date, while Dave tried to quickly end the conversation with Skylar. Nonetheless, Jennifer called them again on November 22, and December 3, 14, and 16.

12

"I wish I had my notary [license], because this guy wants to pay me four thousand dollars," Adam Rohrig said, explaining Skylar's offer to his friend Kathleen Harris.

"I would do that," said Kathleen, who had been a notary for four years.

Adam said he'd set it up, and called Skylar with the news. "I can trust her, she's my friend," he said.

"When can she do it?" Skylar asked.

Adam said he'd get back to him with a time, which he immediately regretted because it turned into an enormous hassle of phone tag. Skylar was calling him even more frequently than usual, so Adam finally gave him Kathleen's phone number.

Jennifer called Kathleen around three o'clock that afternoon.

"I'm a friend of Adam's and he stated that you could notarize something for us," Jennifer said.

"Yes, that's fine," Kathleen said. "When would you like me to do it?"

"As soon as possible," Jennifer said, so they agreed Kathleen would come to their hotel room in forty-five minutes.

When she arrived, the door was ajar, so she knocked and began talking to the baby girl crawling just inside. Kathleen saw Skylar standing by the door, and Jennifer by the back window.

"Those are them," Skylar said, pointing at a semi-circle of documents laid out on the bed.

As Kathleen sat down at the table, Skylar closed the two laptops that were open next to her. She said she only needed the pages she was going to notarize, so Skylar set four sheets in front of her. She noticed they were already signed and marked with the signers' thumbprints, but she didn't look all that closely at the names. The prints were actually supposed to go in her notary book—not on the documents themselves—but she decided not to say anything. In fact, knowing this was a shady deal, she never even pulled the book out of her purse to record it.

Skylar told Kathleen to backdate the paperwork, then Jennifer blurted out the exact date: "November fifteenth," she said.

After Kathleen affixed her stamp and seal, Skylar put an envelope of cash between them, which Kathleen put into her bag.

"Wow, it must be awful to be pregnant and living in a hotel room," she said, trying to make casual conversation.

Jennifer replied that a fish tank had caught fire in their house, and they were staying at the hotel during the remodeling, so Kathleen figured the documents she'd just notarized were related to the insurance.

As she walked toward the door, Jennifer said,

"When all this goes through, we will compensate you more."

Kathleen called Adam to meet her at Poor Richard's in Long Beach to split the proceeds, as agreed, and she was already drinking at the bar when he arrived. As soon as the bartender walked away to fetch Adam's vodka tonic, Kathleen handed Adam a stack of hundred-dollar bills, which he began to count. She usually only charged $50 for her services, so this was a big payday.

"You don't trust me?" she asked.

Satisfied, Adam used one of the bills to pay for their drinks. "How was it?" he asked.

"I've never been that nervous in my whole f***ing life," she said.

Adam reminded her that she'd known this wasn't on the up-and-up.

"Are they stealing money from someone?" she asked.

"What are you talking about?"

Kathleen said she didn't look all that carefully at the documents, but she did notice two names on the power-of-attorney paperwork. "Who are the Hicks?" she asked.

"I don't know who the Hicks are," Adam said, thinking this didn't sound good. He didn't say anything, though, because he didn't want to alarm Kathleen. He simply warned her not to mess with Skylar, figuring it was better for her to be scared and to protect herself than to get herself into trouble.

"Well, he said he'd give us the rest of the money when he found out that the documents went through, that the notary worked," she said.

Kathleen kept asking questions, until Adam told her to forget about it, so they both settled down and had a couple more drinks.

A few days later, Kathleen told Adam she was feeling uncomfortable about the situation.

"When you notarize something, you are supposed to have the signer's signature in the book," she said, worried. "You are supposed to have thumbprints."

"Well, just get rid of your book," Adam suggested.

Kathleen explained that notaries were supposed to mail their books to the California Secretary of State's Office in Sacramento only when they quit being notaries. Adam clarified that he meant they should get rid of the book permanently.

Kathleen promptly put the book in an envelope and took it to the post office, where she paid $6.15 for postage by certified mail, but she sent just the empty envelope. When she met with Adam to discuss how they should get rid of her most recent book, she was so freaked out she gave him all three. He burned them in his fireplace, apparently thinking no books, no crime.

The next time Adam saw Skylar, he inquired about the notarized documents.

"What's this about?" Adam asked.

Skylar explained matter-of-factly that he was taking care of some business for a couple who had sold him their boat and moved to Mexico. He had Mexican citizenship, so he could help them buy property down there. But none of that made sense to Adam.

"What person, whoever they are, leaves a twenty-[five]-year-old in charge of their . . . [stuff], whether he's got dual citizenship or not?" he wondered.

By this point he felt backed into a corner, sensing that he'd gotten himself and Kathleen into something extremely illegal. He figured Skylar was ripping off these people somehow, but he still hadn't connected the power-of-attorney documents with the talk of disappearing someone at sea.

When Adam apologized to Kathleen about getting her mixed up in all of this, she wasn't angry with him.

"No, I agreed to it," she said.

As Thanksgiving came and went, Adam found himself drinking more and more, trying to forget about Skylar Deleon and drown his guilt for involving Kathleen.

Then Skylar called and asked somewhat insistently if Adam would come down to his new boat. Adam felt he had no choice but to agree.

Once they were on board, Adam could not believe how big—or expensive—it was. He got a bad feeling when he saw a giant lock on the door and a business card from the sheriff's department.

"Hey, what's this?" Adam asked, picking up the card. But before he had a chance to take a closer look, Skylar grabbed it, saying he needed to call them, and put the card in his wallet.

Skylar asked him to help bring the kayak ashore, but Adam wasn't big on that idea. The kayak only looked big enough for one, plus he didn't want to lose his keys if they dumped it. Adam said he would rather paddle in on the ten-foot surfboard, so he gave Skylar his sweatshirt, and let Skylar take the kayak.

"You want it?" Skylar asked, once they got to the beach.

Adam had no idea how he would stuff the pointy

wooden boat into his car, so Skylar offered him the
surfboard, instead. Adam didn't know what he would
tell a police officer if he got stopped with the board
sticking out of his window, but he didn't want to
argue.

"Give it to one of your friends if you don't surf,"
Skylar suggested.

So Adam took the board, put on his wet sweatshirt,
and started up Pacific Coast Highway toward Huntington Beach. Along the way, a friend called and
asked if he wanted to drink some beers, which
sounded like the perfect distraction.

Then Skylar called from a few cars away. Had he
been following Adam?

"I have something to show you," he said. "I'm
pulling over right here."

Leaving his car running, Skylar came over and
handed him a color photocopy of two driver's licenses
and a credit card. One was for a man with dark hair
and a mustache; the other was for a woman with curly
brown hair.

"If anybody talks to you, this is what the people
look like," Skylar said.

"I didn't see the people," Adam said. "I wasn't there."

"Well, if anyone asks Kathleen, this is what they
looked like."

"All right."

Things slowly started coming together as Adam recalled Kathleen's question the night she notarized the
paperwork. She'd asked him about the Hickses, and
these people's name was Hawks. As if Adam weren't
uncomfortable enough, he now had two faces to put
to this nightmare. Skylar hadn't been telling stories,
after all. His talk of killing people was real.

He was putting the surfboard into his friend's

garage when he turned it over and saw *Hawks* imprinted on it. Filled with panic, he ran and jumped into the water with all his clothes on. He staggered out, changed into dry clothes, drank too much beer, and talked with his friends about everything *but* what was troubling him.

When he got back into the car and saw the photo-copy again, his first instinct was to get rid of it. So once he got home, he crumpled it up and went for a bank shot into the trash bin between his nightstand and bed.

Adam called Kathleen and gave her a physical de-scription of the Hawkses, as instructed, and warned her again to be careful. Things were going from worse to even worse.

A few days later at the shop, Skylar casually tossed out an important fact as if it were nothing: "You know that guy's brother is the chief of police?"

Adam couldn't understand how Skylar's face could be so devoid of emotion. *He doesn't give a sh***, he thought. *He's a fricking sociopath.*

Adam, on the other hand, was feeling too many emotions. He drank every night until he passed out, and still couldn't sleep. He gave one-word answers to his mother, who could tell that something was wrong but didn't know what. Kathleen, a devout Catholic, felt just as awful, and was drinking too much as well. Adam tried to make her feel better, but he didn't really know how. He couldn't stop thinking that al-though she hadn't hurt the Hawkses, she was in as much trouble as the person who did. And it was all his fault.

PART III

THE INVESTIGATION

13

Dave Byington, a detective sergeant with the Newport Beach Police Department, was washing his Land Rover on November 27, 2004, the Saturday after Thanksgiving, when he got a call from Mario Montero, the only detective working the weekend shift. Byington, who headed the Crimes Against Persons/Economic Crimes Unit, was used to getting weekend calls at his home in Aliso Viejo—it was part of the job. But he had no idea that this one would mark the start of a career-making case.

Montero, a burglary detective, said a missing persons report had come over the fax machine from a Carlsbad sergeant the night before. Only it wasn't your typical report—this one reflected some preliminary investigative work by the sergeant and the victims' relatives, who had law enforcement backgrounds. Such reports didn't get preference, but they tended to have more credibility right off the bat, and this one even identified a potential "suspect": Skylar Julius Deleon.

The report detailed Jennifer's calls to Tom Hawks's brother, Jim, Tricia Schutz's calls to Stockmen's Bank, Skylar's visit and calls to Stockmen's, and Jim's trip to the *Well Deserved.* It also included Skylar's aliases—Jon Liberty, Julius Jacobson, and John Julius Jacobson— and mentioned that he had two other boats registered in his name, a tattoo, and a conviction for armed burglary.

Based on the information known at this time, Sergeant Eppel believes that Thomas and Jackie Hawks are missing and at risk, the report stated.

Byington told Montero to ask the sheriff's harbor patrol to ferry him out to the *Well Deserved,* but once Montero was aboard, he couldn't get inside. All he could do was poke around on the deck, so he called Byington.

"It's locked up," Montero said. "I really don't see anything."

The sergeant asked if Montero spotted any suspicious evidence that would give him probable cause to forcibly enter the boat.

"There might be a bloodstain out here on the deck, on one of the latches," Montero said.

"That's good enough for me," Byington replied. "Break the lock."

Montero gladly did so and entered the rear doors, which led into the salon and galley, and two sets of stairs—one going up to the bridge deck, and the other heading down to the stateroom.

Looking around, he took note of the blankets strewn across the bed, the pillows askew, and the ink pad on the TV in the salon. He also noted that the dinghy, tied up incorrectly, was taking on water. Newport Harbor had a problem with sea lions climbing onto vessels, so the dinghy was pretty trashed. But he didn't see any potential leads—until he found a Target receipt, dated November 17, lying on the floor just inside the door. He called Byington right back.

"What's on there?" Byington asked, listening as Montero read him the items.

"You've got to be kidding," Byington said, thinking that if he were putting together a "kill kit," this is exactly what he'd stock it with: Clorox Wipes to remove fingerprints, blood, or other DNA that he'd left behind, trash bags for bloody clothing or other incriminating evidence, and TUMS for the indigestion that had to come with killing someone. "Track down which Target store the receipt came from."

Montero traced it to a Target store in Long Beach, where he was able to obtain a copy of the surveillance tape capturing the transaction at the cash register. He'd already checked out twenty-five-year-old Skylar's driver's license photo and his mug shot on the state ID computer system, so he could immediately tell that the big-bellied Target customer, who was in his forties and had a mustache, looked nothing like the baby-faced Skylar Deleon, who weighed an athletic 150 pounds.

Montero called Jim Hawks to tell him he saw no obvious signs of foul play—or of Tom and Jackie—on the yacht; then he entered the couple into the National Missing and Unidentified Persons System. After calling Tricia Schutz to gather more details on her banking investigation in Arizona, he was satisfied that he'd exhausted every lead he could on a weekend, so he laid the package that he'd compiled on Byington's desk to deal with first thing Monday morning.

At forty-six, Dave Byington had earned the admiration and respect from the detectives, the prosecutors, and the investigators with whom he worked, and the families of victims whose cases he tried to solve.

At a sturdy five feet eleven inches and 195 pounds, Byington frequently called women of all ages "darlin'," and often reached out to shake hands or slap the back of a male colleague. The charismatic sergeant treated his victims' families with care and thoughtfulness, keeping them up to date on developments, even sending Jackie's family a card and a bouquet of tulips on her birthday. Known to flex a mischievous sense of humor, Byington was also seen as a mentor to his detectives.

Byington was also one of the more handsome officers on the job. His mix of Choctaw Indian, Mexican, and Irish features, the twinkle in his light brown eyes, his thick black hair, and his snappy attire did not go unnoticed by reporters.

Dark skin, 1,000-watt smile, jet black hair combed straight back, nice suit. If he were in "Law & Order" they'd say he was too good-looking to be believable, wrote Frank Mickadeit, the *Orange County Register*'s legal columnist.

But the self-effacing sergeant didn't take compliments well, and besides, this type of media attention resulted in merciless ribbing from his colleagues.

Byington had a habit of talking fast, as if he'd just downed six cups of coffee, and was always juggling twenty things at once. If he remembered, he would return a call *even while getting a tattoo.* These traits enabled him to work on multiple cases simultaneously and assign duties in rapid succession. The multitasking also came in handy while he coordinated what would become a massive case, with nearly forty thousand pages of discovery; six hundred audiotapes, CDs, and DVDs of text, audio and digital-image files; and more than three thousand pieces of evidence, gathered with more than sixty search warrants. He had worked about fifteen homicide cases, but none of them had been as complex and challenging—or had garnered as much emotional buy-in from everyone involved—as this one would prove to be.

Byington and his sister had been raised in East Los Angeles by a single mother, who worked as a Securities and Exchange Commission analyst. As a teenager he got a job at a market where customers often bought milk with food stamps and gangbangers confronted him for beer, forcing him to call the sheriff's department for backup.

"I got my ass kicked by the gangs and I wanted to be in the bigger gang," he said. From the age of eleven, he added, "I couldn't think of a cooler thing to do than be a cop."

At fifteen, he had another important contact with the authorities when he got drunk for the first time with his football buddies in a van parked in Newport Beach, then relieved himself on an unmarked white police car. An angry cop emerged, arrested, handcuffed, and took Byington to jail, where he continued to throw up until his mom and stepdad arrived. Once they got home, his stepdad forced him to chug from a bottle of sickly sweet Napoleon brandy.

"Oh, so you want to be a big guy and drink," his stepfather said, punching young Byington in the gut. The teenager spent the rest of the night outside, throwing up, and trying to sleep off his lesson in tough love.

With one uncle a "ghetto gunslinger" sergeant for the LAPD's Watts division, and the other a city park ranger chief, he followed his role models into law enforcement. After two and a half years as a patrolman in Palos Verdes Estates, Byington applied to the NBPD. His juvenile arrest, of course, came up during his interview.

"I'm seeking revenge because one of your assholes arrested me," he joked.

"What for?"

"Drunk in public."

The sergeant on the hiring committee went to check the files, and after confirming the story, he said, "You were peeing on a police car. You'll do fine here."

And with that, Byington started his career with the Newport Beach PD.

By seven o'clock on Monday morning, November 29, Byington had a surveillance team parked outside what they thought was the Deleons' house, on Grand Avenue in Long Beach. At the time, the two undercover detectives didn't know that the little gray house was actually Jennifer's parents' duplex, that she and Skylar lived in the detached garage in back, or that the entire family was staying at the Extended Stay America hotel. So Detectives Tom Tolman and Dave Moon sat, waiting, on that quiet residential street for most of the day, hoping for some movement.

Newport Beach averaged 1.2 homicides a year, but Byington's team was extremely busy the week the Hawkses went missing, dealing with a murder-suicide, a hostage situation at a jewelry store robbery, and a bank robbery that ended in the thief's death. One of Byington's three homicide detectives was out with an injury, and the other two were caught up in all this chaos, so the sergeant assigned the Hawks case to Evan Sailor, one of his three economic crimes detectives.

"I went to my fraud guy and he turned out to be the best homicide guy I've ever known," Byington said.

The sergeant had intended to work as Sailor's

supervisor, but the case grew so complicated that the two men ended up working more as partners, leading a team of seven primary detectives, with others filling in as needed, and reaching out to local, state, and federal agencies in two countries, several states, three contiguous Southern California counties, and the Pacific Ocean.

In the first day or so, the detectives called the Mexican and U.S. consulates in Mexico to see if the Hawkses could be in jail or injured in a car accident. They flagged their license plate with Immigration and Customs Enforcement officials, whose cameras videotaped cars crossing the border. They put out periodic broadcast calls through citizen volunteers on the shortwave radio system, and they called the missing couple's cell phones, which went straight to voice mail. The last call from either of the Hawkses' phones was made around 7:00 A.M. on November 16 in San Ysidro, the last community north of the border.

They also flagged the Hawkses' credit cards and bank accounts, none of which showed any activity after November 15. And just in case the Hawkses had taken an innocent trip somewhere, detectives checked airline manifests and long-term parking lots at various airports.

Detective Dave White got to work writing warrants for the Hawkses' and Jennifer Deleon's cell phone and landline records. He also went after records for the corresponding cell tower sites to map out the more specific locations of callers and recipients when their phone signals "pinged" off the nearest towers.

As all law enforcement officers know, police come in many varieties, from good to bad, sharp to slow, deliberate and dull-witted to clever and capable. So when Byington called Jim Hawks to follow up, he could sense Jim cautiously assessing him, just as he did when they met later in person.

Byington explained to the retired chief what he and his team had done so far and what other tactics they were in the process of employing. After asking about Tom and Jackie's daily routines and their normal methods of communication, Byington asked Jim to consider the flip side: could Tom and Jackie be hiding out somewhere, or involved in something illegal, such as dealing drugs on their cruises back and forth to Mexico?

Jim knew Byington was just doing his job, so he calmly replied that Tom and Jackie weren't that type of people. He brought the sergeant up to date on the Hawkses' recent cruising activities, however, he acknowledged, "I don't know everything about my brother. They did mention going to Alaska, but it's not like him not to call," or to miss Thanksgiving with the family.

When Byington asked if Jim had any other leads, Jim reasserted his suspicions about the Deleons. "Something's wrong with the wife," he said, elaborating on her calls. "I'm telling you, you need to look at them."

As soon as Tom's sons had learned about Skylar's criminal record, they were chomping at the bit for the police to go after him, because anyone on probation is subject to search and seizure. Jackie's father was pretty impatient as well. But the families had already had several days to digest this information, and Byington's team had only just gotten the case. They hadn't even located Skylar's whereabouts yet—let alone interviewed him.

"I'll try to keep them informed and help them understand the investigative process," Jim said.

The Hawkses seemed like good, law-abiding people with a close, loving family, and Byington's team was determined to help find out what had happened to them.

14

After watching the duplex all day, Detectives Tolman and Moon were relieved to finally see Skylar, Jennifer, and their baby daughter pull up in their red Toyota. The couple ran in to get some things, then sped off.

The detectives followed them to a two-story cream-colored building in a nearby strip mall, where they watched the Deleons park, put their baby in a stroller, and disappear through a glass entryway. Once the detectives saw HOPE CHAPEL on the façade and a white cross in a second-floor window, they realized the Deleons had gone into a storefront church.

Dave Byington and Evan Sailor headed over immediately, arriving at 3:45 P.M. Inside, they climbed the carpeted stairs to the church, which consisted of a small auditorium for services, a main office, and Sunday-school classrooms on either side of a narrow hallway. There, they found Skylar pushing a cart of cleaning supplies, with a pregnant Jennifer, both of whom identified the mustached man in the Target video as Jennifer's father, and confirmed that he'd bought cleaning supplies for the boat they'd just bought from the Hawkses.

"It smelled," Skylar explained. "It was, like, not a moldy smell, but it was, like, a, I don't know, kind of a yucky kind of smell."

After separating the Deleons, Byington spoke with Jennifer in an office, while Sailor took Skylar down to the parking lot, explaining that they were trying to locate the missing couple.

As Jennifer giggled and played with her baby, she told Byington that she and her husband, an unemployed electrician, had purchased the *Well Deserved* on November 15. Earlier in the month, she and her daughter, Haylie, had visited with Jackie on the boat while Skylar discussed a price with Tom. Skylar had handled the transaction, because he took care of the family's finances. They'd ultimately paid $265,000 in cash for the boat and signed papers that were notarized by a friend of Skylar's, whose name she couldn't remember. They'd last seen the Hawkses driving away in their CRV, and they had been trying to reach the couple ever since. But the calls had gone straight to voice mail, so she and Skylar were also concerned about the couple's welfare.

"I would feel the same way if that happened to anybody in my family," she said.

The detectives met up to compare notes, agreeing that the Deleons seemed cooperative and that their stories were almost consistent. Like Jennifer, Skylar had mentioned that the sale price was $265,000, but when pressed, he admitted that he'd actually paid $465,000 for the boat and its mooring. He said he and Tom had agreed to underreport the sale price as $265,000 so they could both get a tax break.

Byington and Sailor decided to switch it up, so each one could interview the other Deleon.

As Sailor gathered financial information from Jennifer, he tried to figure out how such a young couple—with an eleven-month-old and a baby on the way—could have afforded such an extravagant purchase. Jennifer, who'd said they were planning to use the boat as a business investment and a place to live, admitted to lying initially about the $265,000 price, saying she didn't want Skylar to get in trouble for tax evasion.

When Byington asked Skylar to explain the discrepancy, Skylar said he'd actually paid $465,000 for the mooring, the boat, *and* a $5,000 tutorial on how to operate it.

"How is it that you came upon this amount of money?" Byington asked.

Skylar told him the same story he'd told the Hawkses: he'd earned good money during his child acting days, and had supplemented it with profitable real estate deals in Mexico.

Byington said he believed Skylar could've come up with the $265,000, but not the $465,000. He wasn't expecting Skylar's explanation.

"I am embarrassed to say it, but that money is from drugs," Skylar admitted in his calm, childlike voice.

Asked to elaborate, Skylar said the proceeds were a payment from a drug rip-off. "You know about my arrest in Anaheim a few years ago?"

Byington said yes, so Skylar went on to say that some Mexican drug lords had asked him to go to that house and verify the presence of one hundred kilos of cocaine and a bunch of money. That was the end of his role; the drug lords sent someone else to steal the drugs.

"So you got paid nearly half a million dollars for making a phone call?" the sergeant asked, skeptical after working twelve and a half years in undercover narcotics.

Skylar claimed he'd actually been underpaid because the burglary had involved far more money and drugs than he was originally told. But he didn't get any of the money until after he found the Hawkses' boat in a magazine, and called down to have his $450,000 in cash delivered from Mexico.

The story didn't make much sense to Byington. But at the same time, why else would this kid admit to laundering money from a Mexican drug cartel?

Skylar said he was embarrassed about the criminal source of the money, but he assured the sergeant that he'd been clean since his arrest in 2002. He just wanted to provide for his family in legal ways, he said, adding that as a dive master, he hoped to run diving and fishing charters on the boat.

Byington told Skylar he didn't care about his previous criminal conduct; he just wanted to find the missing couple.

Meeting up again, the detectives decided they'd better get the Deleons' statements on tape, but they only had one low-end recorder between them, which Sailor stealthily put into his pocket. Unfortunately, much of the subsequent taped conversation was unintelligible as the four of them walked into the parking lot, engaging in snippets of conversation.

Jennifer and Skylar said they'd just returned from Ensenada, where they'd tried to open a bank account so the Hawkses could deposit the sale proceeds, avoid taxes, and take out a mortgage on some property in San Carlos. But, Skylar said, the bank wouldn't let him do it.

When the detectives asked to see the boat sale documents, Skylar said they were back at the hotel. So Byington radioed the station, saying he and Sailor were heading to the Extended Stay America to check them out.

"That might explain some of this," he said.

The detectives followed the couple back to room 307, which was in complete disarray. Jennifer went over to the chest of drawers and grabbed a manila envelope containing the boat transfer paperwork and documents that gave Skylar a durable power of attorney for Tom and Jackie Hawks, all of which were notarized by "K. Harris" and signed by a witness, Alonso Machain.

From there the group headed down to the lobby to make copies, where Jennifer volunteered that they planned to change the boat's name to *Pure Luck*. Sailor noticed that the paperwork didn't include a bill of sale, so Jennifer said she'd run upstairs to get it.

She came back a few minutes later, saying she knew they had one somewhere, but rather than keep them waiting, she would look some more and bring it to the station the next day.

"Would you do me a favor?" Skylar asked the detectives innocently.

"Don't ask them that," Jennifer said.

But Skylar ignored her, asking whether they would inquire if any of the Hawks family members knew how to operate the *Well Deserved*. He'd never gotten the tutorial Tom had promised, so he had no idea how to switch over the gas tanks.

Byington replied that the family was extremely distraught, and the request would be inappropriate.

Skylar agreed to come down to the station the next day for a more in-depth interview, saying he wanted to help in any way he could.

"Hey, did you have someone following us?" he asked just as innocently.

"Not us," Byington fibbed.

But as soon as the detectives left the building, Byington alerted his surveillance team. "Stay low," he cautioned. "They burned you already."

Neither Skylar nor Jennifer had seemed nervous, and their faces displayed none of the emotions the detectives were trained to recognize as suspicious. Other than offer his screwy story about the drug money, Skylar had done what he did so well—used his charm, his fish tales, and his childlike ways to fool both cops into thinking he had nothing to do with the Hawkses' disappearance.

These people are somewhere. We'll find them, Byington thought at the time. *Not a big deal.*

15

That evening, Skylar called Adam Rohrig, saying he needed a bill of sale before police would release his new boat. Without the document, Skylar said, all the other paperwork looked "weird."

So Adam called Kathleen Harris, but this time she didn't want to deal with it.

"We have to have this, because everything else is notarized," Adam said, repeating Skylar's argument. After Adam explained that they were kind of "locked into this thing pretty good," Kathleen said she understood.

Skylar met Adam at the dive shop and handed over a cheesy-looking typed page. Adam saw Tom and Jackie Hawks's names and a date in the upper right-hand corner, but he didn't want to look any closer.

Kathleen was pissed when they met up in the backseat of her car, but she was even more upset when she saw the document. "There's no f**king signatures on this," she said. "What the f***? There's nothing on here. I can't notarize that."

Adam tried to calm her down, saying they had no choice. Skylar and the dangerous thugs he knew in

Mexico would kill her and her family, probably Adam and his mother, too. Skylar had told him that the Hawkses had stolen money from his family, and Adam didn't know what to believe, but he now knew that Skylar was a man to be feared. For whatever it was worth, Adam conveyed Skylar's offer to pay her more money than the media—or anyone else—if she stuck to her story.

Trying to legitimize the unsigned paperwork, Kathleen pulled out an all-purpose acknowledgment, which she signed and attached. Adam then delivered the papers to Skylar in the Rusty Pelican parking lot in Long Beach, and hoped he was done with this.

But that was not to be. Evan Sailor called Kathleen the next morning, told her that a couple named Tom and Jackie Hawks was missing, and said he wanted to talk to her about the documents she'd notarized for them and the Deleons.

As soon as she hung up with Sailor, Kathleen read the Riot Act to Adam.

"What's going on?" she demanded. "You need to call your friend right away. I need to know what's going on."

All Adam could say was "Holy sh**."

The two of them met later that day at Cal State Long Beach, where he got into her Acura, and recounted what Skylar wanted her to tell detectives. Kathleen was shaking.

"Kathleen, I'm sorry," Adam said. "I had no idea."

As she tried to ask questions, Adam kept saying, "Look at me. Look at me in the eyes. You don't want to mess with this guy."

Kathleen said she was supposed to meet again with Sailor the next morning. Adam tried to calm her down, but they both knew they were up to their necks in something really bad. Adam also had a meeting scheduled with the detective that afternoon, during which he only admitted that he'd referred Kathleen to Skylar to notarize some legitimate documents.

During Kathleen's meeting with Detective Sailor, she relayed Skylar's story as instructed, but the detective wouldn't give up. He kept calling with questions about the bill of sale and asking to see the entries in her notary book. Kathleen told him she'd mailed it to Sacramento, and showed him her postage receipt. But that didn't satisfy him, either. He and another detective showed up at her doctor's office to say that he'd called Sacramento and her book was nowhere to be found.

Asked if it had been returned in the mail, Kathleen said no. By this point her anxiety was ramping up, out of control, but she did her best to stick to her story. Her family's lives depended on it.

16

The day after their police interview, Skylar and Jennifer showed up at the station, as promised, with a single typed sheet dated November 15, 2004, and titled, "Bill of Sale and Release of Liability." It stated:

This is to release ourselves (Tom and Jackie Hawks) from any and/or all liability of the M/V Well Deserved. We have sold this vessel for $200,000 as/is, with mooring additional $65,000, and boston whaler to (Skylar and Jennifer DeLeon). We have come to agreement that we will provide suitable assistance instructing the new owners of minor details of the M/V Well Deserved. Please Note that new owners have agreed to give Tom and Jackie Hawks sufficient time to remove personal items not included in sale. Time not to exceed 2 weeks from 11/15/2004.

A document, known as a "California All Purpose Acknowledgment," was attached, with the same notary's signature and stamp. Unlike the other paperwork, the bill of sale had no fingerprints or signatures from the Hawkses. By notarizing and attaching the acknowledgment, Kathleen was declaring that she'd witnessed the couple executing the sale.

Sailor had been planning to do the second interview

with Skylar, but he and a team of investigators had already left to search the boat more closely for fingerprints and DNA, and to collect the GPS equipment for forensic analysis. So Dave Byington took the new paperwork without looking at it, and while Jennifer waited in the lobby with Haylie, he led Skylar into an interview room equipped with a hidden microphone and a camera disguised as a clock.

Skylar seemed no more nervous than the day before, leaning confidently toward Byington on the couch as he answered the sergeant's rapid-fire questions. Byington still believed Skylar had nothing to do with the Hawkses' disappearance, but he hoped Skylar would provide some helpful leads, given that he and Jennifer were the last people to see the couple alive. The sergeant also needed to get Skylar's official statement on tape.

Trying to get Skylar to open up, Byington reiterated that he wasn't interested in any probation violation, financial or tax crime that Skylar may have committed. He was just trying to help Tom and Jackie's family find them, so he asked Skylar not to hold anything back.

"It's been fifteen days—you can imagine. They have adult children. They have grandchildren. They're going nuts. . . . Everybody is saying, 'Well, that Skylar and his wife, they have to have something to do with this.' I tell you what—before I talked to you yesterday, I thought that was the case."

But, the detective said, he now thought it was possible that the Hawkses had gone off on their own, or that maybe someone other than Skylar had had something to do with their disappearance. "What I need from you is the exact truth," he said.

"No matter what the truth, it will come out, no matter what," Skylar said.

Byington asked Skylar to run through the whole story again, starting with where he learned that the *Well Deserved* was up for sale.

Skylar said he saw an ad in *Sport Fishing* magazine, thinking the yacht would work as a home *and* a business.

"Whatever I can do to make money," Skylar said, laughing.

Skylar said he was somewhat familiar with the vessel because Tom had taken him on a minicruise, although he did little more than touch the throttle to feel how the boat handled.

"Was this on a sea trial?" Byington asked.

"No," Skylar said, insisting that he'd never left the harbor with the Hawkses. He mentioned that he'd brought a buddy with him on one short trip they all took "to the whatchamacallit, to do the crappers."

"And this buddy is who?" Byington asked.

"Alonso . . . ," Skylar said.

"Alonso?"

"Machain."

Skylar said Alonso came along because he knew something about boats. Skylar readily supplied Alonso's phone number, explaining that he was trying to get a job with the sheriff's department. Byington said maybe he could give Alonso a few pointers.

Surprisingly, Skylar didn't need much prodding to elaborate on the details of his illegal money-laundering scheme or the underreporting tax arrangement that he and Tom had made.

"I have a bunch of money that I have no way to spend, and if I bring it here, I'm going to get in trouble," he said, explaining he couldn't go get it from

Mexico because he was on probation. "So . . . I'm kind of in [between] a rock and a hard place."

Skylar said he first spoke to Tom by phone a week or two before the transaction, in early November, and Tom invited him to "come down, take a look. . . . He seemed like he was really cool. And then he was . . . like, you know, 'If you get this, I can work something out with you.'"

So Tom took him out to the boat and asked how he wanted to pay for it. "He's like, well, you know, 'Cash, money order?' And I was like, 'Oh, cash. You know, you get a better deal for cash?' And he started laughing. He's like, 'Is it good?'"

Skylar said he assured Tom he wasn't talking counterfeit money. "And he's like . . . 'If you're going to go ahead and get it . . . I can save a little bit of taxes.'"

"So he brought that up about the taxes?" Byington asked.

"Yeah," Skylar said, explaining that Tom said he could write out the sale paperwork to reflect a much lower price than what Skylar would actually pay. "He's like, you know, 'Maybe twos, threes,'" meaning in the $200,000 or $300,000 range. "So I was, like, . . . 'This is perfect.'"

After that, Jackie suggested that Skylar bring his wife down to take a look, which Skylar was planning to do, anyway. "I can't do anything without my wife," he told Byington.

"Smart man," the detective quipped.

Skylar said he also told Tom that he wanted to talk to his accountant to make sure he didn't get into any trouble. "I don't really want to give him all this money, and then all of a sudden, I'm screwed."

Byington asked if the Hawkses had questioned Skylar about the source of his money.

"[Jackie] had asked . . . and I told her, I said, 'Well, you know, I did acting and, you know, stuff like that,'" Skylar said. "'I did real estate over at Ditech' . . . and she said, 'Oh wow.' . . . I told her I did *Power Rangers*."

Skylar said he and Tom discussed raising the price to include the mooring, which reminded him that he still needed to talk to a guy Tom had mentioned, who had a spot at the 15th Street dock where Skylar could tether the dinghy. Skylar had been worrying that he would get a ticket, or the dinghy would be impounded if he left it at the dock, so he'd been using the kayak to go back and forth to shore.

"That explains why the kayak's on the shore," Byington said. "This is all questions that we had. Great."

Skylar said he brought Jennifer down to the boat to meet the Hawkses, and to show her that Haylie would be safe living there. "They were pretty much mainly just talking to Jenn."

Skylar explained that he was interested in checking out the condition of the hull, so the Hawkses showed them a video of the boat being serviced in Mexico.

"I might not even think about that," Byington said, "but that's smart."

Skylar said he and Jennifer asked about taking the boat out for a trial run that day, but the Hawkses had other plans. However, Tom did start up the engine so Skylar could see there was no black smoke, and Jackie showed them pictures of their new grandson. Skylar and Tom talked more about the final purchase price to include basics such as dishes, the ham radio, and binoculars, which Tom and Jackie agreed to leave behind.

Byington noticed that the sales figures kept changing as Skylar told his story. He initially said, "despite what our paperwork says—we spent like four eighty-five on it." Later he said they paid "an extra five grand for the computer" and at least a week's tutorial on driving the boat, which came to $495,000.

Asked if there was any paper trail, such as a wire transfer, for the money he'd paid Tom, Skylar said no. He'd given Tom a briefcase of $100s, stacked in $10,000 bundles.

Byington asked about the surfboard, omitting the family's allegation that Tom and Jackie never would have left it behind. Skylar admitted that Tom had said he wanted to keep the board, but when he didn't come back to claim it, Skylar had given it to a buddy. Skylar said Tom also had wanted to take the two wet suits, one of which had been made especially for Jackie, along with her scuba gear, her buoyancy compensator, and an extra outboard motor for the dinghy.

"Besides the surfboard, the stuff is still on there," Skylar assured Byington.

Skylar mentioned again that Tom had talked about getting a smaller boat—a trawler or catamaran in the thirty- to forty-foot range—and a house in San Carlos. This prompted a more in-depth discussion about Skylar's offer to help Tom open a bank account in Mexico with the power-of-attorney documents and the Mexican citizenship papers Skylar said his father had helped him obtain sometime ago.

"I don't know the 100 percent legality of my citizenship, but . . . my dad had paid some other people a long time ago, and I got a full citizenship down there."

Wondering if Skylar might flee to Mexico, Byington

asked if he'd ever tested them out, or used them to purchase a house down there. Skylar said no, but he'd used them to work and live there in 1999 or 2000.

He said Tom invited him to do a final check on the yacht, once he and Jackie got back from a weekend cruise to Catalina with Tom's brother. "He's like, you know, 'We'll take care of some stuff and . . . you can drive it a little bit,' and I was, like, 'Sweet. I'm on my way.'"

Skylar said he was running late after setting up the services of "some notary girl" he'd found through a friend at Pacific Sporting Goods. He'd asked the friend to recommend someone who wasn't "going to get us in trouble for, you know, paying all cash, or who's not going to be like, 'Whoa.'"

So Skylar said he called and offered her "like three something," meaning $3,000, and she agreed to meet them all at the dock: Skylar, Jennifer, Haylie, Tom, Jackie, and Alonso, who had driven his own car.

Leading Tom over to the Toyota, Skylar said, he opened the briefcase and let Tom scan the stacks of cash with a special pen for identifying counterfeit money.

"He just went right across the tops and was, like, okay," Skylar said. "He was excited, but nervous. . . . He was just, like, 'Let's just close this up. . . . If it's not there, I'll let you know.' . . . I was, like, 'I guarantee you it's here.'"

The notary, Skylar said, didn't look in the briefcase. She just took Tom's word that the money was all there.

"Her impression was it was two-something," Skylar said.

"The two sixty-five?"

"Yeah."

Then Tom showed her the certificate of documentation and his and Jackie's IDs.

"And you presented her with a power of attorney, too?"

"Yeah."

"She said, 'You guys just got to sign it in front of me, and that's it,'" Skylar said.

Skylar explained that Tom and Jackie had given the power-of-attorney documents to him after he offered to open bank accounts for them in Mexico. So after the sale he took the trouble to go to their bank in Kingman, Arizona, where he also recorded the sale documents, then went to a bank in Ensenada to try to open an account.

"So he didn't seem to have a problem giving power of attorney, then?"

"No," Skylar said. "He's like, you know, 'Just don't . . . screw me over.'"

The whole Mexican bank account thing didn't work out, though, Skylar said, so he threw away the voided check that Tom had given him. "I said, 'Screw this . . . I'm not doing this. This is too much dang drama. . . .' I try calling him. He's not answering his phone. He's not doing any of this stupid stuff. So I was like, you know what? This is just—"

"It's too much work?"

"Yeah . . . I thought it was going to be a lot easier than it was."

Skylar said Alonso was the one who actually put the power-of-attorney document together because "he deals with realty and all that kind of stuff," and had Mexican citizenship as well.

"Alonso seems like a talented man," Byington said. But, he added, "Just to get this correct—because this is a big stumbling point for the family—they said that there's no way that their family members would give power of attorney to anybody."

But Skylar stuck to his story, saying Tom and Jackie said they were going to "take care of some stuff," and would see the Deleons the following week. Then they drove away in some type of SUV.

"Did it look like it was loaded up with stuff? Look like they were ready to take off somewhere?" Byington asked.

Skylar said he couldn't really tell, but when he went back to the boat, he thought some of the Hawkses' clothing and personal items had been removed. He was a little irritated, he said, because they'd left without giving him a key to lock things up.

Byington said Skylar's phone records showed he'd received a call from Jackie Hawks on November 16 at 7:00 A.M.

"Did you get a message from her? Did you talk to her?"

"No," Skylar said. "I had a missed call from them, but that's it."

"So you never spoke to them again after that point?"

"No . . . I tried to get ahold of them, I think, the next day."

"And no answer?"

"No, no answer. . . . I think I left a message, just saying, 'Hey, give me a call.'"

Asked if he'd taken the boat out yet, Skylar said yes, he'd taken his father-in-law, brother-in-law, and cousin out to San Clemente Island using the autopilot, and everyone got sick.

"All right. You then return home. . . . Next thing you know, the police are knocking at your door."

"Then we get a contact from his brother, asking if we knew where he was, or anything," Skylar said. "And I believe my wife told him that . . . as far as we know, he's in San Carlos right now. . . . From what I've gathered from him, I would almost guarantee he's down there."

"Causing you all this grief."

"Yes. I would just guarantee it."

As they were finishing up the two-hour interview, Byington promised Skylar that they'd release the boat to him by the next day, if possible. He also said the police had taken the GPS equipment off the yacht, but they needed Skylar's written permission to analyze its data because it technically involved a search. Skylar gave the okay.

Anything to help get his dream boat back.

17

Once Detective Sailor got a chance to examine the Deleons' paperwork in more detail, the economic crimes expert started looking into the backgrounds of the notary, Kathleen Harris, and the witness, Alonso Machain, who had signed the documents. Neither had a criminal record.

During interviews, Kathleen and Alonso both backed Skylar's story that they'd watched the Hawkses sign the paperwork at the 15th Street dock. Everyone was nervous during the transaction, Kathleen said, but excited.

Alonso volunteered that he'd met Skylar while working as a jailer at the Seal Beach facility. He claimed that he'd created the power-of-attorney documents on his computer, then ridden to Newport with Skylar to witness the sale, which didn't jibe with Skylar's story that Alonso had driven his own car. If Skylar had gone out on the boat right after the sale, as he'd claimed, then Alonso would have had no way to get home, Sailor realized. Alonso also said he saw the Hawkses return to their boat in a dinghy after the transaction, while the Deleons had claimed the couple drove away in their CRV. When Sailor called Alonso back for clarification, Alonso said he was mistaken, confused because of his many trips to the boat. He *had* driven himself to the dock, and he *had* seen the Hawkses drive off in their CRV.

At this point the detectives saw Alonso as a naïve, not very bright guy who wasn't as believable as Skylar, but who wasn't involved in the Hawkses' disappearance. A couple red flags did arise concerning Kathleen, though. She gave a faulty description of Jackie as having long, curly brown hair, when, in fact, she had short, spiky blond hair. And Kathleen's story about her notary book didn't check out.

After talking to the Secretary of State's Office in Sacramento, Sailor learned that her claim she'd mailed in her book wasn't exactly kosher—notaries were only supposed to send their books to Sacramento once their licenses expired, or they were done being notaries. When Sailor asked Kathleen for proof, she produced a certified-mail receipt for the exact weight. The woman simply would not move off her story.

Sailor and Byington were also growing more suspicious of Skylar's story. First, why would the Hawkses put their fingerprints on the power of attorney when they belonged in the notary's register book? Second, why hadn't the Hawkses signed the bill of sale? And perhaps, most important, why would they give such sweeping legal and financial control over their affairs to a twenty-five-year-old stranger? It didn't make any sense.

The Hawks family agreed. Their reaction to Skylar's claim that Tom and Jackie had signed over power of attorney to a convicted felon on the hood of a car, and sold their boat for a briefcase full of cash: "No freaking way."

Tom had habitually tried to cut costs. Jim lovingly called his brother "notoriously frugal," joking that he'd always looked forward to the day when Tom would pay for lunch.

When Tom decided to sell the boat without a broker, it wasn't the first time he'd tried to avoid paying such fees. He'd sold his bar in Prescott—Matt's Saloon—without a broker, which meant the sale fell in and out of escrow several times after buyers defaulted, but it finally went through in the end.

"Tom did his own wheeling and dealing in real estate stuff, and it worked well for him," said Tom's former coworker, John Ryder, who used to tell Tom that "he was a cheap bastard sometimes." John hastened to add that he, too, was a "cheap bastard," and proud of it.

John described Tom as "a little bit of a maverick when it came to doing business. . . . If there was a way to get less taxes, yeah, he'd do that." But Jim disagreed, saying his brother would never have done anything as blatantly illegal as submitting false information to the IRS.

From his long police career, Jim knew the majority of missing persons cases proved to be unfounded, but he felt in his gut that Tom and Jackie weren't coming back. The Newport police were being responsive to his suggestions and leads, but, he said, "I knew it would take a while for them to get to the point where I was."

Slowly but surely, Byington and Sailor were listening more closely to the family's assertions. But for the moment, they still didn't have enough evidence to make this a homicide. Nonetheless, Byington figured it was time to alert the Orange County District Attorney's Office, so he called prosecutor Matt Murphy, who handled all homicides in Newport Beach, Costa Mesa, Irvine, and Laguna Beach.

"What do you need?" Murphy asked.

The sergeant told Murphy what he knew so far. "This is starting to turn south, and it's looking like this may be a homicide," Byington said, asking for advice on how to proceed.

"I'd like to come down and talk to you," Murphy said.

The two men decided to meet for a strategy session the next day at the police station. But in the meantime, Murphy told him not to arrest anyone, and to make sure he documented, audiotaped, and videotaped everything he could.

By this point, Byington was thinking that Skylar was too much of a wuss to kill the Hawkses himself, but he might have the cojones to hire someone else to do it for him. Perhaps someone from Mexico, where his father had drug connections.

Looking back later, Byington said, "Best move I ever made was getting Matt on early and listening to him."

The DA's homicide division was known as "a vertical unit," which meant that Murphy and his investigator, Larry Montgomery, worked closely with police detectives from the very beginning of an investigation, starting at the crime scene if possible. Bringing a prosecutor into a case early cut out unnecessary delays that could occur, for example, when a defense attorney shut down an interview because he wanted to strike an immunity deal for his client, something detectives couldn't do on their own.

This team approach not only helped relations between the prosecutor and the detectives, but it also helped them all put together a winning case for court. In this particular case, Murphy had weekly strategy sessions with detectives, and sat in on important interviews with witnesses and suspects. Montgomery, who had worked thirty years as a police officer—twenty as a homicide detective with the Irvine Police Department—conducted the questioning, while Murphy took notes, forged his legal strategy, passed notes, and suggested questions.

It wasn't until Murphy walked into their first strategy session that Byington realized he'd already had met the tall, lanky attorney.

Byington had responded to a homicide call one night in May 2002, and was walking the detectives through the search warrant process while they ate their pizza dinner—right next to the victim. Forty-three-year-old Paul Strazicich had been shot eight times, the last time in the chest, lying on the kitchen floor. Pornography was everywhere, in what later proved to be a staged scene by his married lover, who then bludgeoned a friend and fatally shot herself a week later. Byington would always remember the look on the rookie prosecutor's face when he walked in and saw the detectives nonchalantly munching away next to a corpse.

"He was putting on his best 'been there, done that' face, but it was not fooling anyone," Byington said.

The sergeant was right. It *was* Murphy's first homicide case and the only dead bodies he'd ever seen were at funerals or traffic scenes. He'd initially thought Strazicich was asleep, until he saw the clear liquid on the floor. When he realized it was bodily fluid, he almost threw up, but was saved by his own fear of embarrassment.

The detectives were somewhat stymied by their witnesses, and the Hawks family was growing increasingly frustrated by the investigation's limited scope. So the Hawkses tried to help move things along, as did their friends and colleagues.

From Newport Beach to the Tijuana border, the senior volunteer patrol for the Carlsbad Police Department checked hotels and posted flyers about the missing couple, and Jim Hawks's former police union put up a $1,000 reward for information.

"This was a way for us to show the [Newport] police department that this was a *serious* missing persons case," Jim said.

Recognizing the value of these efforts, Byington and Sailor decided to use the Hawks family as a resource and coordinated a media push to pin down the whereabouts of the missing couple or their car, with the help of Tom's son Ryan.

Ryan Hawks had recently switched careers from engineering to the more social job of medical equipment sales. After dabbling in modeling he was comfortable in front of the camera, so he willingly took on the role of family spokesman, a duty that would repeatedly put him on national television in the coming years. With his square jaw, wide smile, and dark brown hair, he looked so much like his father at the same age that someone comparing their photos might have thought they were twins.

The hardest thing for Ryan to do in the weeks and

months after his parents' disappearance was to fall asleep. So he made himself available for media interviews, poured himself into his new career, and spent half as many hours again designing and updating a website about the case: the Tom and Jackie Hawks Official News Site.

The NBPD kicked off the media push on December 1, 2004, holding three news conferences in as many weeks, and releasing descriptions of the Hawkses and their CRV.

By December 13, the story had captured the national media's attention. Ryan made appearances on three network morning shows, as well as MSNBC's *Deborah Norville Tonight* and FOX's *On the Record,* with Greta Van Susteren.

"One month ago tonight the Newport Beach couple sold the yacht they had been living on for four hundred thousand dollars," Van Susteren said. "They reportedly planned to buy a second home with the money, but they were never heard from again. And tonight there's no sign of the couple, the cash, or their car. Their son is hoping for any clues."

Immediately after Ryan's appearance on the national stage, heart-wrenching messages poured into his website's "guest book" from all over the globe. Many were from adoring women, including this one from his birth mother, Dixie: Our boys are devastated now.... Ryan and Matt worship you, Tom; love you, Jackie, and my heart aches for them to be without you

18

On the evening of December 4, a middle-aged woman called 911 from a pay phone in Westminster, California.

"Please tell me first that the call is recorded, and then secondly, tell me how I would find out how I can try to get some information regarding the missing couple, which was recently in the newspaper, who had a boat that was in the city of Newport," the woman said.

"Yes, the line is recorded," the dispatcher said. "Do you have information on that?"

"I have a family member who most of our family are very concerned about and afraid of, who has been bragging a lot lately about having received over half a million dollars in cash," the woman said. "His name is Skylar Deleon, currently, which is a changed name. His original name was John—"

"Okay, ma'am, hold on, hold on, just one second. Was he bragging just about the cash? Or was he bragging that he murdered these people as well?"

"He did not mention anything about the people. . . . I'm very concerned, because if he knew that I was making this call, my family and myself could be in danger by him or by someone else."

"Okay, well, you haven't given me your name or anything, and you're calling from a pay phone, so don't—"

"He has been bragging about having—"

"And his name is Skylar Deleon?"

"Skylar Deleon is the name he's changed to within the last few years. . . . John Jacobson is his name originally, and his birth name. He lives in Long Beach and he doesn't live far from the 405 Freeway. But he has recently acquired many, many, many possessions, and one of them is this boat, and a relative of mine just told me about the story in there, and the boat was the same boat that he acquired. And I'm told the cash that he's received—"

"It's the same type of boat?"

"It's the same boat exactly."

"And how much cash did he receive? A half a million?"

"He has received over a half a million, so he brags, and now he's also bought the boat and many other things, and is in the process, with his in-laws, of buying property."

"Okay."

"He's living in the home with his in-laws and his wife, or so we're told it's his wife, although there are two or three different wedding dates from the two."

"Do you have any information on them?"

"I know that he is married to a young girl. Her name is Jennifer and I'm not sure of the last name. . . . They have a little girl and she's pregnant. They're living with their in-laws in a duplex. I'm just very concerned about the child who's living in the home with them, and I don't know if he's involved with something regarding these missing people. It's strange to me that he would be actually owning the boat now, or so he said, that he recently said had been gone over by the police."

"Where's the boat at?"

"In the city of Newport," the woman said. "It is the same boat that has been talked about, with the missing couple who previously owned it. So if you could please check into this . . . I'm going to hang up because I can't take a chance with anybody being aware, and I'm sure that you can probably figure out quickly who we are. But more importantly, I don't want any of my family to get hurt."

Newport police would later learn that this woman was Skylar's aunt Colleen Francisco, but well before the 911 tape made its way to them.

On December 15, Skylar left a message for his probation officer, requesting early termination for his probation so he could travel and work outside the United States. The next morning he was told that only the court could grant permission, so he went to the courthouse, where Judge Gary Ferrari granted his request to work at a resort in the Bahamas. Skylar's probation officer called to alert the NBPD of Skylar's apparent escape plans.

At nine-twenty that same morning, an American woman living in Ensenada called Sergeant Steve Schulman, the NBPD's public information officer, and reported that she knew the location of the silver CRV they were looking for. Schulman immediately called Sailor.

"I found your car," he said, passing on the woman's number.

Byington and Sailor's desks were within shouting distance, so Sailor was able to relay the woman's comments directly. Apparently, her boyfriend had seen a story about the Hawkses and their missing car on FOX News the night before.

"I'm looking at it right now," she said, explaining that it was in the parking lot of her trailer park.

Byington's heart started racing. "Can she go out and verify the plate?"

Sailor asked the woman to e-mail him a photo of the license plate, and when it landed ten minutes later, the two detectives celebrated their first big break in the case.

Although prosecutor Matt Murphy felt in his gut that Skylar had killed the Hawkses, he knew they didn't have enough evidence to arrest him for murder yet. But faced with the likelihood that their prime suspect and his wife were about to flee the country, he knew they needed to do something. They could jam Skylar up with a probation violation, but because he'd also admitted to money laundering, Murphy figured that was the best way to go, partly because it would save them from tangling with the Los Angeles County probation system. So Murphy gave Byington the go-ahead.

"Rip him," he said.

The detectives immediately put a surveillance team on Skylar, and Sailor lured him to the station at 11:20 A.M. by promising to release the boat.

The ruse worked, except that Skylar brought his baby daughter with him. Sailor and Byington led them into the interview room, where Skylar looked right at the camera in the wall clock. This time he

was definitely *not* comfortable, realizing that the two
detectives were turning up the heat.

"This is the big urgency we have right now," Byington said. "These people are still missing—"

"Uh-huh," Skylar said.

"I'm fearful that they are not alive," Byington said, because the Hawkses still hadn't contacted police, Skylar, or their family.

Byington laid out two possible scenarios: "Either they're dead and you have something to do with that, or your story . . . about getting this money brought up, then that's the truth. . . . We need to verify one of those two things."

"Okay," Skylar said noncommittally.

"You're saying you have nothing to do with their disappearance."

"No."

"As far as you know, they're alive."

"Yes."

Well, then, Byington said, Skylar needed to provide them with names and phone numbers to prove it. "You're looking at either homicide, which you claim you have nothing to do with . . ."

"Uh-huh."

". . . and that may very well be true, because this is quite a tale you have weaved about this money coming across."

As Byington continued to hammer at Skylar, the color slowly drained from the suspect's face. Perhaps the baby could feel his tension, because she abruptly spat up on his shirt.

"Oh, baby," Byington said.

"You got tissues there?" Sailor asked. "No tissues?"

Clearly looking for an excuse to get out of there, Skylar said Haylie needed some water out of her sippy cup, which was in the car, so Sailor followed him out to the parking lot, continuing to ask questions.

Skylar said his attorney, Ed Welbourn, had told him not to talk to police, but he'd come, anyway. He really wanted to help, he said, but he couldn't give up the names of the Mexicans who had paid him the money. It was just too dangerous.

"My family is in jeopardy," he said. "My dad is behind all this. I can't tell you. Jenn, I, and my kid will die."

Skylar said his father, John Jacobson, would "bury him in a day" if he found out he'd given any names to the police. Calling him "John," Skylar said he wanted to distance himself from the man who had sold drugs, had been involved in organized crime, and still had connections in Mexico. In fact, he said, John was his liaison with the Mexicans who'd brought him the money.

Asked if he thought John was responsible for the Hawkses' disappearance, Skylar said his dad was definitely capable of making them disappear. Since Skylar had bought the boat, his father had been calling three to five times a day, telling him not to talk to the police or use his cell phone, which he was sure the police were tapping. Skylar even let Sailor listen to a couple cell phone messages from John, which he offered to let Sailor tape.

"Would there be any reason we would find your DNA inside their vehicle?" Sailor asked.

Skylar said, no, although he may have rubbed up against the exterior while they were doing the transaction on the hood. Sailor used that opportunity to ask Skylar for a DNA sample, and Skylar agreed.

With that, Skylar drove away, clearly unhappy to be leaving once again without "his" boat.

* * *

About fifteen minutes later, Jennifer Deleon called Byington in a huff.

"What's going on?" she demanded.

Byington, who was antsy to get to Mexico to process the CRV for evidence, gave her the same bottom line: either Skylar was responsible for the Hawkses going missing or being killed, or he was telling the truth about the laundered money from Mexico.

The problem, Byington said, was that reporters were asking lots of questions about the boat buyers paying in cash, and as long as Skylar and Jennifer were cooperating witnesses—not suspects—he wasn't going to give out their names. But that could change. She needed to be aware that reporters had all kinds of resources, including people who were paid to find out such things.

"That can ruin my business," Jennifer said.

Skylar, he went on, could be liable for lesser charges, such as money laundering or tax evasion, but he also could be liable for homicide if his story wasn't true. So Byington asked again: "How is it that he got the money?"

"From the people, I don't know their names, but—"

"Okay, well, but . . . tell me how the process worked."

After Jennifer repeated the same cockamamie story about Skylar getting paid by the Mexicans for breaking into the Anaheim house in 2002, Byington explained the main problem with it: Skylar had refused to identify the Mexicans who supposedly brought him that money.

Also, he said, some curious new facts had emerged earlier that day. Skylar's father had been in town the day before they'd bought the boat, so he was aware of this money and that they were going to buy the boat with it.

"Did you know that?" Byington asked, saying he'd had the impression that she and Skylar were at odds with John Jacobson.

Jennifer didn't remember if John had been in town at that time, but, she said, "I personally don't care for him."

Asked about the Deleons' initial statements that John had been involved in some illegal dealings in Mexico, Jennifer said, "Oh, I don't know anything about that. I know he's . . . I mean, everybody has a past."

"Sure," Byington said, coaxing.

"But as far as I know, he's been really clean and straight for—"

"So why is it that Skylar is so afraid of him?"

"Because he's an asshole, basically. And we don't like to deal with him," Jennifer said, adding that he'd be nice one day and be "ripping into" Skylar the next. "And who wants to deal with that? . . . They've never been close."

Byington said Skylar mentioned that John had visited with the kids at their place the day before they bought the boat. "Do you remember seeing him?"

"Honestly, right now, I don't remember, but that doesn't mean that, I don't know. I, right now, I can't remember yesterday. I mean, I don't know if you've heard, but I'm not doing well," Jennifer said, claiming that the situation was stressing out her entire family and was affecting her pregnancy.

"The primary thing is your health, okay, and your baby's health," Byington said, but the fact remained that she and her husband were the last people to see the Hawkses alive, and this was a "potential homicide."

"I completely understand that," Jennifer said, growing agitated again that the police hadn't released the boat as promised. "But at the same time . . . I'm getting wise to you, too. . . . I talked to the other detective, and he's like, 'We're gonna give it to you, yadda, yadda, yadda.'" She didn't want Skylar driving down there again for nothing. "If you just want to talk to him, just tell him that."

Byington started to say something, but Jennifer cut him off. "Don't bull, you know what I mean? . . . I feel like you're just like, 'Okay, well, yeah, you're gonna get it, you're gonna get it, I'm a hundred percent [sure],' and then—"

"Jennifer, my other alternative is placing the handcuffs on him, and that's not what I want to do," he said.

If he could definitively say Skylar had nothing to do with the Hawkses going missing, and that he wasn't going to "drive off somewhere," Byington said, the police would be happy to release the boat. But they couldn't do that right now. "'Cause the last thing I want to do . . . is release the vessel to you and then we come to find out that somehow . . . you or your husband have a hand in this. . . . We need to put some pieces of this puzzle together and you hold most of the pieces. We have an incomplete picture without your statements. You have a way to talk to Skylar, and you have a way to maybe convince him. . . . Please talk to your husband. See if you guys can come to some consensus."

* * *

Byington was nervous about going without a gun or backup to Ensenada, where he didn't speak the language, had no jurisdiction, and didn't know the area. So he hooked up with California Highway Patrol (CHP) Officer Ignacio "Nacho" Garnica in San Diego County, who was part of the International Police Liaison Officer association, a group of representatives from thirty U.S. and seventeen Mexican law enforcement agencies.

Byington also chose to bring Detective Keith Krallman, who was six feet four inches tall and part Hispanic, and had five years with the LAPD's gang and undercover narcotics units. Krallman had been Sailor's partner in the economic crimes unit before being transferred to robbery/homicide, but he was new to this case.

So at 1:00 P.M., Byington, Krallman, and Crime Scene Investigator (CSI) Don Gage headed south, picked up Garnica, and continued on to Ensenada, about ninety minutes south of the border.

Garnica had called down to alert his Mexican colleagues of their mission, and at the request of the state police's homicide chief, they met up at the beach around 6:00 P.M. Garnica translated for Chief Jose Luis Mena-Jaloma, who said that for the past four hours, he'd had his men surrounding Villa De San Miguel in the El Sauzal trailer park, watching the CRV and a white couple inside.

Great, Byington thought, *the Hawkses are here*. If it *was* them, he thought, he was going to punch them out for costing him a whole week's sleep.

Byington felt relieved when he saw the CRV was still there. But he had a tough time letting the local police handle the situation because they obviously hadn't received the same training. When he saw people running out the back door, for example, no one was there to stop them. So Byington huddled below the front porch and tried his best to let his Mexican colleagues do their job without his interference.

He heard Mena-Jaloma knock on the door and engage in conversation with the fifty-something Latino man who opened it, Diodoro Valenzuela-Salido. Byington could only understand snippets of Spanish, but he distinctly heard the man say, "Skylar Deleon."

"At that moment I knew that Skylar killed these people," Byington said, knowing in his gut that the Hawkses were *not* the white couple to whom Mena-Jaloma had referred.

But there was more. As soon as he heard the man say, "Jennifer," he thought to himself, *She's good for it, too.*

Salido told police that his family had known Skylar since 1999, when Skylar had met Salido's sons, Jose and Luis, at the beach. Skylar had introduced them to his own father, who had visited several times, and the two families surfed together. Skylar didn't seem to get along very well with his father, Salido said; the two seemed distant with each other.

"[Skylar] would stay with us during the time he was here, about two days, which was about once or twice a year," Salido said. "We became friends since he did not seem to be a bad person. He always had money, he drove different cars, which were fairly new."

Jose, who was now twenty-one, had become close friends with Skylar, and two years ago, Skylar had said he would give Jose his car as soon as he got a new one, to repay the family's kindness.

On November 26, 2004, Skylar showed up around noon in the CRV, with his wife and daughter driving separately in a red car. When Salido and his family came out to greet them, Skylar handed Jose the keys to the CRV.

"Here are the keys to your new car," he said.

"I asked him who the owner was," Salido told police, "and Skylar answered, 'For Yoyo.' That is my son Jose Diodoro. So I thanked him for bringing a gift for my son. I was not surprised because he did have money and boats . . . and according to him, he had million-dollar insurance."

Jose told police the same thing. "I asked him if there were any problems with the car. Skylar replied that . . . the car was okay and he would give me the title later, because he owed some money to the person who had the title."

Next, Skylar said he wanted to open a bank account, so Salido and his son accompanied the Deleons on a ninety-minute trip to a bank downtown. The Mexican family spoke no English, so they didn't understand what Skylar was saying during the several phone calls he made there, but they could tell that he was unsuccessful. They went back to the house for dinner, after which the Deleons went off by themselves to talk in the red car for about an hour, then drove away.

After the interviews, Byington was eager to get the CRV back to Newport.

"We need the car," he told the chief.

But Mena Jaloma wouldn't allow it. "You've got to leave the car here," he said. "We need to go back to the office and do paperwork."

This not only went against every chain-of-evidence instinct Byington possessed, but it also prompted fears of further contamination. He and Krallman looked at each other, as if to say, "You've got to be kidding."

"We can't leave the car here," Byington pleaded. "It's a homicide."

Garnica said they had no choice. Byington needed to come back the next day with letters from the Newport police chief and Jim Hawks, spelling out why the Mexican police should release the car for transport across the border.

So they followed Mena-Jaloma to the Ensenada station, where they went back and forth for the next several hours. Byington finally managed to persuade the police to allow his team to go through the car before it was towed to their yard—in case it had disappeared by the time he returned.

Byington was right to worry about evidence going missing. Before they went to the station, he'd seen some freshly dry-cleaned clothes on the CRV's backseat, and it was gone by the time they returned. He wasn't about to have the rest of his evidence tainted, so he did what he had to do. The Salidos wouldn't allow their photos to be taken, but after some discussion they did allow police to take mouth swabs to exclude them as suspects. And although the Mexican police didn't want Byington's team to remove anything from the car, CSI Gage managed to sneak the floor mats under his shirt and took swabs off everything he possibly could.

"What, you want the heater knob?" Gage asked.

"Yes, I want the heater knob," Krallman said, explaining later that it was lucky they did, because they found traces of Skylar's DNA there.

Byington reluctantly started the drive home with his team, updating Sailor and Murphy as soon as he crossed the border—and had cell phone reception again—around midnight.

"Skylar is good for this," he said, noting that Jennifer had also been seen at the house, so she was likely involved as well.

Before finding the CRV, the detectives had theorized that Skylar had killed the Hawkses, dumped their bodies, then got rid of the car. After visiting the *Well Deserved* four times, looking at the for-sale photos Tom Hawks had posted online, and interviewing his family, Sailor had realized that the lighter of its two anchors was missing. The seventy-seven-pound CQR was still there, but the sixty-six-pound Bruce was gone.

CSI Gage found absolutely no blood, fingerprints, or DNA anywhere on the boat—even from the Hawkses—a sign that it had been carefully wiped down. The detectives theorized that Skylar could have dumped the bodies somewhere in Mexico, or maybe at sea, using the anchor to weigh them down so they didn't float to the surface. Finding the car only solidified their hunch that Skylar had been lying. Murphy had independently come to the same conclusion.

"We can't let this guy go," Sailor said. "We've got to arrest him and keep him from fleeing."

Sailor had met with Murphy earlier that day to prepare the arrest and search warrants, intending to bring Skylar in for money laundering as soon as they found the car. Given the latest developments, Sailor arranged to get a judge to sign off on the warrants and pick up Skylar ASAP.

As Sailor and his team were putting their plan into motion the next morning, Byington, Krallman, and Garnica set off on their second trip to Ensenada.

When they arrived, they had to pull a high-ranking woman in the Attorney General's Office out of a family Christmas party to sign the car paperwork. While the woman yelled in Spanish about the pompousness of Amercan law enforcement, Byington and Krallman kept their heads down as Garnica calmly tried to apologize and convey the seriousness of their case.

After that, they had to wait at the police station for ninety minutes before Byington was told to sign a stack of documents separated by sheets of carbon paper and written in Spanish he couldn't understand. Byington signed blindly, hoping he wasn't forfeiting his life away.

While the Mexican authorities continued to process paperwork, the detectives went to a seafood restaurant nearby, analyzing the evidence they had so far.

Krallman expressed his gut feeling that Kathleen Harris could help break the case open. "The notary is lying," he said. "There's no way she's telling the truth."

Frustrated by the CRV situation and the flood of suggestions from all sides, Byington wasn't very receptive to this one. "I don't need people telling me what our problems are," he said. "I need people to give me solutions to our problems."

"If you want solutions," Krallman said, "let me interview Kathleen Harris. I'll get her off her story."

"Fine," Byington grudgingly agreed. "You want to interview her, I'll arrange it for you to interview her as soon as we get back."

Happy at last, Krallman went back to the meal, a pleasant respite from the bureaucratic mire of the past two days. But it wasn't over yet.

Byington had hoped to bring the CRV back with a tow truck, but the Mexican authorities were uncooperative once again, ordering him to drive it himself. So he pulled down his sleeves and put on a pair of gloves, trying to leave as little of his own DNA as possible in the vehicle.

When he got in the car, he realized it wasn't only a stick shift, but its fuel tank was also on *E*.

Byington radioed Krallman in their gray Astro police van nearby. "I need gas," he said.

"We can't stop here," Krallman said, relaying the message from Garnica.

"Dude, I'm on empty."

"We can't stop here," Krallman repeated, explaining that they couldn't take a chance of getting pulled over by a different Mexican police agency.

Luckily, Byington had enough fuel to get to a gas station just outside the city limits. From there, he drove to the border, filled with dread that he would get stopped and have to explain to the Mexican police why he was driving a car registered to two people who were presumed dead. Also, because they'd issued an all-points bulletin (APB) on the car, and publicized its license plate so widely, he was also worried that he'd get stopped at the border crossing.

Thankfully, they made it back to the station without incident.

Meanwhile, Detectives Mario Montero, Jay Short, Joe Wingert, and Dave White went undercover to watch the duplex on Grand Avenue and tail Skylar if he tried to go anywhere before the judge approved the warrants.

Once Sailor was on his way with the warrants, the detectives were authorized to pick up Skylar on the spot. A couple of narcotics detectives headed over to assist in the arrest if necessary, and Lieutenant

Richard Long came to oversee what was expected to be a highly publicized news event.

When Skylar, Jennifer, and Haylie Deleon emerged from their studio at 4:10 P.M. and started loading their car, Wingert handcuffed and arrested Skylar. Wingert was patting him down, when he felt some weird padding around Skylar's butt. Was the kid trying to hide something inside his pants?

"What the hell is this?" asked Wingert, a direct, no-nonsense guy.

"It's a diaper," Skylar replied.

Wingert was not the type to curse on a regular basis, but this occasion got the better of him. "What the f*** you got a diaper for?" he asked, confused.

"I'm incontinent."

Wingert put Skylar into the back of a patrol car, while the other officers led Steve and Lana Henderson out of the duplex and secured the area.

Skylar and Jennifer kept asking what the charge was, but Wingert wouldn't say. "Detective Sailor will be here in a minute, he's going to explain everything to you."

When Sailor arrived at 4:30 P.M., he opened the back door of the police car to talk to Skylar.

"What's going on?" Skylar asked.

"We got a warrant for . . . right now, it's money laundering. I don't know if you want to talk with me or not."

The detective heard Skylar sigh, clearly relieved that the charge wasn't murder.

"I have nothing to say," Skylar said, other than he wanted to speak with his attorney.

Learning that the police had already obtained a no-bail probation hold on him, Skylar said, "This is ridiculous. I sit and try to help you guys out and then

I get in trouble. On what grounds do you have for arresting me?"

"I can't discuss it with you now," Sailor replied.

Jennifer was indignant, saying she couldn't believe this was happening. When her mother tried to ask questions, Jennifer snapped at her, too. "Can you not, please, just be quiet? Thank you."

"Can he kiss his daughter good-bye?" Jennifer asked Sailor.

"Not at this point," he said.

Jennifer also complained when police seized the original boat documents from the Toyota. "Will those copies be available?" she asked, concerned that the police wouldn't release the boat to her without them. Assuming this was how she typically conducted herself, the detectives could see who the dominant party in her marriage was.

Sailor and Long confronted her with what they knew about the Deleons' recent trip to Ensenada, encouraging her to look at the bigger picture.

"We've got the Hawkses, who are missing," Sailor said. "They're probably not alive anymore, so laundering the money and the boat are the lesser of the two evils. What I need you to do is start being more forthright with me and start telling me what you really know."

"It's not going to happen right now," Jennifer said. "I just don't, I—I'm not in the state where I really need to be there right now, but we'll get there. I'm not trying to put it off and be—"

"But if you . . . were involved with their disappearance or their demise," Long said, "it would be perfectly sensible for me to think, 'Well, she doesn't want to tell us all of what she knows,' but if you're not involved . . ."

"I understand that and I know how that looks, but at the same time, we've been honest, you know, in many other things, and still gotten questioned and I'm going to just leave it at that," Jennifer said, adding that she wanted to talk to her attorney.

"Tell him to come down so we can all talk," Long said.

Long meant well and tried to look out for his troops, but he didn't help matters by telling Lana that her daughter was a "coldhearted murderess bitch."

Jennifer told the detectives they weren't going to find anything of interest in the search, other than some laundry and baby stuff. "There's absolutely nothing in there," she said.

However, as the police searched the studio, they found a cache of incriminating evidence: two attaché cases filled with the Hawkses' personal papers, their Hi8 digital recorder, with some recorded tapes, Jackie's laptop, and, curiously, a business card for Jose Bahena, the LAPD's Interpol liaison officer.

Short, who was in charge of coordinating the search, turned over the card to Sailor the next day as he was processing the evidence. Sailor, in turn, told him to give it to Krallman because of his history with the LAPD.

In the Toyota they found Jackie's cell phone battery and the Hawkses' MCI calling card. And in the living room of the duplex, the detectives found Skylar's camouflage backpack, which contained more of the Hawkses' paperwork, Jackie's Arizona voter ID card, and an insurance card for the CRV. They found Skylar's military discharge papers, which they later learned had been doctored, and a notebook in which he'd been writing chord progressions and song lyrics about partying in Mexico with salsa and tequila sunrises, forgetting bills and the past: *Wine Dine 69 Cheap Thrills and a Bottle of Wine . . . That's all it's gona* [sic] *take to make you mine.*

Police found a rifle and a shotgun in the rear bedroom of the duplex, which Steve said they could take for forensic testing. He also signed a consent form for them to obtain his bank records.

In the meantime, Steve showed Sailor the ledger for his checking account, which reflected several transactions from $4,000 to $6,000, with notations of Skylar's and Jennifer's names. He explained that he'd paid off the kids' credit card debts and had also covered payments for Skylar's work-furlough program, none of which they had repaid him, even after he'd taken out a second mortgage on the duplex. He said he earned about $100,000 working for BP, but Lana only made $12.50 an hour as a receptionist.

The detectives weren't thrilled that Long had encouraged Jennifer to invite her attorney over while they were trying to conduct the search, but they were even less pleased when Jennifer *and* Skylar's attorneys showed up around 7:30 P.M.

After Long tried giving Jennifer's lawyer, Michael Molfetta, the "do the right thing" speech on the front porch, Molfetta spoke privately inside with his client. Afterward, he said she didn't want to talk to them. But, he added, "I can guarantee you guys, she didn't murder anyone."

Prosecutor Matt Murphy and the detectives believed that Jennifer was the lightweight in the case, so by phone that night he offered Molfetta a deal for immunity in exchange for her testimony against Skylar.

"Look, man, somebody's going to talk," Murphy said. "I'm going to you first. Let's get her on the witness bus."

But Jennifer refused to help prosecute her husband. "She's got nothing to say," Molfetta told Murphy.

In spite of being deeply in debt, the Deleons had purchased the red Toyota for $31,475 on October 22, bringing their total debt to more than $100,000. The detectives had the car impounded and towed to a lot in Costa Mesa, finally finishing the search around 8:30 P.M., when they gathered in a circle, their stomachs audibly growling, to discuss where to eat. Annoyed with the lieutenant's meddling that day, they fell quiet when he came over.

"Is anyone hungry?" Long asked, saying he wanted to take the team out to dinner.

No one said a word, so Long asked again. The detectives grudgingly agreed, so they caravanned to a hamburger joint nearby. As Long walked into the restaurant, stoic and proud, he looked at the waitress and pointed to one of the TVs that hung from the ceiling.

"Me and my boys just handled a big operation and we might be on the evening news," he said. "Could you please change the channel?"

The waitress declined, saying the TVs were only capable of playing video, which, at that time, featured a surf contest. The detectives were amused, especially when no media had shown up at the Deleons' house, anyway.

News of Skylar's arrest soon spread, however. And, thanks to the Internet, it became an international story. Skylar's brief stint on *Mighty Morphin Power Rangers* made his involvement more interesting to the media, particularly to the entertainment gossip sites and boating communities. Some websites misidentified him as one of the actual Power Rangers, and ran the wrong photo of him. Anyone who has been on

TV and is then accused of a crime—particularly murder—is deemed more newsworthy than regular folks these days.

Skylar Deleon was finally achieving the recognition and attention he seemed to be craving. It's doubtful, however, that this was how he'd imagined it all playing out.

19

Two days after Skylar's arrest, Jennifer and Lana visited his grandparents, Marlene and Jake Jacobson, in the front room of their daughter Colleen's house in Westminster. The older couple lived in one part of the house; Colleen and her husband, Dean Francisco, in the other. Dean, who was livid about the whole situation, left the room after telling Jennifer what little he thought of her husband.

Colleen came in toward the end of the conversation and could see that everyone had been crying. They'd all been shocked to see stories about Skylar's arrest on TV, although the Jacobsons already knew he was in jail because he kept calling the house collect.

Colleen, who later described the conversation to Sailor and testified about it in court, was worried how Jennifer might be taking the news. She was prepared to comfort her, but Jennifer didn't seem all that upset. Colleen thought it odd that she seemed more emotional than Skylar's own wife.

Jennifer said their church friends were praying for them and had taken up a collection to help with legal expenses. Lana described her humiliation as the police rifled through her family's personal things. And Colleen apologized to the group for Skylar and what he might have done.

"We tried really hard to get him straight as a teenager," she said, explaining that she and Dean had also tried to protect Skylar from his father's bad influence.

Jennifer said she thought that police—or someone else—had tailed her and Lana to the Jacobsons' and predicted things would only get worse. Scared that she'd end up giving birth to their second child in jail, she'd already begun making arrangements for Haylie and her unborn son to live with her parents.

"Did Little John kill someone?" Colleen asked.

Jennifer just looked at Colleen, so Colleen tried again. "Did you kill anybody?"

Jennifer just looked at her again, only this time Colleen could have sworn that Jennifer was smirking.

When Colleen tried to ask more about what had led up to all of this, she said Jennifer simply replied: "We needed the money."

As Jennifer and Lana got up to leave, Colleen hugged Jennifer and asked if she needed money or anything.

"No, we are going to be okay," Jennifer said.

Afterward, Colleen and Dean had a talk with her parents. Marlene had been taking calls from Skylar on one phone, and relaying the information to Jennifer on the other. But Dean put a stop to that, saying they could use their own phone to accept Skylar's collect calls, but not the Franciscos'.

Colleen spent the next couple hours going over the strange conversation with Jennifer, still not believing what she'd heard. After getting past the thought that this was out of her control, she decided there was something she could—and should—do.

If Johnny was a murderer, then who knew what he might do to her, to her grandchildren, or to Marlene and Jake. So she called the police again, but she didn't do it anonymously from a pay phone this time.

About six weeks earlier, Jake had told Marlene that he wanted to help out Skylar and Jennifer.

"I talked to the kids and they need to borrow some money," he said. "They are having a hard time."

Marlene said she was against loaning them the $3,000 they'd requested. "We have gotten stuck from your son," she said, referring to her own son John, who had stiffed them on the $7,000 he'd borrowed.

Jake just laughed, saying, "The kids wouldn't do that to us."

So Marlene and Jake withdrew the money from the bank on October 29 and gave it to Skylar and Jennifer at the boatyard.

When Jennifer volunteered that they would repay them $500 a month, Marlene was surprised. "You feel you can, really?"

"We have got a large sum of money coming in," Jennifer said confidently. "We will pay you back the money."

Marlene believed her, but had the Deleons sign a promissory note, anyway. "We felt we could trust them. They were our grandchildren," she said later. "But this came out of what was left of our savings, so we just felt that we needed to get the money back."

Skylar showed them the boat he'd just bought, which he was having repaired and cleaned.

"We were standing right next to it," Marlene recalled a few years later. "Skylar was up with the man that was doing some cleaning inside of this boat, and . . . he said he was going to use it to take people out in the ocean, and for scuba diving and that type of thing."

Skylar had always complained about money to Marlene. "I don't know just what he expected out of life, but I have been brought up that when you want money, you work for it," she said. "You earn it. So maybe that's 'small townish' or something, but that's the way it always has been. And he expected everybody to do everything for him. So he was a very spoiled child.

"I asked Jennifer at one point why she married him, and she looked at me and went like this," Marlene said, rubbing her thumb and fingers together. "I said, 'Money?' And she said, 'Oh yeah.' But then, at other times, she told me how wonderful he was and how much he protected her and he loved her and was good with the baby, and took the baby so she could do things. So she was . . . on top of the world with him."

On the evening of December 17, Sailor received a message at home that Colleen had contacted the station, so he called her back.

Colleen said she'd raised Skylar since he was thirteen, and that he and his father had recently reunited after not talking for quite some time. The two of them had been calling her house all day, because Skylar and Jennifer were supposed to have a conference call with John and Marlene that evening at seven-thirty to discuss whether they should talk to police. John lived out of state, but Colleen suspected he was involved in the boat transaction as well. He'd told her this never would have happened if Skylar had talked to him about it first, but she believed that Skylar would set up his own father if he could.

Although the detectives found no independent evidence of this, Colleen claimed Skylar had tried to commit suicide by cutting his wrists and suffocating himself. She also noted that John had talked about shooting himself, like his brother Jerry.

She said Skylar had also told her that he had more than $1 million, had given money to the Hendersons to invest in property, had started the fire in their house so they could collect insurance money, had had a sex change operation, and had assassinated people in other countries.

A couple days later, Sailor and Byington met with the Franciscos, both of whom said John was capable of killing or having someone killed, and that Skylar could have been involved in transporting narcotics, describing him as a sociopath, cheat, liar, and thief.

Sailor would have nine conversations with Colleen, who would end up being one of the prosecution's key witnesses.

After Sailor's second interview with Alonso Machain, his view of the young man had changed. Alonso still seemed naïve and gullible, but not so innocent.

"It was obvious he was lying to me," Sailor said.

By December 22, Detective White had carefully scrutinized Alonso's and Skylar's cell phone records for the months of October and November, and saw a high number of calls between them. So Sailor called Alonso down to the station to put some pressure on him, while a team of detectives searched his house. They didn't find anything of note, but his financial records did prove useful later on.

Alonso tried to pass off his relationship with Skylar as a casual friendship, saying they only talked once in a while. So Sailor confronted him with the phone records, noting that he and Skylar had exchanged 123 calls between November 1 and December 1, averaging four calls a day.

"That's more than an occasional friendship," Sailor said.

Alonso was visibly shaken. His head down, he stumbled over his words, trying to talk his way out of it, but he had no feasible explanation.

"We knew something was up," Sailor said later. But at that time, "We didn't know it was murder."

Drawing on his four years as an economic crimes detective, Sailor also analyzed the Deleons' financial records, looking for leads and a motive.

Skylar had earned $26,600 at Ditech in 2002. After he got fired and went to jail in 2003, his net income dropped to $9,678; Jennifer's was only $9,000.

The Deleons still owed $27,000 to Steve Henderson as of November 1, 2004. In addition, they had ten credit cards stacked with $25,000 in debt, with the largest minimum payment being $120 a month. Skylar's share was $16,000 on six cards and Jennifer had $9,000 on her four. They owed Skylar's grandmother $3,000, and they also had a $12,000 credit line with Bank of America, with a monthly payment nearing $500. In addition, they were responsible each month for payments of $687 for their new Toyota Highlander, $494 for Skylar's Ford truck, $400 rent for Jennifer's chair at Little John's Salon, and at least $100 in cell phone bills.

On October 15, 2004, the balance of their joint account was $556. By November 13, it was overdrawn by $52.

After reviewing one hundred checks written against that account, Sailor found that Jennifer had signed every single one of them, showing that she—not Skylar, as they'd told police—was in charge of their finances. Clearly, the Deleons were under the kind of financial pressure that any couple would want to relieve. It was just a question of how.

20

On the afternoon of December 20, Detective Krallman called the number on the business card for LAPD Officer Jose Bahena that they'd found in Skylar's things, and got an interesting briefing about the abbreviated homicide investigation into the death of JP Jarvi.

Afterward, Krallman turned to Byington, whose desk was catty-corner to his, and said, "You're not going to believe this."

"What?"

"Well, this officer up in L.A. was assisting the Mexican authorities with a murder involving an American citizen, and guess who's involved in that homicide?"

Byington waited with anticipation.

"Does the name 'Skylar' ring a bell?" Krallman asked.

"You're sh***ing me."

"Nope."

"Holy moly," said Byington, launching into one of his mile-a-minute commentaries. "Run with it. See what you can get. It's your baby."

Byington soon learned that Mena-Jaloma, the Ensenada homicide chief who had helped them recover the CRV, was the same detective who had interviewed the Deleons nine months earlier in the Jarvi case. Why hadn't Mena-Jaloma mentioned that to him? Was it because he'd dropped the ball? Or was it something more insidious? Byington always wondered if Skylar had known Mena-Jaloma personally, especially in light of a comment Skylar had made to a codefendant about putting a dead body in the trunk of his car and dumping it in Mexico.

During a 7:00 A.M. meeting with Officer José Bahena two days later, Krallman learned that he'd assisted the two Ensenada detectives in locating Jarvi's van at City Loans, an auto pawnshop in Long Beach.

When Jarvi took out a loan using his van as collateral, City Loans installed a GPS tracking device, known as an Aircept, in case of nonpayment. The repo men activated the device soon after Jarvi was murdered, and it "pinged" in front of the Hendersons' house on January 1 and 8, 2004, then at Jet Automotive, a repair shop in Long Beach, on January 13. The repo men took it the next day.

On January 28, Greg Logan, the shop's owner, told the Mexican detectives that Skylar, a customer and acquaintance, had dropped off the van—with the keys inside. Logan gave them Skylar's home address, where Bahena helped translate a conversation with Jennifer. She admitted that she'd gotten into the van, which Skylar had brought home, but said, "We got rid of it," saying they should talk to Skylar about all of this. She gave them his cell number, and they interviewed him later that day at his TWI work site, Terminal Island in Long Beach.

Skylar, Bahena said, had someone fax over his cell phone records, which Bahena forwarded to Mena-Jaloma. That was the end of his involvement, and, as it turned out, the end of the case. Bahena gave Krallman copies of the same records.

After going to City Loans to get details on the van and on the company's tracking devices, Krallman called Sailor to say he was headed over to Logan's shop.

"That's funny," Sailor said, "I just got a call from Long Beach police officers about a Greg Logan who knows about Tom and Jackie Hawks, and said that Skylar was inquiring about money laundering."

Logan, a tall guy covered with tattoos, told Krallman that he'd worked on Skylar's F250 truck engine a year earlier. Since then, Skylar had called or come by every few months to chat about problems with the truck, to invite him out on his boat, or for nothing at all. Logan said he socialized with some customers, but not Skylar.

"It's just that his personality is, I don't know, kind of flaky," he said. "Seemed like a lot of bullsh** out of his mouth all of the time, and I don't need that."

Skylar brought his fishing boat to the shop one day, saying he was getting the motor and upholstery redone, and had all the workers come out and look at it. Logan had no idea how Skylar made his living, but he was always talking about his hobbies, his business ventures, and his plans to buy a house in Mexico and start a fishing business, so Logan "just assumed he was rich."

Skylar had called about six or eight months ago to ask if Logan had room on his lot to store a buddy's van for a few days. The guy had taken off to Mexico, and Skylar needed to move the van because of street sweeping. Logan agreed, so Skylar dropped it off.

The repo guys towed it away a few nights later, but when Logan notified Skylar, he didn't seem to care much. A couple weeks later, two guys from the Mexican consulate office in L.A. came by to ask questions about the van.

"They told me they found the [owner] guy with his throat slit in Mexico," Logan said.

So he called Skylar again, but got the same response. "I don't think he had a reaction," he told Krallman.

Sometime later, Skylar told Logan he was coming into a lot of money. He didn't want the government to get it, so he proposed buying three of Logan's vehicles and transferring the money directly into Logan's bank account. But when Skylar asked for the routing numbers, Logan suggested he get a cashier's check, instead.

Skylar never actually used the words "money laundering," but Logan figured that was what he was hinting at.

"He talks, like, in riddles. . . . I thought he meant, how do you get around not paying the tax, to buy the boat, and not pay the tax?" Logan said.

Skylar had always been a car buff. One time he asked Logan to borrow his 1995 Viper, saying he wanted to take his wife out for their anniversary. He left his wife's Honda behind in its place, but Logan still kicked himself all night. Thankfully, Skylar brought it back in one piece the next day, then he asked to borrow it again to drive down to Newport.

"He said he was going to meet somebody on a

powerboat," Logan said. Skylar had also said he was
going to buy a boat, but Logan had long quit paying
attention to his stories by then.

Not long after that, he saw on the news that a yacht-
owning couple from Newport were missing. After
Skylar's arrest, Logan remembered Skylar's request
about the Viper, put it together with their money-
laundering conversation, and called Long Beach
police, thinking the information might be helpful.

"Do you think Skylar had anything to do with the
disappearance of these people?" Krallman asked.

"I don't know. I tend to think that people are
good," Logan said. "I think he's full of sh**. I think
he's maybe got some kind of complex. He has to be
something bigger than what he really is, but I think
he's a nice person."

The next day, Krallman interviewed JP's mother,
Betty Jarvi, and she told him about the condo transaction she'd cosigned for JP's $50,000 "investment."
Among the materials he collected from her were JP's
phone records, which showed that he and Skylar
had exchanged seven calls in the last couple days JP
was alive.

Krallman also spoke with JP's brother, Jeff, who
had heard some talk about JP and a boat, but said it
didn't make sense because there was "nothing nautical" about JP. After reading a newspaper article a year
after his brother's murder about a missing couple
who had owned a boat in Newport Beach and something about Mexico, Jeff had a gut feeling they were
all related, so he'd alerted a Newport police officer.

"I told him that had something to do with my brother, and I was right," Jeff said.

Slowly, a whole new set of investigative dominoes was starting to fall, and once again, Skylar was looking good for the murder.

21

As often as she was allowed, Jennifer Deleon visited
Skylar in the men's jail across the street from the
courthouse in Santa Ana. Inmates were permitted to
have three weekly visits, one each on Fridays, Satur-
days, and Sundays that lasted up to sixty minutes.
Hoping to gather some information while Jennifer
was out and free to incriminate herself, Newport
police monitored tapes of any visits with Skylar and
also of Skylar's collect calls to her. They also read
every letter that Skylar sent or received.

The jail's visiting areas consisted of partitioned
booths, where inmates and visitors sat on metal stools
on either side of a clear glass or plastic pane, and
communicated through telephone receivers. Presumably because of his incontinence issues, Skylar was
soon transferred to the medical unit, where he spoke
to visitors in a separate room adjacent to the other
booths, with a door that had to stay open. It was unclear whether this separation was for privacy reasons,
because Skylar was a high-profile inmate, or if it was
merely a case of "first come, first serve."

The Deleons must have been aware that their

conversations were being taped, because the tape picked up snatches of incoherent whispers and frequent periods of silence between their cryptic partial sentences, when they were likely mouthing words to each other.

On a half-hour visit the day after Christmas, Jennifer and Skylar talked in their own special code, declaring "I love you" to each other five times. But rather than Jennifer giving instructions, which police believed was the couple's usual dynamic, Skylar was acting as the mastermind, only now he was coordinating things from behind bars. He coached his wife on whom to call and what to say—even what other people should say, including his father. Jennifer appeared to be the eager follower, taking direction as needed.

"You need to give permission to your attorney to talk to mine," Skylar said. "That way they can work together."

"I can do that today," she said.

"No, not right now, talk to John first. . . . Tell John that they may try and . . . charge me with something stupid. Let him know that what he has to do is go there and say that (whispering) . . . Okay?"

"Okay."

"You got to tell him that. I don't know if you have or not."

"Well, it didn't really come to that," she said.

He told her to get a "very, very recent picture of Justin" in what seemed like a scheme to claim his half brother was involved, to get his father involved, or to give Skylar an alibi of some sort. "Tell him to talk to my attorney, but he has to tell my attorney (whispering) . . . I was just trying to help him," Skylar said. "Tell him (whispering) . . . we'll change the name, tell him . . . we'll fight for him. . . . He's gonna lose his business. Tell him I will fight for his business."

"He keeps saying that he loves you," Jennifer said. "You know what I found out? Your grandma called the detective. He didn't call her."

"I know, she's just stupid," Skylar said.

"That's what John was, like, 'She's pissing me off,' I'm, like, 'He's mad at her right now.'"

"Ed [Welbourn] was saying, he's, like, we got a really good chance of beating this," Skylar said. "We can one hundred percent beat it if John just says that (whispers)."

"What if he doesn't?"

"He's all fifty-fifty. . . . He's, like, if he says that, alone, they'll have to drop the charges."

Jennifer said Skylar's father thought she was stupid. "But then he said that you told him once before that I'm not as naïve as I look."

A few minutes later, the visit was about to end. "It'll be okay, baby," she said.

"I can't wait to see you, to hold you again," he said.

"Okay, that's us, I love you."

"I love you, sweetheart," Skylar said.

"I'll talk to you in the morning. Be strong."

"I want to see my new baby."

"You will."

Prosecutor Matt Murphy was nothing if not fair and professional. He was used to winning, but that didn't mean he didn't work for it. For him, the murder of Tom and Jackie Hawks was the most horrific crime, and one of the most complex cases, in all his years at the DA's office. And he was determined to win a conviction for the Hawks and Jarvi families.

Nonetheless, he played by the rules, so he felt ethically obligated to drop the money laundering charges against Skylar because he knew in his heart that Skylar had never exchanged any cash with the Hawkses.

"You're supposed to be right, especially in a vertical unit, and most especially with a homicide unit, you've got to be one hundred percent sure that the guy is not only the right guy, but you've got him with the right charges," he explained.

However, Murphy couldn't let Skylar go free, so he needed another way to hold him while he and the detectives continued to build their case.

One of them found the answer in a public record search in late December: a civil lawsuit filed by Morris "Mo" Beck six months earlier, which led Murphy to file grand theft charges against Skylar on December 28.

Beck said Skylar had come to him in December 2003 for an insurance estimate to repair the stern drive of his Sea Ray. After taking a look, Beck recommended an overall "repower," which also meant a new engine and transom assembly.

It would cost more, but the boat would run better, he said, and Skylar would only have to pay the difference his insurance didn't cover. Skylar agreed, saying he also wanted some hull work done later on. Once Beck ordered all the parts, Skylar brought in the boat.

Beck was willing to take a deposit, but Skylar insisted on paying off the whole job the afternoon of Friday, December 26, with $17,000 in hundred-dollar bills. At that point he asked Beck to install a water heater, a bait pump, and some sophisticated navigational equipment designed for global travel—even though the boat wasn't capable of cruising much past Catalina Island.

Then, one subsequent Monday morning, Beck found the lock on his yard had been cut, and Skylar's boat was gone. So Beck sued, seeking the outstanding amount Skylar still owed, plus interest and punitive damages. Skylar responded that he'd paid his bill, but Beck had tacked on additional charges.

The civil case dragged on for more than a year.

Detective Sailor had been playing phone tag with John Jacobson, who kept referring Sailor to his attorney, so the detective decided to get tough. The same day Murphy filed the grand theft charges against Skylar, Sailor had a patrol car pick up John on a traffic warrant so he could try to squeeze a story out of him in person.

Skylar kept blaming his father for everything, and the Hawkses' car had been found in Mexico, where John had drug ties, so Byington thought John might be involved in one or both homicides. John claimed he'd been traveling in Arizona when the Hawkses were murdered, and police couldn't disprove his alibi.

"I thought Dad was good for something," Byington said, "Skylar was never the type of guy who did anything alone." But, he added, "We didn't know. We had no clue. . . . We heard about big, bad voodoo daddy . . . and you get him in there, and he's just a big tub of goo."

The jail deputy called a little while later, saying that John had decided he wanted to talk, after all. So Sailor put him in a white brick interview room with a hidden camera and microphone and brought Byington to witness the juicy statement he thought they were about to get.

But before either one could say much, John immediately started complaining about being held for the past two hours. "I've been more than cooperating," he said. "They want to look in my truck, I say go for it. . . . I got the money to bail out right now, I should be allowed to bail out. I should be allowed to make a phone call. . . . You want my cooperation later on with my attorney, then stop with the games."

Byington could not believe what he was hearing. "So that's what you called us back down here for?" he asked, incredulous, feeling his blood pressure rising.

"Huh?" John asked innocently.

"It took you that long in that pea brain of yours to figure out that you wanted to get some cooperation from *us*?" Byington asked. "You'll get your opportunity to post bail. You'll get your file. In case you haven't seen these, these are the two missing persons," he said, holding up the Hawkses' photos.

"No, take a look at 'em, 'cause, apparently, you've got these big, giant balls—that's what everybody tells me. You're this tough guy, back there, wherever you live, and that everybody is afraid of you. Well, guess what, your kid is responsible for their death, and you know [something] . . . about it. It's about time for you to step up and be a father."

As John stared at Byington, looking shell-shocked, the sergeant told him to cut the garbage about his rights being violated and face up to the reality of the situation. "These people are dead. They've got grandkids, they have brothers, sisters, parents."

"I'm just saying—" John tried to interject, but Byington was on a roll.

"You don't want to be a dad once in a while. . . .

Your kid's laying you out, I could give a sh**. . . . Keep looking over your shoulder, 'cause the warrant will come. . . . If you want to worry about this crap. . . . Fine. Worry about it."

"No, I'm just saying—"

"Keep it to yourself," Byington barked. "Nice talking to you. I appreciate you calling us back down here."

John tried to shake it off, as if he'd heard it all before. Turning to Sailor, he said he knew Byington was pulling the old "good guy/bad guy routine."

Byington, who had just closed the door behind him, ripped it open again. He couldn't let that one pass.

"'Good guy/bad guy'?" he asked, ordering Sailor to pull his file and go. "We don't need to talk to your ass," he told John. "I thought you wanted to say something."

"I'm just saying there's no need to play games," John said. "I said I'd talk to my attorney."

"Good riddance. Talk to your attorney. No good guy/bad guy," Byington said, slamming the door behind him.

That same week, Steve Henderson found a threatening note tacked to the door of the duplex's front unit, indicating the author didn't know where the Delcons lived. Written on a color Xerox copy of a news story about the Hawkses was this message: *Jennifer, do the right thing or else.*

Jennifer believed that John Jacobson had left the note, so she turned it over to Long Beach police.

* * *

On January 2, 2005, Haylie's first birthday, Jennifer was back to visit Skylar with her father and daughter. Jennifer took the baby into the booth, and waited a few minutes for Skylar, who came in crying.

"She knows her daddy," Jennifer said, cooing, as she passed on hellos from a neighbor and several people from church while making ga-ga noises at the baby. Back to a more serious tone, Jennifer asked about Skylar's health issues.

"They're taking my blood pressure and stuff twice a day," he said, sniffling.

"You need it," she said firmly.

"I don't have any choice," he said. "They wake me up at four in the morning and do blood pressure checks."

"Whatever, whatever," she said matter-of-factly. "It's okay, because you're going to calm down, and it's going to be okay. Everything will be all right. I'm going to get everything taken care of tomorrow. Everything."

"We need to just tell the truth on this, and it will be a lot better," Skylar said, still sniffling.

Skylar's latest story was that he was being held on trumped-up charges and was going to be released after ninety days, the penalty period for being arrested, which was a probation violation.

Skylar had explained to Jennifer and her parents that they didn't have the assets to cover the deposit for the $250,000 bail that would allow his release any sooner, but that his lawyer, Ed Welbourn, was optimistic, seeing that it was Skylar's father who had caused all this trouble by threatening them and forcing Skylar to do something bad.

"If all we did is, we got threatened, he's, like, no jury in the world is going to convict . . . especially if they can get the guys from the strip club to say they've gotten threatened," he told Jennifer, alluding to John's strip joint in Arizona. Skylar noted that John's criminal history was added proof.

Jennifer got up so her father could come in. Skylar tried to talk about being falsely accused, but Steve Henderson had other plans. He wanted to give Skylar a religious lesson before the Lord threw him away like "a piece of trash."

"So you said you're crying out to the Lord," Steve said. "You know, it's one thing to cry out to Him when you're in trouble, it's another thing to cry out when you're not in trouble. . . . There's two ways you can go through, my friend. . . . One path leads to where you are . . . and another path that doesn't. . . . I can just say He'll be there for you if you want Him to be."

"I do," Skylar said, adding that when he got out, he wanted to work with kids, maybe in a youth ministry.

"Sounds like it could be a long time," Steve said. "I want you to think about love. Love doesn't allow things like this to happen to family." Then his tone lightened a bit. "I seen you on TV," he said, laughing.

"What are they saying?"

Steve said it was something related to Skylar's arraignment.

Skylar said his lawyer predicted that all the charges would be dropped; the authorities had no real evidence, they were just being "hateful." The attorney also said that charging him based on a civil case was "absolutely ridiculous" and one of the dumbest things he'd ever seen.

Skylar explained that he and Jennifer had an alibi—they were together the whole day in question, and now "there's a witness that's seen somebody else down there and can fully identify that person."

Returning to his whiny "victim" voice, Skylar said, "I don't like this and I can't handle being away from Jenn and Haylie. . . . I just sit here and cry for hours."

Steve, who was clearly uncomfortable with this show of emotion, seemed determined to make a quick exit. "Yeah? I'm sorry to hear that. I'm sorry it has to be this way," he said.

A couple minutes later, Jennifer came back with Haylie. "It's okay, baby," she said soothingly to Skylar, her other baby, asking if Steve had upset him. "He didn't yell at you or anything, did he? I love you, 'kay? And we're going to be okay."

Sniffling again, Skylar cooed at his little girl, "Happy birthday!" and she responded with her usual chipper "Hi! Hi!"

"Everybody is praying for you," Jennifer said. "So you just have to be strong and patient for the truth to come out, 'kay?"

Her tone serious again, she explained that John had called her. Skylar said, irritated, that his father wouldn't visit, he'd simply declared the whole mess an "interstate thing" and planned to leave California so police couldn't pick him up.

"That's what he told me, too," Jennifer said, adding that he "knows about the note on the house. Lisa told him. . . . He goes, 'You know I didn't do that, I'd never do that.'" Jennifer suggested that Skylar keep such details to himself next time, and not tell his stepmother or half sister "anything of value."

Skylar had been busy working on a plan to kill two birds with one stone: create an alibi and up the ante on the "blame John" game. The witness he'd mentioned to Steve was inmate Danny Alvarado, whom he'd met on the bus to court and was being held for having a knife in his vehicle.

On December 30, while they'd been waiting in adjacent holding cells at the courthouse, Alvarado had overheard Skylar talking about the Hawks case. Alvarado was originally from Prescott, Arizona, so he was curious. On the bus back to jail that evening, he and Skylar got to chatting. Skylar said he and his attorney could help Alvarado if he was able to help Skylar with an alibi. Skylar gave Alvarado one of Welbourn's business cards and promised a financial reward.

They couldn't talk in detail, because too many people were around, but they got another chance on a subsequent court date. Skylar persuaded Alvarado to tell police that he'd been fishing at the 15th Street pier in Newport, when he saw Tom Hawks get into a dinghy with a black man and a white guy named John, who fit the description of Skylar's father. Only Alvarado wasn't supposed to know they were related. The black man was a big, burly guy, six feet two inches tall, with fat on top of muscle, in his midfifties, with a receding hairline. John had a noticeable scar from his eyebrow to his hairline. Alvarado had learned his name because he'd tried to bum a cigarette off him, and he remembered him because of John the fisherman in the Bible.

Skylar claimed that John had murdered the Hawkses, and was now trying to frame his own son for it. So, even more important, Skylar said, he needed Alvarado to find someone to kill John Jacobson.

22

Skylar came to attorney Ed Welbourn on a referral from the civil lawyer who was defending him against Mo Beck's boat repair lawsuit. Welbourn had worked cases of attempted murder before, but this being his first murder, criminal defense attorney Michael Molfetta, his former employer with whom he shared office space, agreed to advise him.

The two attorneys sat down with Skylar and Jennifer before he was arrested. As they told their story, Molfetta immediately sensed that Skylar had murdered the Hawkses, whereas Jennifer didn't seem the killing type.

For a while, he and Welbourn didn't know whether Jennifer would be arrested, so they worked under the premise that Molfetta would assist with Skylar's case unless or until Jennifer's situation changed. As the evidence continued to mount, Matt Murphy told Molfetta it was no longer a question of *if*, but *when*, Jennifer would be arrested. So Molfetta broke away and worked her case alone, splitting his retainer with Welbourn, who, in turn, joined forces with his attorney father, Robert Welbourn.

Molfetta was convinced that Skylar was headed for a death sentence, and the sooner he could persuade Jennifer and her family of that, the better. So he sat Jennifer down in his office—twice—and gave it to her straight.

"The sun will go down and Skylar will be on death row," he said. "So do what's best for your kids and get off this ride."

But Jennifer wouldn't accept his advice. Sometime after she rejected Murphy's immunity offer, Molfetta said he asked Murphy if he would renew it and went back to Jennifer with a second chance, which she also refused. (Murphy's memory differs on this issue; he says there was no second offer.)

At times, Molfetta said, Jennifer would tell him things indicating "she knew exactly what was going on and what had happened to the Hawkses," and that Skylar was complicit. But two minutes later, she'd say, "Skylar wouldn't kill anyone."

Molfetta voiced his next suggestion even more forcefully: file for divorce, and don't write or visit him ever again. Jennifer ignored that, too. Ultimately she would visit Skylar thirty-four times and exchange 2,300 letters with him, sometimes three in one day.

Michael Molfetta was a beefy guy who exuded testosterone and confidence. Unafraid of offending anyone, he was known to go after opposing counsel in court like a pit bull. Lauded for being one of the county's best lawyers, he was also known for having one of the sharpest tongues in the courthouse. Although he always shot for a straight victory, sometimes winning meant a hung jury or a mistrial.

Born in Italy in 1964, Molfetta moved to Manhattan

with his family when he was a baby. His father started the Mezzaluna restaurant chain, the Los Angeles franchise of which later employed waiter Ron Goldman, who was murdered along with O.J. Simpson's wife, Nicole.

After Molfetta's parents got divorced, he spent five years in Carriacou, an island in the West Indies, before going to boarding school. He then attended Occidental College, went on to Southwestern Law School, and played professional football in Helsinki during his first summer break.

Molfetta clerked at the Orange County DA's Office after law school, where he discovered the only vocation that could rival the rush he got on the football field.

"It's the only place I could end up in a street fight without ending up in handcuffs," he said. "It just suited my personality."

He joined the DA's office in 1991, and after learning the ropes, he was asked to mentor two newbies, who were clerking during law school. One was a young woman who would later become his second wife and mother of his three children. The other was Matt Murphy.

All good attorneys have an MO and an image that reflects their personality, which they learn to project in the courtroom. If they tried to be something they aren't, the juries sensed it right off. Molfetta's schtick was humor and sarcasm, and oftentimes deprecating humor.

Molfetta loved to rib Murphy about the two cases in which he had outlawyered his former student, so Murphy had been hearing "teacher two, student zero" for more years than he liked to admit. One day, he told Molfetta, he would be better than his teacher. And they were about to find out if he was right.

Murphy's image, Molfetta said, was the credible "handsome good guy," but he wasn't all that humble.

Murphy was educated in an all-boys Catholic prep school in Los Angeles, the California penal code was now his bible, and he found satisfaction in exposing hypocrisy in criminal defendants who claimed innocence because they were good, practicing Christians and would never lie—let alone kill anyone.

The son of a doctor and a nurse, Murphy was born in Taiwan in 1967, while his father was in the U.S. Air Force.

He studied political science at the University of California, Santa Barbara, became vice president of his fraternity, and worked with handicapped kids. The rape of a close friend prompted him to start a mandatory program on campus—Greeks Against Rape—and inspired him to go to law school at the University of San Diego. After his DA clerkship, he was hired full-time in 1993, piling up victories in the juvenile gang, felony, and sexual assault units before he was moved to the homicide unit at age thirty-four.

Standing at a very lean six feet two inches, Murphy had an acerbic wit and cutting sense of humor. But he usually held those traits back from the jury, coming across so calmly that sometimes his voice could barely be heard in the back of the courtroom.

That's because his focus was on the jurors, to whom he made a habit of talking in a simple, direct, sincere, and respectful manner. His goal was to help them understand the gravity of the matter before them, and notice when he raised his voice, "fired up" at opposing counsel or an uncooperative witness during cross-examination or in his closing argument.

Murphy's ties were never loud, either, and although he had a winning smile, he rarely flashed it during the proceedings, only when he checked in with victims' families, his colleagues, or key reporters at the breaks to see how his witnesses and evidence were playing. If they weren't persuaded, the jury might not be, either.

Although he described himself as a "lifer" in the DA's office, some wondered if Murphy had aspirations to be district attorney someday; Murphy insisted he did not.

During a trial, Murphy tried not to make objections because he believed that arguing in front of the judge was disrespectful. Besides, Murphy wanted to look as if he was above losing his cool, always portraying the confidence of anticipated victory. Only when his opponent didn't play by the local rules of gamesmanship, tried legal stunts, or dragged out the proceedings did Murphy's body language reveal any frustration or antipathy. On those occasions he walked back to his table from a sidebar with the judge, his long neck craned and head cocked like a tall bird, his lips pursed with determination to come back—no matter what the setback. And he usually did.

Murphy had the ability to remain extremely focused—working hard and ignoring the rest of his life while in trial, using his time on the freeway while driving home or to his gym to talk to Byington or reporters. Murphy was a bachelor at heart, even when he had a girlfriend, watching most, if not all, of his friends get married.

"He's got hot- and cold-running women, whenever he wants them," Byington joked.

Murphy loved surfing and golfing with friends, but he had to admit that prosecuting cases was what he did best.

23

In early December, Adam Rohrig was working his bartender job, listening to a friend from the dive shop talk about the *Well Deserved,* when Skylar popped up on the TV news, which described him as the last person to see the missing yacht owners alive.

"That's Skylar!" the friend exclaimed.

Adam scrambled for an innocent explanation, but inside, he knew the truth: *These two people are dead.*

After another night of drinking with Kathleen Harris, Adam called her with some advice: "Don't tell them where the bodies are," he said.

Kathleen thought he was joking, but she couldn't be sure. "I don't know where the bodies are," she said, hoping that Adam didn't know, either.

As Christmas approached, Dave Byington followed up on Keith Krallman's challenge to interview Kathleen. "Okay," he told Krallman, "it's your turn."

For the next hour, Krallman sat across from the notary in the interview room and let her run through her story once again. She seemed comfortable until he looked her in the eyes and spoke calmly but firmly.

"I don't believe anything you're saying," he said. "And if, in fact, I'm able to obtain evidence that you're being less than truthful or lying, I'm going to come after you to the full extent of the law."

Kathleen stared down at the floor, her eyes growing watery as she took several deep breaths and grabbed at her purse. But, still, she wouldn't admit to anything.

Krallman felt like a failure and apologized to Byington for letting him down.

A few days later, Krallman was at home watching TV with his wife when Byington called.

"Hey, I just wanted to let you know you did a great job," he said. "Congratulations."

"What are you talking about?" Krallman asked.

"You did it. You just made this a double homicide. Kathleen Harris went out and got an attorney. Everything she'd been telling us was a lie. You read it correctly. You're the only one who came to me and spoke your mind. I'm proud of you."

Adam was happier than usual to take his usual year-end trip to San Francisco to see his father. At this point, it was a most opportune reprieve. Or so he thought. Jennifer Deleon, the next-to-last person he wanted to talk to, interrupted his temporary escape with a phone call.

"I have all of Skylar's dive stuff," she said. "I'm wondering if I could sell it back to the shop, what could I get for it?"

"We don't buy back gear," he replied.

Jennifer asked how much the equipment cost the dive shop in the first place, so Adam told her: $1,500.

"Well, that's not very much money," she said. "I guess I'll just hold on to it. When are you working next? Give me a call when you get back to town."

On Christmas Eve, Kathleen had told him she'd hired an attorney. After speaking with one who had represented Skylar before—and said he had killed twenty-one people when he was in the military—she knew she should come clean, but was even more petrified of Skylar than before. Her parents were frightened, too, so they put her into hiding. She then hired attorney Paul Meyer, who advised her to stop talking to Adam.

Nonetheless, Adam gave Kathleen a call to wish her happy birthday and tell her about his strange conversation with Jennifer.

"It's not Skylar who you have to be scared of," Adam said. "It's his people. I'm not scared of what will happen to me. I'm scared of what's going to happen to my mom."

"I'm going to talk to the detectives and tell them everything," Kathleen said. "You need to get an attorney."

"I have no money," he said. "My mom has no money."

Adam realized that he couldn't run from the law for much longer. If someone was going to go down in flames, it should be him. He tried to tell himself that he hadn't killed anyone or caused them to die—that perjury was his only offense. But he knew his friend needed to protect herself, no matter what that meant for him.

"Fine, Kathleen," he said resignedly, telling her to do what she needed to do. "I have to go."

Adam lay in bed, emotionally and physically paralyzed, for the rest of the day. When his mother asked what was wrong, he just batted her away.

Kathleen and Meyer met with detectives and the prosecution team at the DA's office on January 4, 2005, shortly after she'd talked with Adam. In what would be the only such deal in this case, Meyer was able to get his client immunity from prosecution for the fraudulent notarization, a misdemeanor, as well as the felony charges of accessory after the fact and aiding and abetting.

Kathleen gave them a more truthful version of events, and although she wasn't good with dates and times, her confession gave detectives the wedge they needed to break open the case and spark a series of crucial witness statements and arrests.

They couldn't be sure if Kathleen had a bad memory, if she was trying to protect herself and Adam by minimizing her involvement, or a little of both, but some of her statements conflicted with each other, and also with Adam's. And some were outright lies.

She came back two days later to clarify some details and correct her false statements. "I lied to you because I was trying to cover Adam," she said. "And I'm sorry. I didn't want him to get in trouble for burning the books. And when I did go notarize those documents . . . I thought it was going to be illegal, because there was a lot of money involved. But I didn't know what it was."

Kathleen had lied so many times, her credibility was tainted, so DA investigator Larry Montgomery asked if she'd neglected to tell them anything else.

"All I know is that I did not meet with the Hawks," she said. "I met with Skylar and Jennifer. I messed

up. I notarized something that I should not have
notarized, and I got caught up in something that's
really awful, and I'm sorry that I lied to you about
that. I don't know what else to tell you."

The morning after talking with Kathleen, Adam
was still lying in bed depressed. Things were bad
enough without having to work for the next seven
days. But it only got worse when Sailor called to ask
for a meeting at the closest Starbucks.

Adam was walking to his car to head over there
when Byington's team pulled up, swooped in, and
frisked him. Although he wasn't pleased that Sailor
had lied to him, Adam agreed to give them and Byington a statement, including a description of the color
photocopy Skylar had given him.

"What did you do with it?" Byington asked.

"I threw it away. I didn't want anything to do with
it," Adam said, adding that he'd tossed it somewhere
along the road in Huntington Beach.

A few minutes later, Detective Short took Byington aside to show him a crumpled wad of paper. "Hey,
look what we found under the bed," Short said as he
revealed the photocopy Adam had described.

Jackie's photo was taken before she'd cut her hair
short and dyed it blond, so it finally made sense why
Kathleen had given police the wrong physical description.

Byington had a short fuse that day, frazzled after a
month of losing sleep over this case, and erupted at
Adam. "Quit f***ing around with this!" he screamed.
"You f***ing son of a bitch, what the f*** is this doing
in your room if you threw it away?"

Adam replied that he'd truly believed that he'd

tossed it where he'd said, but, apparently, he'd missed his usual bank shot into the trash bin, and the wad had rolled under the bed. Observing Adam's obvious embarrassment, Byington believed him.

Adam would prove to be a far more credible and consistent witness than Kathleen. During his ten interviews with detectives, he fleshed out the timeline and content of Skylar's scheme, and his litany of lies.

Now armed with Kathleen's and Adam's statements that the boat sale transaction had never occurred, the detectives were ready to turn up the pressure on Alonso Machain. Although they still had no direct evidence that he was involved in the murders, they definitely had him for fraud, so Sailor called to ask him some questions the next day. When Alonso wouldn't talk, Sailor headed down to his office at Absolute Mortgage in Irvine to arrest him.

A clerk led Sailor back to Alonso's desk, where he was talking on the phone. His eyes widened with fear as he saw Sailor approach.

"Hello, Alonso," the detective said, walking behind him. "Hang up the phone, you're coming with me."

Allowing Alonso a modicum of dignity, Sailor led him past a half-dozen curious coworkers into the hallway before arresting him for conspiracy to commit fraud.

Down at the station, Alonso was far more nervous than before. He finally admitted that Skylar had paid him to back up his alibi by signing the power-of-attorney documents, and that he had never witnessed any transaction. But he still claimed he knew nothing about the Hawkses' disappearance.

His attorney, Roy Peterson, said Alonso was willing

to cooperate. So agreeing that he would make a better witness than defendant, Murphy and Byington agreed to drop the fraud charge.

"No harm, no foul, we knew where he was at," Byington recalled thinking. "But it bit us in the ass, because a day later he was in Mexico."

Alonso's parents were very religious, and like him, they had been born in Mexico. After Alonso told them what he'd done, they drove him to Tijuana, where he took a bus to stay with relatives in the state of Chihuahua, knowing that the Catholic nation of Mexico would not extradite one of its citizens to face the death penalty.

24

About a month after Skylar's arrest, Byington got a call from a sheriff's sergeant at the courthouse who reported that an inmate named Danny Alvarado was carrying a suspicious folder of materials relating to the Deleon case. When Byington sent Detectives Short and Prouty down to check it out, they found it contained news articles about the Hawkses' murder, Ed Welbourn's business card, and a physical description that fit John Jacobson.

Alvarado tried to sway the detectives with the alibi story that Skylar had supplied him with, but it didn't go over very well. Once Short and Prouty told him that the area near the dock, known as Balboa Island, had Neighborhood Watch cameras that would have captured his alleged meeting with Skylar's father, Alvarado realized they had him cold.

"I was pretty much choking myself with the bullsh** story that [Skylar] had asked for me to give," Alvarado testified later. "I was going to get deep and hang myself in this, and I didn't want to be any more implicated, so I decided just to start telling the truth."

After he came clean, the big question for the

detectives was why Skylar would throw a burly black guy into the mix. Was he trying to throw them off, or was there a sliver of truth to this story?

Skylar had better luck with the Henderson family, who was lining up with his "John Jacobson made me do it" story. Lana volunteered to an interview with Sailor at her office on January 27, 2005, where she claimed that John was responsible for the Hawkses' murder. Skylar's cousin had told her that John used to put toothpicks under Skylar's nails, and both of John's ex-wives said he'd beaten them. Everyone was frightened of him, she said.

"John's a scary person," she said. "He is a piece of work."

She'd met him only once in person, but she'd spoken to him several times on the phone after Skylar's first arrest in 2002, and he had falsely accused her of calling him "an f-in' SOB," Lana said.

"He is an instigator, and he's a troublemaker," she added.

Lana said she was surprised when John told her that Skylar was trouble and untrustworthy, but even more so after she challenged his lack of paternal allegiance. When he still wouldn't stop badmouthing Skylar, Jennifer told Lana to hang up.

Lana said she was praying for the entire Jacobson family, who weren't "upstanding people." Marlene Jacobson had called Jennifer after Skylar was in jail, claiming that the police had a warrant out for Jennifer's arrest. This upset Jennifer so much she went into premature labor.

Jennifer, she said, had a good explanation for why she and Skylar had lied to police: "They're afraid of

John. . . . He forced their hand in this situation, to where they were afraid of bodily injury from him if they didn't do this."

"Does he say, 'I'm going to kill you'?" Sailor asked.

"No," Lana said, "she just said, 'He's going to hurt us.' And I said, 'Even Haylie?' And she said yes."

"And she knows that you're going to come forward with this information?"

"Yes, yes."

Lana said she didn't think Skylar knew where the Hawkses were. "'Cause I flat out asked him, and every time . . . I ask my kids something, they tell me . . . Skylar has lied to me, but I don't think he's lying about this. . . . I know in my heart that he did not do this, if he didn't have to."

Jennifer told her that Skylar had loaned John his cell phone, which he'd taken it out on a boat ride with the Hawkses. Skylar didn't go because he had the baby that day.

"How come you didn't tell me that before . . . he was arrested?" Sailor asked, noting that it seemed "pretty relevant."

"I don't know," she said.

Asked why she hadn't discussed this directly with Skylar in jail, she said, "Because the phones are tapped. . . . I write him letters, but I don't write about this, because I know that things are read."

"What do you think happened with the Hawks?" Sailor asked.

They'd either gotten the money from John and were in hiding or scared, she said, or they could be dead. "I wouldn't put anything past John."

But none of this changed Sailor's mind about Skylar's guilt. "He's not going to be getting out," he said firmly. "My other concern is your daughter. Your daughter has helped him to set up a transaction, knowing she was not supposed to. . . . Charges are going to be coming down, Mrs. Henderson. I am going to be arresting your daughter."

If Lana had come forward with this information at Skylar or Jennifer's request, Sailor said, "You will be charged. So I'm hoping, by all means . . . you are here out of the goodness of your heart. . . . This isn't some petty theft of a candy bar out of a candy shop. This is two people's lives."

"I understand," she said. "I pray for those people, hoping that they're still alive."

"You need to pray for your daughter and your son-in-law," Sailor said.

"Like my husband told you, we, every day, constantly, we are praying that the truth comes out, because we don't want any harm to anyone, and we raised our daughter the same way. And I know for a fact that she would not harm anyone. . . . I know in my heart that Skylar did not hurt those people. . . . I love Skylar, I do. . . . I love him, just like I gave birth to him. . . . I know he didn't kill them."

Kaleb Julius Deleon was born on Valentine's Day, with his father in jail and his mother under suspicion for murder.

Jennifer brought the baby, swaddled in a blanket, to an on-camera interview with KCAL-TV. She held the baby in her arms as she spoke to the reporter, once again using her child as a prop to gain trust and credibility.

Asked to describe Skylar, Jennifer said: "Fun-loving, genuine guy. Love him. This is really hard not having him, and having the baby without him. My daughter misses him extremely. This is very difficult."

"Is he capable of killing Thomas and Jackie Hawks?" the reporter asked.

Jennifer would not—or, perhaps, could not—give a straight answer. "I don't even know how to answer that," she said, breaking eye contact with the reporter.

Curiously, she had been much more straightforward in a conversation with her friend Meghan Leathem only two months earlier.

"Meghan, he is innocent. We are going to be fine. This is all a misunderstanding."

The detectives, who had been keeping tabs on Alonso Machain, grew concerned when they stopped seeing activity on his ATM and credit cards, his original cell phone and the new one he'd gotten after his arrest. Matt Murphy could tell from talking to Alonso's attorney, Roy Peterson, that Alonso had gotten cold feet, but the detectives suspected it was more than that.

"It was like he'd fallen off the face of the earth," Sailor said.

The detectives had located Skylar's Hatteras at a dock in Long Beach, where they learned that he and Alonso had offered the workers $100 to take a stun gun hit. So Sailor decided it was time to serve a second search warrant at Alonso's house to look for a stun gun, and see if, in fact, Alonso had left town.

When they arrived at 7:00 A.M. on February 22, Alonso's stepfather was just getting ready to take his two younger sons to school. Clearly uncomfortable, he opened the house for the search and said he'd be right back. Alonso's mother had already left for work.

The family lived in a lower-middle-class residential neighborhood, which was relatively quiet, although gang shootings broke out occasionally a few blocks from their house.

Alonso was four when his mother married his stepfather, in Mexico, and when the family moved to the United States in 1989, Alonso retained his Mexican citizenship. Twenty-two-year-old Alonso had shared a bedroom with one of his half brothers, but the room showed no sign of him. His drawers were empty, his clothes were gone, and his stepfather was evasive about his whereabouts. All that remained was his car in the garage, and it had a flat tire.

Alonso's stepfather said he didn't mean to be disrespectful, but their lawyer had advised the family not to talk to police. So Murphy, figuring Alonso was with relatives in his birth country, called Roy Peterson again.

"Look, we can put him out at sea on the boat. We know he's been lying, we know he's in Mexico. I know how to get people from Mexico—Google me," he said, referring to a juvenile murder defendant he'd prosecuted recently. "We will find him."

Murphy said Alonso could spend the next few months or years looking over his shoulder, or he could take the offer to come back within seventy-two hours and give a statement, knowing the death penalty was off the table and that nothing he said could be used against him, known as "use immunity." If Alonso didn't lie and he testified in court, Murphy said, "then you and I will talk about a disposition, after it's all done."

In the meantime, he said, Alonso would be arrested and held on two counts of conspiracy to commit murder, a crime equivalent to murder under the law.

Meanwhile, a team of six detectives searched the Hendersons' house and the Deleons' studio. Krallman wore a wire as he interviewed Lana and Jennifer.

The detectives were looking for paperwork regarding Skylar's sex change and any evidence related to the Jarvi homicide. They also planned to seize Jennifer's platinum wedding ring, and the anal-sex machine Skylar had purchased online from jail the same day they believed he'd killed JP Jarvi. They found the sex machine in a box, which Lana watched them carry outside.

"I want you detectives to know, that's not mine," she said.

Krallman got the feeling that Jennifer wanted to talk, so he called her that afternoon, hoping she would open up. Early in their ninety-minute conversation, Krallman felt Jennifer was being guarded and less than truthful. When he threw out incriminating details to expose her lies, she got quiet. "I think she knew the gig was up," he said.

Topics ranged from her conversation with the Mexican detectives about Jarvi's van to Skylar's habit of exaggerating and telling stories, even Jennifer's need to be in control.

"I have a little bit of a control thing, where I like to know everything and . . . to say that I can have a little bit of say in everything, but I'm learning that I don't, and that's my struggle right now," she told Krallman. "I'm definitely being tested. . . . We're not praying for patience anymore, because I can't."

Jennifer repeatedly tried to get off the phone,

saying she wanted to talk to her attorney so she could "do it the right way" without "blurting everything," but Krallman used his smooth interrogation techniques to keep her talking.

"For my own peace of mind, did you have anything to do with the Hawkses' disappearing or missing?" he asked.

"No."

"Nothing at all? Okay. . . . See, I know you're crying right now."

"I'm trying not to," she said.

"No, it's okay to cry."

"It will spoil my milk," she said, a little giggly.

Krallman appealed to her religious beliefs, which almost seemed to work.

"I want this over. . . . I want to be an honorable godly woman," she said, her voice breaking. "That's really what both of us want. If you only knew, Skylar wants to talk to you so bad, but Ed doesn't want him to *yet*."

"Then I think that starts right now," he said, "because the man upstairs, God knows what's going on. He knows the truth. . . . It's just whether or not we confront those demons."

Reminded that they were talking about a double homicide, Jennifer said she was well aware this was a serious matter, and that's what scared her. "This isn't something piddly that's going to go away, and I know that," she said. "I don't think I've done anything." Still, she could "anticipate what the next step would be. . . . More charges. For Skylar. Potentially myself."

Using the good cop/bad cop approach, Krallman apologized for his lieutenant's recent comment that she was a coldhearted, emotionless murderess; Jennifer said she was still smarting from it.

"I'll be honest with you. I have trust issues right now, and I have for a little bit of time," she said.

"Does that include Skylar?"

"No, him and my family and my kids are all I have right now."

She told Krallman she didn't know the name of the van's owner. Skylar, or maybe it was the detectives, simply told her they were investigating the murder of a guy in Ensenada. When she questioned Skylar about the people he was associating with, he maintained his ignorance. And given that the police never pursued the matter further, she believed him.

"Have they got ahold of him yet?" she asked innocently.

Every so often, Krallman would interject a few blunt questions, but he would do so calmly and softly, or with levity.

"Did you kill Tom or Jackie Hawks?" Krallman asked, chuckling.

"No."

"Did Skylar?"

"No."

When that didn't work, Krallman asked if she could tell him what she thought might have happened to the Hawkses.

"I don't know," she said.

Moving on, he asked if she'd ever been "dumbfounded" or "absolutely shocked" to learn something about Skylar.

"Have you ever caught him in a lie?" he asked.

"He exaggerates," Jennifer replied. "I pretty much, as soon as it comes out of his mouth, just tell him to knock it off, because I can tell. But it's always about stupid things."

Asked for an example, Jennifer said, "He'll take a

little situation, 'Oh, I got this call from this job,' and he'll talk it up so much that before he realizes it . . . all of a sudden he's got the job, and he's going to be working, you know, all these hours and making all this money, or whatever, and turns out he's just got a second interview.

"It's not something that's life-or-death," she went on. "He wants to appease. He wants to look good to people that he admires."

Jennifer said she'd seen the same behavior in his aunt and grandmother. "He's breaking that habit, but it's taken some work. . . . He didn't learn it in a day, he's not going to get rid of it in a day. . . . It's been three to four years and we're doing better [with it]. . . . It's never been anything super important, so it doesn't really affect our marriage. . . . Because me and him are honest, and I don't feel that we have a problem with that. I think that he does it more with other people. . . . So he lies a little bit here and there. . . . I don't want to come across that, you know, my husband is a pathological liar, but at the same time, that's the type of people he was raised around."

Jennifer said she was scared to say more because Skylar's father had threatened her.

"He tells me accidents happen," she said.

Krallman said she should tell him if this happened again, so he could protect her. He also said he knew that she and Skylar had driven the Hawkses' CRV to Ensenada after telling police they'd seen the couple drive away in it.

"I know. It doesn't look good," she admitted.

"This might be a horrible example, but maybe in order for you to relate, let's just say your mom and dad came up missing," he said.

"Well, I wouldn't want you to do anything different than what you're doing for them," she replied.

But as much as she said she wanted to help, Krallman wasn't able to get her to admit to any criminal wrongdoing.

"I got the sense that she was about to, and that she wanted to tell the truth, but she was scared to because of the ramifications," he said.

By the end of February, Murphy was ready to charge Skylar with murder, publicly disclosing for the first time that Skylar was also a suspect in the murder of an unidentified man whose throat was slashed a year before the Hawkses were killed.

Mark Hulce, one of the Hendersons' church friends, took a walk with Steve one afternoon in March. Glancing back toward the duplex, they saw that a tall, skinny, suspicious-looking guy had approached Lana at the front gate, so they headed over to check it out.

"Does Jenn Henderson live here?" the long-haired Hispanic man asked Steve.

"Yeah, she does, but who are you?"

Steve feared the man was a gangster, especially when he said he was a friend of Skylar's from jail, and had been told Jennifer would pay him $10,000 to give Skylar an alibi.

"We were, at that point, very scared," Steve testified later. "We had no idea what this man's intention was or anything, but we told him that he needed to leave."

As the man walked away from the house and down Pacific Coast Highway, Steve and his friend followed from a safe distance, intending to write down his license plate number. They pursued him for a good mile before he disappeared, so they figured he'd ducked into a business to hide.

What they didn't know was that he was wearing a wire and had been sent to the Hendersons' by three Newport detectives who were listening from down the street. The man was Danny Alvarado, the same guy Skylar had recruited to put a hit on his father, and the detectives had hoped he would draw Jennifer into an incriminating conversation.

When things didn't go as planned, Alvarado snuck into a car dealership, where he was eating donuts when the detectives picked him up.

25

By March 1, 2005, Murphy had reached an agreement with Alonso's attorney. Alonso was back from Mexico, but he wanted to spend one last night with his family before turning himself in. Just to be safe this time, however, undercover detectives sat on the Machain house overnight.

But Alonso didn't try to flee again. His conscience had been bothering him, and he wanted to do the right thing.

"What I did was going to haunt me for the rest of my life," he said.

So, on the morning of March 2, after stopping at church, he and Roy Peterson headed down to the Newport Beach police station.

Knowing this would be a key interview, the detectives rigged up a sound system in the former lieutenant's office, where Detectives White, Weinert, Krallman, Short, and Prouty stood ready to cross-check Alonso's statement with records and other evidence they'd collected.

White and Short had lined the walls of the office, which had become known as the "chart room," with the cell phone and tower records they'd arranged into three- by five-foot charts. As callers were identified, photos and names on yellow stickies were added.

They were able to pinpoint Skylar's whereabouts with the cell tower records, which showed that he made several calls from Newport early in the day on November 15 and late that night, and one from Catalina somewhere in between, and that Alonso made calls from Newport and Lantern Bay/Dana Point.

Tracking the layers of the emerging murder conspiracy was no small task. White, who was charged with writing warrants for a growing number of relevant phone numbers, was a little overwhelmed. Starting with the records for Tom, Jackie, Skylar, and Jennifer's phones, he had generated several dozen numbers, from numerous carriers, from the day the Hawkses were murdered. Short had asked White to prioritize a few particular numbers, including two that exchanged thirty calls with Skylar around the day of the murder, twelve on November 15 alone. Those numbers also called each other, and exchanged some calls with another number quite a few times on November 15 and 16.

Sitting around the police chief's conference table, which was equipped with a hidden microphone, were Byington and Sailor, Alonso and his attorney, Murphy and his investigator, Larry Montgomery. Sailor brought in some phone records from the relevant dates to prompt Alonso.

Montgomery asked Alonso to go back to the very beginning, when he'd met Skylar at the Seal Beach jail in the summer of 2003. For six long but fruitful

Skylar Deleon always had a thing for boats, so he and his wife, Jennifer, had a second, formal wedding on the *Spirit of Newport* in March 2003.
(Author photo)

Tom and Juckie Hawks on their fifty-five-foot trawler, the *Well Deserved.* *(Photo by Charles Silvers)*

Tom Hawks *(right)* and his brother, Jim, on their farm in Chino, California, in 1954. *(Photo courtesy of Jim Hawks)*

Tom was voted "Best Looking" during his senior year at San Dieguito Union High School in Encinitas, California, in 1965. *(Yearbook photo)*

Jackie O'Neill celebrates her third birthday in Mentor, Ohio, in 1960.
(Photo by Jack O'Neill)

The O'Neill women, wearing their Easter best in 1974: *(left to right)* Kathleen, Beverly, Jackie, Gayle and Jenny.
(Photo by Jack O'Neill)

Tom and Jackie were married on July 29, 1989, in Prescott, Arizona. (Photo by Jack O'Neill)

Tom faithfully practiced a work-out routine to stay in shape during the two years he and Jackie cruised around Mexico. (Photo by Charles Silvers)

Jackie plays with a butterfly in Punta Mita, Mexico, in December 2003. (Photo by Charles Silvers)

Skylar and his father, both born named John Jacobson, eat Christmas dinner with the Jacobson clan in 1991. *(Photo by Bryan Brah)*

As a child actor in the early 1990s, Skylar went by the name of Jon Liberty.

Jennifer Henderson graduated from Millikan High School in Long Beach, California, in 1999. *(Yearbook photo)*

Skylar and Jennifer got pregnant with their daughter Haylie immediately after their second wedding in March 2003. *(Photo by Picture People)*

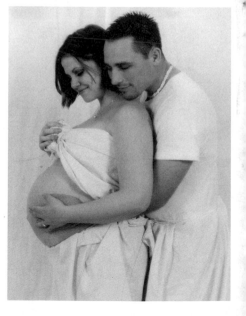

After Skylar was arrested for armed burglary, he met Jon "JP" Jarvi at the Seal Beach jail in the summer of 2003. *(Photo courtesy of Betty Jarvi)*

JP *(left)* and his brother, Jeff, grew up in Anaheim, California. *(Photo courtesy of Betty Jarvi)*

In his early twenties, Captain Jon Jarvi flew small private planes for a living and was an announcer for Team America. *(Photo courtesy of Betty Jarvi)*

In December 2003, Skylar took his cousin, Michael Lewis, and JP Jarvi on a "surfing" trip to Ensenada, Mexico, where Skylar slit JP's throat. *(Photo courtesy of Newport Beach Police Department)*

Alonso Machain, a guard Skylar met at the Seal Beach jail, later helped him kill the Hawkses. *(Photo courtesy of Newport Beach Police Department)*

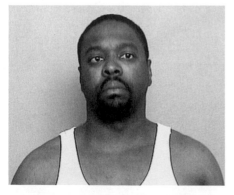

Skylar met Myron Gardner while working for Total Western, Inc., as an electrician's assistant. *(Photo courtesy of Newport Beach Police Department)*

Myron hooked Skylar up with John F. Kennedy (JFK), a Long Beach Insane Crips "OG" (original gangster). *(Photo courtesy of Newport Beach Police Department)*

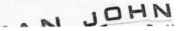

About ten thousand boats are moored in the exclusive Newport Harbor in Orange County, which feeds into the Pacific Ocean. *(Photo courtesy of Newport Beach Police Department)*

Skylar and JFK overpowered Tom Hawks in the bedroom of the *Well Deserved*. *(Photo courtesy of Newport Beach Police Department)*

Alonso grabbed and handcuffed Jackie in the galley. *(Photo courtesy of Newport Beach Police Department)*

On deck, Skylar tied Tom and Jackie to the anchor and threw it overboard; then JFK pushed the couple through this gap in the railing. *(Photo courtesy of Newport Beach Police Department)*

Detective Sergeant Dave Byington *(right)* and Detective Evan Sailor, now a sergeant, led a team of more than eleven detectives in investigating this complex homicide case. *(Author photo)*

The Deleons claimed the *Well Deserved* sale was notarized near this 15th Street dock, after which the Hawkses drove off in their silver CRV. *(Author photo)*

Skylar was arrested for money laundering on December 17, 2004. *(Photo courtesy of Newport Beach Police Department)*

The day of Skylar's arrest, Newport Beach police detectives searched the Deleons' cramped studio in Long Beach. *(Photo courtesy of Newport Beach Police Department)*

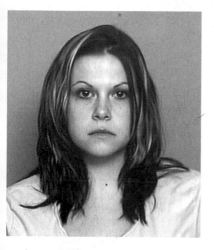

Jennifer Deleon was the final defendant to be arrested for the Hawkses' murder on April 8, 2005. *(Photo courtesy of Newport Beach Police Department)*

Jennifer at a court hearing in October 2005. *(Photo by John McCutchen)*

Skylar looked increasingly thin and feminine as he appeared with his attorney, Gary Pohlson, for pre-trial hearings. *(Photo by John McCutchen)*

In three separate trials, Orange County prosecutor Matt Murphy won murder convictions against Jennifer, Skylar, and JFK *(Author photo)*

Jennifer's attorney, Michael Molfetta, argued that she was just another one of Skylar's victims. *(Photo by John McCutchen)*

Skylar's defense team: *(left to right)* investigator Nicole Fischer and attorneys Richard Schwartzberg and Gary Pohlson, Skylar's primary counsel. *(Author photo)*

JFK's defense team: Winston McKesson *(right)*, JFK's primary counsel, and Charles Lindner (seated), both Los Angeles attorneys. *(Author photo)*

Ryan Hawks speaks to the media on April 10, 2009, after Skylar is sentenced to death. *(Author photo)*

Matt Murphy answers reporters' questions at a news conference after Skylar's sentencing. *(Author photo)*

hours, Alonso poured out the explicit details of the crime that Murphy and the detectives had been hoping to hear for the past three months. It would be the only first-person account they would get of what transpired on the boat. Alonso also outlined the events in the months leading up to the murder and the subsequent cover-up, detailing all the machinations Skylar went through to find the "third man," along with a suspect description, and purchase information for the stun gun and handcuffs.

During previous interviews, Alonso had been "jumping around like a cat on a hot skillet," as Murphy put it, rubbing his hands nervously and avoiding eye contact. But this time, he looked them in the eyes, teared up at appropriate points in the story, and never minimized his involvement as he explained how he helped Skylar groom the Hawkses for the big day.

In the end, the detectives couldn't find any major holes or contradictions in his statement.

"There was nothing that he lied about," Sailor said.

Among the most important details were the name and description of the middleman who helped Skylar find the "muscle" he was seeking. Alonso identified him as a black man named "Byron" or "Myron," an electrician foreman at Total Western, who had a lazy right eye and was in his thirties or forties.

Alonso described the third man—whom Skylar persuaded to join in his scheme within twenty minutes of them meeting—as a black man, about six feet tall, bald, not very clean-cut, with an old faded gold car.

"I don't remember his name," Alonso said, "if it was JT or TC or CT, something like that."

It was difficult for the detectives in the other room

to follow the conversation because Alonso's voice often dropped to a low mumble, but his taped confession provided them with key plot points in the development of the conspiracy. Matched against phone records, these enabled detectives to create a chronology of events—including calls from Skylar reporting to Jennifer after each significant act—and a map of the travel route the killers took on the *Well Deserved*. Also, by correlating Alonso's story with the GPS data, detectives determined that Skylar set the waypoints when he disappeared to the bridge to set the autopilot, and that the Hawkses were thrown overboard at a spot dead even between Catalina and San Clemente Islands.

Although Alonso didn't hear Skylar's conversation with Jennifer right after the murders, he noted that Skylar had "told me prior, that every time that he did something like this, he—he would call his wife and let her know that . . . he was okay."

"Out of all the times that you talked to Skylar, do you get the impression Jennifer was aware of what he was doing?" Byington asked.

"Yes."

Asked if Skylar had mentioned telling her about this plan specifically, Alonso said, "Not directly, but conversations he had with her [by phone] while I was in the car with him led me to believe that she knew something."

But the biggest surprise for the detectives was that Skylar and CJ had tied the Hawkses to the anchor and tossed them overboard—*alive*.

"How was Skylar acting while this was happening?" Byington asked. "Did he appear angry? Was he matter-of-fact?"

"No. He was—he was calm. . . . It was like the most normal thing."

"How about when you were driving back? How was his demeanor then?"

"The same."

"Did he show any remorse? Did he seem like he was sorry for what had happened?"

"No."

"Did he appear afraid or nervous?"

Alonso shook his head.

Murphy was so fascinated that he stopped taking notes a couple hours into the interview, and just listened, doodling an intricate shark on his coffee cup. As Alonso described Skylar's call to Jennifer to come down to the boat with Haylie to put the couple "at ease," Murphy's brain was spinning.

Holy crap, she used her kids to help commit this murder! he thought, feeling a tremendous relief that she hadn't accepted his immunity offer. *She was up to her eyeballs in it, if not the mastermind of the whole thing.*

Afterward, Murphy almost felt disappointed. He'd had visions of rising to the legal challenge of proving in court that Skylar was on the boat, simply based on cell phone records and other forensic evidence the detectives had collected. Now it was almost going to be too easy.

Byington had suspected it would be a brutal story, but he wasn't prepared for his internal brutality monitor to hit an all-time high. What kind of people were the Deleons?

"My mouth was on the floor," he said. "I was physically ill by the end of the day."

26

The way Alonso explained the events leading up to the murders, Skylar took him on November 3 to buy two stun guns for $175 at Sword in the Stone at Lakewood Mall, where he tried to get the salesman to take a hit to prove that the device would truly incapacitate someone as advertised. The salesman refused, so Skylar offered $100 to some boatyard workers, joking that he'd made a bet he could handcuff a buddy if he shot him with the stun gun. When that didn't work, he even tried asking the day laborers at Home Depot. He finally told Alonso that he'd tested the gun on a friend and it worked.

Skylar told Alonso to buy the two pairs of handcuffs on his own. As a former jail guard, Alonso was able to purchase the cuffs for $63 without raising any suspicions at Uniform Express in Montebello two days later.

Their trip to the yacht on November 6 turned out to be more of a reconnaissance than a murder mission, but Skylar made sure to keep Alonso invested in the job by telling him afterward that Tom Hawks must have taken enough money or screwed somebody over badly enough to get killed for it. How else could a retired probation officer afford such an expensive boat? Even if it was paid for, Skylar said, the maintenance was still pretty expensive. He also noted that the Hawkses had contradicted themselves by saying they wanted to be closer to their new grandson in Arizona, yet they were planning to buy a house and a smaller boat in San Carlos, Mexico.

When Skylar proposed wiring money from his bank in Mexico to the Hawkses' in Arizona, Alonso said, Tom suggested that he and Skylar could save on taxes if he underreported the purchase price.

"You could say you paid me four hundred thousand dollars in cash payment for the boat, and then I'll give you a slip that says you only paid two hundred," Tom told Skylar.

Alonso and Skylar made another trip to the *Well Deserved* a few days later, just a little ride around the harbor so Tom could teach Skylar a bit more about operating the boat and emptying its sewage tanks. They didn't even bring the stun guns or handcuffs.

In the meantime, Alonso said, Skylar had been trying to line up a third man to help them. His first attempt was a guy he said he'd worked with before— a middle-aged white man, about five feet five inches tall, with blue eyes and a big belly, who drove around in a yellow truck that looked like a U-Haul. Skylar didn't tell Alonso that this was his father.

They met up with the belly man in a beach parking lot after their first meeting with the Hawkses on November 6, and drove around while Skylar briefed him on the plan. Then he and Skylar went off to talk out of Alonso's earshot. Skylar reported back that the guy was going to think about it.

A day or so later, Skylar met up with the same guy at the boatyard, where they chatted privately some more. Afterward, Skylar told Alonso the guy didn't feel comfortable with the situation—or with Alonso, because he didn't know him—so he was out.

Next, Skylar went through a middleman, the electrical group foreman at Total Western, to try to find some "muscle."

"Does he know who I am?" Alonso asked.

"No," Skylar replied. "I didn't tell him who you were."

"Why not?"

"Because he doesn't need to know."

On November 14, Skylar said he'd found a guy to help them, took the guy clothes shopping that evening, and told him to meet them at 8:00 A.M. on November 15 at a liquor store parking lot at the northwest corner of Martin Luther King Jr. Boulevard and Pacific Coast Highway in Long Beach. But the guy never showed up.

Skylar couldn't reach him, so he left a voice mail. When the guy called back, he said he was going to be late; he had to get a haircut.

When he still didn't show up, Skylar called him again, and this time his girlfriend answered, saying she couldn't get hold of him. Impatient, Skylar got Myron on the phone.

"What's going on?" he asked. "Your guy is not showing up. I've been calling him and he won't pick up."

Myron promised to try to send someone else. He and Skylar talked a couple more times over the next half hour, and Myron finally told Skylar to look for a black man in a white T-shirt.

While they were waiting in the parking lot, a young man fitting that description approached. Skylar got out of the car and was talking to the guy when a green Jetta rolled up. Four young black men got out and walked toward them.

"What's going on?" one of them demanded, clearly wondering what this white guy was doing in Long Beach Insane Crips' territory.

"No," the T-shirt guy said. "Everything's good."

But it turned out that this wasn't Myron's T-shirt guy, who showed up shortly thereafter: he was a heavyset, muscular, dark-skinned black man; his hair was so closely cropped that he looked bald, and his goatee was braided into a six-inch tail. Skylar started filling him in on the plan, while Alonso waited in the car. A few minutes later, Skylar and the man, who went by "CJ," got into the car. Skylar showed him the boat interior photos on the laptop, pointing out where in the stateroom they would take down Tom Hawks, while Alonso restrained Jackie in the galley. CJ just listened, acknowledging with the occasional "Okay. Okay."

"You get seasick?" Skylar asked, "because we're going to go out to sea and we might even come back the day after."

"No, man," CJ replied.

After the briefing, CJ said he needed to get something out of his car, a faded gold Cadillac that was parked a block and a half away. CJ was going to pose as Skylar's accountant, so they drove to his apartment, where he changed into a more respectable outfit: a green sweater, some slacks, and a pair of dress shoes.

In addition to working for the city of Long Beach as a contractor for the gang intervention unit, the father of three had also been doing quite a bit of church work in recent years, and was a month away from becoming a minister. So CJ was used to appearing respectable when needed, which meant he sometimes rolled up his long braid and tucked it under his chin to look like a straight goatee.

By 1:30 P.M., they were heading south to Newport in Skylar's car, and Skylar called Tom from Huntington Beach to tell him they were on their way.

Skylar parked near the 15th Street dock, but after all the hoopla earlier that day, they'd walked all the way over there before he realized that he'd forgotten to bring the folder containing the power-of-attorney documents. So he sent Alonso back to the car for it.

Once they were on board, Tom gave them another tour for CJ's benefit as they prepared to head out for the sea trial. Tom, who was wearing shorts and a T-shirt, let them know that they needed to get going. The boat didn't move all that fast, and knowing that Skylar wanted to dive down and inspect the hull, Tom said they needed to clear the harbor, where the water was murky, before the sun set or Skylar wouldn't be able to see anything.

Alonso hung out at the stern while Tom and Skylar were on the bridge, as they headed out to sea. They'd cruised out of the harbor a little ways when Tom shut down the engines. Wearing the Hawkses' wet suit and mask, Skylar jumped over and went underneath to take a look, holding on to a hard line attached to the boat.

"Why don't you put on your wet suit and go under with him?" Jackie suggested to Tom.

Recalling Skylar's original plan, Alonso thought to himself that Tom had better not, or he might not come back.

While all of this was going on, CJ pretended to be seasick and went to lie down in the stateroom. So after Skylar finished his hull inspection, he got changed down below, where Tom joined them, while Alonso chatted with Jackie upstairs in the galley. During a break in the conversation, she made a cell phone call, saying they were out on the sea trial with the prospective buyers.

She and Alonso were talking again when a couple of loud thumping noises erupted from the stateroom. Jackie rushed toward Alonso and tried to peer down the stairs.

"What's going on?" she called out.

But by this time, Tom couldn't utter a sound because Skylar and CJ were holding him down. Tom had kicked something as he tried to fight back, so CJ had punched him in the nose, which was now bleeding down his chin and onto the quilt.

Alonso jumped to attention, pulled out the stun gun, and tried to use it on Jackie while she struggled to get away, but he couldn't get it close enough to work. Thinking quickly, he grabbed the handcuffs from his back pocket. Using his jailer techniques to twist her arms behind her and snap the cuffs on her wrists, he then walked her downstairs to the stateroom. Skylar told him to get some duct tape from the engine room and wrapped several pieces loosely around the couple's eyes and mouths. Skylar instructed Alonso to babysit while he took care of some things, so Alonso grabbed some tissue and tried to wipe the blood off Tom's nose and chin.

While the Hawkses were lying on the bed, Skylar went upstairs to the bridge to program the GPS system so they could cruise on autopilot to a point about forty miles out. The sky began to grow dark as the yacht made its way out to sea.

Then came phase two of the plan. They took Jackie back upstairs to the galley, where they took off her cuffs and peeled the tape back from her eyes enough to see. CJ held her in case she tried to run away, while Skylar put the documents in front of her.

"You need to sign this, and if you cooperate, we'll let you go," he said.

Scared and shaking in her sweatshirt and jeans, Jackie signed her name on the boat title, which Skylar had found in an office cabinet. She also signed one of Skylar's power-of-attorney documents and initialed all the boxes. After staining her thumb with the black ink pad Skylar had bought at Staples, she left her thumbprint on them as well. Skylar asked for her Social Security number and other banking information, which he then typed into his laptop.

Finished with Jackie, he and CJ brought Tom up from the stateroom, but before they uncuffed him, Skylar gave him an ultimatum. "If you try anything funny, I'll hit you over the head with this Maglite," he said.

"Okay," Tom said. "I'll sign."

Once they were all back in the stateroom, Jackie tried to appeal to Skylar's conscience. "How could you do this, Skylar?" she pleaded through the loose tape on her mouth. "You brought your wife and baby on the boat. We trusted you."

Jackie said she wanted to see her new grandchild again. "I don't want to die. We don't have any money," she said, adding that she and Tom would do whatever Skylar wanted.

However, nothing would change his mind. He simply shrugged off her comments. Tom tried to tell his wife to calm down, that everything would be all right if they just cooperated. But it was no use.

As they lay back to back on the bed, Jackie cried and shook uncontrollably. Despite being handcuffed, Tom managed to maneuver into a position where he could stroke his wife's hand from behind his back, the only semblance of physical comfort he was able to offer.

Alonso watched over them again as CJ and Skylar searched for a third anchor that Skylar was convinced was around somewhere. They couldn't find it, though, so the two of them grabbed the lighter of the two anchors from the front of the boat and carried it to the back deck, dragging the chain along with some rope.

Skylar promised to free the Hawkses so they would go up to the top deck without a fight. "Don't worry," he said. "We're going to drive you to Mexico, but this boat is too slow, so we got to switch boats."

From Alonso's vantage point, just inside the salon door, he could see the fear emanating from Tom and Jackie as they were brought up separately. His own fear was certainly palpable. He wasn't even half CJ's size, and he was worried that his partners would decide they didn't want to split the booty three ways after all. Once the Hawkses were dead, what would stop them from killing him, too?

"What's going on?" Tom and Jackie asked once they were both up on deck. "Why are we at the back of the boat?"

Skylar ripped off some new duct tape and wrapped it even tighter around the couple's mouths and eyes. He tied their arms behind each of them separately, then, with Jackie's back against Tom's chest, he tied them together.

Although Tom was blinded by the tape, he must have sensed Skylar behind him, because he simultaneously pushed and kicked backward as hard as he could, his foot landing solidly in Skylar's groin with such force that Skylar was thrown into the air, landing in one of the deck chairs.

Skylar just laughed, and CJ responded with a massive swing to the side of Tom's head. If Tom hadn't been tied to Jackie, he would've fallen to the deck. Instead, he slumped against her, dazed, and made gurgling noises.

After he recovered, Skylar tied a rope under the Hawkses' armpits and attached it to the anchor's chain. The boat was moving at a pretty good clip in the darkness, but there were no lights on the back deck. Only above, shining into the black night.

Alonso couldn't believe what he was seeing. Skylar went over to a hatchway in the railing and opened it up. He heaved the sixty-six-pound anchor overboard, the weight of it stretching the rope taut. As the anchor quickly sank, the couple was pulled toward the railing and Jackie's head made a crunching sound as it slammed into a door on the way toward the hatchway. CJ pushed Tom and Jackie the last bit through the opening, which allowed them to be yanked into the water.

It was all over in an instant.

Without missing a beat, Skylar started issuing orders. He had each of them put on a pair of gloves and told them to wipe the boat down with T-shirts, erasing any fingerprints or DNA they might have left behind. Skylar handed his stun gun to Alonso and told him to throw his overboard as well, then to dump all the medicine vials in the bathroom cabinet into a trash bag.

Meanwhile, Skylar tossed Tom's probation retirement plaque and some other personal items, as well as the handcuffs and the keys to unlock them. Searching around for the keys to the Hawkses' CRV, Skylar pulled the bloodstained quilt off the bed, so they could dispose of that, too.

The three of them had already gone through the boat once, looking for money and valuables, but Skylar had them do it again. This time Alonso found several thousand dollars in an envelope in a bedroom drawer. Skylar divvied up the cash, handing Alonso and CJ their $1,300 shares.

Alonso called his parents and girlfriend, and told them he was out to sea with Skylar. They had no idea what he was doing out there, and he didn't want them to know. Skylar was trying to get ahold of Jennifer, but he couldn't get any reception, so he made the call with Alonso's cell phone.

With the boat still on autopilot, the *Well Deserved* made its way back to Newport Beach. CJ grabbed a beer from the fridge and a fishing pole, and sat silently, fishing off the back deck. As they approached the shore, CJ called to check his voice mail at 12:38 A.M., the signal pinging off a tower atop Jack's Surfboards on Newport Boulevard. A whole slew of messages had piled up while they were out at sea.

Once Skylar and Alonso finished mooring the boat, it was nearly 1:00 A.M. The three of them got into the dinghy with the bag of medications, which they threw away, then drove back to Long Beach in Skylar's car. No one talked much. The only substantive discussion was about Tom being such a strong guy that it was a struggle to control him. Skylar also said he was going to come back with some help the next day to wipe the boat down more thoroughly.

As they were dropping CJ off at his place, CJ said, "Just talk to Myron about my cut."

From there, Skylar drove Alonso back to the duplex on Grand Avenue, where Alonso's car was parked. Alonso didn't want to go home, so he and Skylar just sat there for a while.

"You can stay at my house. I'm going off to the hotel," Skylar offered in a voice no less calm than he'd been on the boat.

But Skylar had a job for him first: drive Jackie's cell phone to Tijuana and use it to call Skylar's phone, so it would look as if the Hawkses had taken off to Mexico. So Alonso hopped in his car and drove the couple hours to San Ysidro, where he arrived around 7:00 A.M. Still upset from the events on the boat, he called Skylar as instructed, but he didn't cross the border. Instead, he broke the phone and tossed the remnants into a trash can near the freeway before starting the drive home.

A few days later, Skylar met with Alonso at a gas station near Lakewood Mall to sign the power-of-attorney documents. Skylar was going to have them notarized, and told Alonso what to say if the police contacted him. Besides the whole notary story, Alonso was supposed to say that the Hawkses never showed up to get their stuff the day after the sale, as planned.

After Detective Sailor called Alonso to ask about the discrepancies in his first interview, Alonso went straight to Skylar's house for instructions. Jennifer waited in the living room while they talked privately in another room.

But again, Skylar didn't seem the least bit concerned. "Don't worry about it," he said. "When you call them back, tell them it was just an honest mistake and that you kind of got the days twisted."

Shortly after that conversation, Skylar asked Alonso to meet him at the same gas station, where he showed him a stack of documents he'd found on the boat, including bank statements, stocks, and bonds. The two of them drove to the beach, where they burned the paperwork in a fire ring. Although Skylar never threatened him, Alonso didn't feel it was safe to refuse any of Skylar's requests.

For the same reason he never asked for the rest of his payment. Skylar called one day to tell him he was on his way back from Mexico, where he was unsuccessful in accessing the Hawkses' bank accounts, but Alonso never got more than the initial $1,300. He could never be sure if Skylar or CJ had found other cash on board, but that didn't appear to be the case. On November 19, Jennifer deposited $1,338 in cash into their joint account.

27

Alonso's description of "Byron" sent the Newport Beach detectives scrambling to determine Byron's last name, and to develop a list of black gangsters from Long Beach who fit his description of the third man and who went by similar initials.

Late in the interview, cell phone subscriber information for a Deneen El came over the transom. El was the registered owner of the cell and home phones that exchanged the thirty calls with Skylar between November 14 and 16, and DMV records showed she was a black woman who lived in Long Beach. Detective Short wondered why Skylar would be calling this woman, until he recalled the interview with inmate Danny Alvarado, who had linked Skylar's alibi to a big, burly black man. At the time, it didn't seem relevant, but it was starting to make more sense now. From Short's experience with gangs, he knew that the men commonly had their girlfriends buy or register phones in their names, to hide the men's involvement.

While Short did some computer searches, Sailor checked Alonso's description with the Long Beach gang detectives. The Newport team found that Deneen El was also the coregistered owner of a vehicle with a Myron Gardner, who, records showed, also shared the same phone numbers and address. The forty-one-year-old black man had a rap sheet ranging from voluntary manslaughter to narcotics possession, burglary, and spousal abuse. Figuring this had to be "Byron," they decided to pay him a call the next morning.

But Sailor and Short could find no gangsters with the right initials who had lived close to the liquor store, and weren't in prison or dead. So Byington asked Short, Wingert, and Prouty to dive deeper and connect the dots. This assignment would open up yet another branch of the investigation, taking the Newport team into the heart of Long Beach's black gang culture, a world where members resisted acknowledging names or relationships, went by initials based on nicknames, and changed monikers like dirty socks.

The next morning, Wingert and Prouty went to Total Western to talk to the human resources folks about Myron, while Short stayed behind to write a search warrant for Myron's house and car.

Wingert and Prouty learned that Myron was working at the NRG Energy Inc. plant in El Segundo, where they interviewed him while another detective searched his vehicle. They found a standard green notebook in which Myron had doodled *Myron* and *CJ* on one of the pages.

"We were grabbing at anything with initials," Short recalled.

Myron admitted that Skylar had asked him to come out on a boat, and also had asked him to help with a drug deal in Mexico. Myron said he refused both proposals, but told Skylar to contact a twenty-eight-year-old black guy named C-Dog, Treach Dog, or Trench, in the Whistler Liquor parking lot that Alonso had described.

C-Dog had been in prison, Myron said, and was a member of one of the local Crips gangs, the 20s or the Insanes, abbreviated names for the Rollin' 20s and the Long Beach Insane Crips, also known as the ICG. Myron acknowledged that C-Dog backed out of the deal with Skylar, but he wouldn't answer any more questions about the final third man.

"We weren't getting anywhere with him," Short said.

It wasn't much of a story—and they later learned that he'd mixed up the physical description of C-Dog with one of his friends—but his statement otherwise corroborated Alonso's, and gave police enough cause to arrest Myron for conspiracy to commit murder.

Short wrote down every contact and any other information he could glean from Myron's cell phone, including a CJ whose number later proved to have exchanged numerous calls with Myron on November 15 and 16.

On March 4, Short received the subscriber information for another number that exchanged ten calls with Myron on November 14 and 15, registered to Antoneisha Farrington, whose DMV photo showed that she, too, was a black woman from Long Beach.

Four detectives headed over to interview her, learning that she had a child with Insane Crips member Orlando Clement, who was in North Kern State Prison in Delano.

She sent them on a wild-goose chase with a long

story about the phone that had exchanged the ten calls with Myron, saying it was one of three cell phones she'd given to her girlfriends. Detectives found one of them in her apartment, as well as a number for CJ, which was scribbled on some paper, and letters that Orlando had written to her from prison, naming CJ as his possible father. One of Farrington's girlfriends had the second phone, and the third, which actually exchanged the calls with Myron, was never found, but police believed that Orlando had thrown it out his car window in January. The relevance of all these details was still unknown to the detectives, but that would soon change.

On the morning of March 7, Short and Wingert met with Long Beach gang Detectives Sean Hunt and Jim Kloss, briefing them on the leads from Alonso's statement, and brainstorming about potential gang members who fit his description of the third man. The Long Beach guys said they knew Myron as "Fly," an OG, short for original gangster, from the Insane Crips, who was no longer active. They then drove the Newport detectives around the neighborhood surrounding Whistler Liquor, including Grandma's House, a well-known Insanes hangout.

Given that the third man was older than the typical gangbanger, and was willing to help Skylar murder two complete strangers after knowing him for only a few minutes, Kloss initially suggested "Crazy John" F. Kennedy, who fit the physical description and went by "CJ."

After going through all the potential suspects, the detectives came up with a list that also included ten guys who went by C-Dog, three CTs, one CD, and two JDs, all of whom were Insanes affiliates.

Kloss said he'd seen Crazy John on the street recently, noting that he'd previously dated Orlando Clement's mother and was thirty-nine, close to Myron's age. Hunt said he'd arrested Crazy John several times, and Kloss recalled a confrontation with him a year earlier after CJ's nephew was murdered. Considered a ruthless street fighter and well-respected OG, Crazy John had often been seen driving by gang-related murders minutes after they occurred. He also was known to frequent Grandma's House.

His rap sheet went back to 1980, when he was sent to a detention camp for receiving stolen property, battery, and exhibiting a deadly weapon at fifteen. He broke a boy's jaw after only a few days, and was transferred to a California Youth Authority prison for a year, spending another three years there for stealing a car. In 1985, he moved up to adult prison, where he spent much of the next decade on charges of possessing and selling various forms of cocaine, and the attempted murder of a couple. He was arrested for murder in 1988, but the charges were dropped for insufficient evidence.

Meanwhile, his problems with substance abuse continued. In 1995, he got in a car crash, and was so drunk the officers didn't even bother to do a sobriety test. After they found a bottle of Cisco Black Cherry in the car, he jumped up and danced, then sat back down and stared blankly, saying he thought he was still driving. He was also booked for being high on PCP.

By the end of the day, Kloss was ready to put his money on Crazy John as the third man. Given the suspect's unique name and the fact that he went by initials, everyone involved in the case subsequently referred to Crazy John F. Kennedy as "JFK," even though he in no way resembled the former president.

Two days later, the Newport and Long Beach detectives made the three-hour drive to Delano to interview Orlando Clement, who wasn't all that cooperative. He refused to admit that he knew Myron Gardner or anyone named Fly, even when they showed him a photo lineup that included Myron's photo. He'd only admit to speaking by phone to "G-Homey," an older guy from the neighborhood who asked Orlando to go on a "business trip" with a white guy who needed some "help."

G-Homey told Orlando he'd have to get dressed up to look presentable, but he wouldn't tell him what he had to do or how much he'd be paid. Orlando agreed to meet the white guy at Whistler Liquor.

When they met up, the white guy said he was a former U.S. Navy Seal who lived in Newport Beach and worked oil platforms. He refused to say anything about the job other than that Orlando would act as "security" while he bought an expensive boat. They'd talk money later.

Asked if the white guy was Skylar Deleon, Orlando said, "It's a possibility."

That afternoon, Orlando said, the white guy took him to the Lakewood Mall to buy an outfit with shoes, socks, and a belt, which came to about $100. He was supposed to meet the guy the next morning, but decided not to go and exchanged the clothes for baby stuff for his kid. Shown a photo lineup with Skylar's picture, Orlando said he couldn't identify anyone.

Confronted with phone records proving he'd exchanged numerous calls with Myron, Orlando insisted that the only calls he'd gotten were from G-Homey. After he was also confronted with the calls to and from CJ, Orlando grudgingly admitted that CJ was a father figure who was very close with his mother, but contended he had no involvement in the scheme.

The detectives didn't believe him. As soon as they were back on the road and heading home, Short called Byington.

"What do you think?" the sergeant asked.

"We need to show Alonso JFK's photo," Short said.

Byington and Sailor wasted no time calling back with the good news. Alonso had instantly pointed to JFK's driver's license photo in position #2 of the six-pack, which showed JFK wearing a goatee. Alonso said he thought JFK had a goatee the day of the murder, but he wasn't sure. Nonetheless, they had their third man.

"That car got loud real quick," Short recalled. "It was a celebration with the four of us."

Sailor wrote up JFK's arrest warrant and faxed it over to the Long Beach station, where Short and the other detectives were heading. Hoping to get JFK into custody as soon as possible, they presented the case at that night's briefing for plainclothes and uniformed officers, who immediately headed out to search the streets for their suspect.

Short also spoke that night with Long Beach Detective Rich Conant, who had forged a relationship with JFK's family after his nephew was shot. Conant showed Short some photos from the nephew's murder scene that featured the faded gold 1988 Cadillac that JFK had been driving. It proved to be registered to one of his family members, and was yet another point of corroboration with Alonso's statement.

Conant agreed to call JFK's sister, Javana, and ask her to bring him to the station the next morning for an interview. Unbeknownst to her, this was a ruse so the police could arrest him, so Javana agreed.

28

The next morning at ten, JFK's sister came alone, which meant that he was still on the loose when Short and Wingert showed up. Luckily, though, a police unit reported seeing him driving away from a house, so the detectives hopped into a car, eased up behind JFK's Cadillac, and pulled him over at 11:30.

Searching his vehicle, they found a stack of photos from a Carnival cruise to the Bahamas four days after the murder. The photos showed JFK posing with a female companion, who was not the woman he lived with—the mother of one of his three children. In one photo he was standing at a bar with yet another woman, both of them curving their fingers and thumb into a *C*, which the officers took to be a Crips gang sign.

In an interview that afternoon, JFK insisted that he'd never been to Newport before—let alone murdered anyone there.

JFK said he'd been in some trouble before, but he'd gone straight, and had been trying to help the youth of Long Beach get "on the right track," just like he'd done with his own life. He acknowledged that he had "ticked off" the police with the "little work" he'd done in the now-defunct gang intervention program, but he was no Malcolm X, so he didn't understand why he'd been arrested.

"Being in the church and everything, I ain't even been involved in no negative activities," he said.

Short said he'd be happy to explain. After he outlined the basics about JFK's involvement in Skylar's case, JFK claimed he'd never met the guy.

"I'm giving you the truth . . . you know what I'm saying?" JFK said. "But I don't know no Skylar. I never had a meeting with him."

Furthermore, he said, "I don't even hang around with no—not [to] be, uh, racist or nothing, but . . . the only white friends I know is people that work, you know, in the city [of Long Beach] and stuff, like, but, outside of that, I don't associate with white people like that at all, period."

He claimed to have an alibi for the day of the murder, saying he'd been doing a three- or four-day job painting a fence at a duplex in Long Beach, where he often did work for the property manager. He said he was even painting while talking to Myron on the phone—all sixteen times—that day. JFK shrugged off their unusually high number of calls, saying, "It's coincidence."

Myron had been a friend since 1979, when he went by "Superfly," JFK said. But now he was just "Fly." They normally talked three or four times a week, mostly to sell Myron some Viagra or Cialis.

"It's illegal, but it's no major [deal]," JFK said. "For the young people Cialis—it's a sex thing, you know. . . . I can buy a pill for five bucks and . . . sell it for fifteen."

Asked about his income, JFK said he was on unemployment, earning $1,640 in state benefits each

month, but he admitted he was also doing odd jobs
and claimed he made an additional two hundred dollars a week on his drug business.

Short and Wingert told him that they'd already
talked to Myron Gardner and Orlando Clement.

"There's a reason why it's led to you," Short said.

But JFK consistently denied any involvement in the
Hawkses' murder. "I ain't got nothing to do with it,"
he said.

"These people are saying you did some terrible
things," Short said.

"I'm not a terrible person."

Wingert chimed in, "So, when this thing plays out
and we go to court, we're sitting in front of a jury, and
our people are marching up there and testifying on
the stand that . . . these are the things you did . . .
you're going to sit there and go, 'I don't have anything to say. I don't know anything about it.' How do
you think that's going to play up to a jury? You don't
even give them an excuse. You don't say, 'Hey, this is
not what I thought it was going to be.'"

"I just hope that they do the right thing," JFK said.

Despite a search warrant for JFK's person, he refused to submit to a DNA swab—twice that day—
although he relented a week later at the courthouse.

On the surface, anyway, JFK appeared to have been
trying to do the right thing for some years. He'd spent
the last seven of them earning a total of $159,000 as
an "outreach" consultant under contract with the
Gang Intervention and Prevention Program, within
the city's Department of Parks, Recreation and
Marine. Although program officials claimed these
consultants were interacting with local gang members

to stem violent incidents before they occurred, the city's gang detectives alleged that the program operated more as a covert gang *recruitment* unit. Of the program's eight consultants, five had been accused or convicted of crimes by June 2005, prompting the city council to halve the program's $700,000 budget.

JFK had been taken under the wing of the Reverend Leon Wood, pastor of the North Long Beach Community Prayer Center. Wood, a gentle, well-meaning, and well-dressed man, saw JFK as a leader in his community who could be influential in luring young gang members to church before the gang life usurped their hopes and dreams.

As they had continued to work together for the past three years, Wood said, he saw JFK develop into the man he'd hoped he would become. Wood had been training JFK to become a licensed pastor and take over the church, which had JFK ministering to the old and sick in nursing homes. Playing up his church involvement, JFK named his own business Christian Hands Handy Service.

But he'd still been having trouble with the law. He'd been caught twice carrying marijuana and PCP while working in the gang program, and two months before his most recent murder arrest, he was served with a gang injunction against the Insane Crips, barring him from engaging in "gang activities" in certain target areas. This came five months after his confrontation with police at the scene of his nephew's murder, where JFK had been shot into compliance with a Taser and jailed for several months, costing him his job with the city.

His nephew, Aviante Hale, who also had been an Insane Crips member, had been living with JFK. And although JFK claimed he was no longer an active member, he still followed the street "code" by refusing to reveal the rival gang shooters' names.

"You got a gang counselor who can't even keep his nephew out of gangs, and now fails to cooperate with a homicide investigation?" police Lieutenant Gary Morrison told the *Press-Telegram.* *"In our opinion, he never stopped being a gang member."*

Although one of JFK's daughters was enrolled in college in San Diego, his seventeen-year-old son, Jonathan, was following in his father's footsteps as a self-admitted member of the Insanes.

About a month after JFK's arrest, the Newport and Long Beach detectives drove back to the prison in Delano for a follow-up interview with Orlando Clement.

Only after they showed him the front-page story about JFK's arrest would he agree to identify Skylar in a photo lineup and to identify Myron as "Fly."

As they went over his statement about meeting Skylar in more detail, Orlando said Skylar told him he was in the "boat business," and while they were in the car together at Whistler Liquor, Skylar talked to someone on the phone, saying, "Hold on, be patient. I'll call you in a little while." It was Jennifer.

Orlando recalled thinking that Skylar must be crazy to come into an all-black neighborhood at night by himself.

"You're pretty bold," Orlando said. "Do you have a gun on you?"

"No, but I have this," Skylar said, reaching under his seat for his stun gun, which he handed to Orlando and told him to try it out. Orlando pulled the trigger, causing a loud clicking sound and an electrical arc, then handed it back to Skylar.

Skylar was so cold and emotionless throughout their exchange that Orlando figured he had to be getting into something really bad, because Skylar didn't seem to be scared of anything. Orlando was a towering six feet four inches tall, with a criminal history of dealing drugs and stealing cars, but he'd never committed murder—and he knew better than to get involved with a guy who handed his weapon to a stranger in a dark parking lot without even blinking.

Asked about his numerous phone calls to JFK on November 15, Orlando said JFK had promised to give him $40 the day before, but all his calls to JFK kept going to voice mail. So around 3:00 P.M., Orlando said, he started looking around the neighborhood for JFK, to whom he usually spoke with every day. However, no one in the neighborhood had seen him. Unaware that he was helping police dispute JFK's alibi, Orlando said he was still calling and searching for JFK around 11:00 P.M.

Orlando said he finally ran into his "old homey" on November 18 at a friend's garage music studio in Long Beach. JFK was quiet and subdued as he watched TV, so Orlando didn't bother him.

Asked if he felt JFK was capable of murder, Orlando replied, "Maybe or maybe not. He used to be an Insane gang member, but now he's a preacher."

Short and Wingert tracked down the property manager who had allegedly hired JFK for the painting job at the duplex. After checking her records, she said he did paint the fence—but not until December

2004, a month after the Hawkses' murder. So much for his alibi.

The detectives also monitored JFK's phone calls from jail and heard an interesting exchange with a female friend.

"What are you doing?" he asked.

"I'm at home," she said.

"I know you're at home. Who are you with?"

"No—nobody."

JFK told her to go to the computer room and directed her to a spot on his bookshelf. "Let me see . . . my brown little—little record book right on the bottom shelf . . . I need to put that somewhere safe."

"Okay."

"I might have to use that."

"Okay."

"They will probably be over there after a while, I guess," he said, referring to the police. "Please don't be crying. Put that in a safe place because I'm going to need that when I get some . . . representation."

Prosecutor Matt Murphy and the detectives figured this was code for "hide the record book."

"There was something in there that he didn't want us to find," Murphy said.

29

It's not necessary, but it's certainly easier to win a homicide case when the jury has proof of what happened to a victim's body. Byington had heard about the navy's Unmanned Vehicles Detachment and Deep Submergence Unit, which searched the ocean floor for airplane wreckage and other items, so he met with its commander in San Diego. They forged a deal to search for evidence of the Hawkses' murder as a training run on March 28, 2005, which would be cost free for the NBPD.

Using the waypoints Skylar had entered into the GPS system, the unit was able to plot a two-square-mile search grid. They assumed Skylar drew from his diving experience in selecting this area, where the ocean floor dropped steeply to a depth of 3,800 feet.

The naval ship dragged a sonar system to the spot, where they let it roam back and forth in a pattern of overlapping paths across the floor, searching for metal objects of interest. Once the sonar maps were analyzed, a submarine the size of a MINI Cooper was deployed from its storage container on the ship's top deck, and steered to the marked areas by remote control and video cameras.

Detective Short went out with the unit for a two-day search, but came back empty-handed. So Detective Joe Cartwright, who had just joined Byington's unit, jumped at the chance to try again on June 20.

It wasn't a perfect science. The submarine was finicky, and it didn't have the capability to effectively communicate where the objects were located, so "it was kind of a needle in a haystack," Cartwright said. "They had a large margin of error, so sometimes they'd see something, but just couldn't find it."

The search team, which included the sonar expert who inspected the *Titanic* wreckage using these same methods, often found objects boaters had tossed away, from floor buffers to shopping carts. The likelihood of finding any trace of the Hawkses' remains was practically nil, because they likely had been absorbed into the ecosystem—i.e., consumed by sea creatures— within a few days. And at that depth, the constant motion of the ocean currents would have rubbed their bones together until they'd disintegrated into nothing. So in this case they would be happy just to find the anchor chain, handcuffs, duct tape, nylon rope, or one of the stun guns.

Several days into the search, Cartwright heard an alarm sound, and saw the submarine rise to the surface. "The submarine just died," he said. "It was broken and we just couldn't use it anymore."

"We know what happened from Alonso and putting things together," Cartwright said later, "but it would have been nice to come back with something to make it tangible, at least for the family. But it didn't work out."

* * *

Gary Pohlson, a former prosecutor turned criminal defense attorney, was one of the few lawyers in Orange County who was eligible for appointment to capital cases on the taxpayers' dime. So after the Welbourns stepped down after the prelim, Pohlson took over and appeared in court for Skylar Deleon at the end of August. As usual, he chose longtime friend and colleague Richard Schwartzberg as his second chair. At the time, Pohlson didn't even know about the Jarvi case.

Pohlson was a balding, ruddy-faced man with a kind smile. Although he bustled around the courthouse, he maintained a very easygoing countenance for the jury, speaking in casual and simple language, as if he were one of them. An everyday Joe, like your favorite uncle. He was rarely aggressive, at least in this case.

This was the sixteenth death penalty case for Pohlson, who had been an attorney since 1975 and started doing death cases in 1983. Since then, he'd been voted "Criminal Trial Lawyer of the Year" by the county's Trial Lawyers Association, headed the bar association, and taught law courses.

He wanted to win for his client, of course, but he always had empathy for the murder victims, especially after having had his own share of tragedy. His father had been murdered, and his niece was killed by a drunk driver.

After three years of studying to be a priest at St. John's Seminary in Camarillo, he decided to change directions so he could have a family. Quoting the familiar saying, he quipped, "Many are called, but few are chosen. . . . I realized it wasn't for me."

So he graduated from Santa Clara University, earned a law degree from the University of California, Los Angeles, then spent three and a half years as a prosecutor in Orange County. But his goal had always been to be his own boss, so he left and formed his own firm with a colleague.

"I like being in trial. I like the contest, the competition, all of that is exciting to me," he said. With some of the would-be priest still inside him, he said, "I think of this as a vocation rather than just a job. That may sound pompous, but . . . I just love what I do."

His personal opposition to the death penalty, he said, stemmed in part from his seminary background.

"I just don't think it's a good thing for America," he said. "I think it's demeaning for all of us," not to mention "unbelievably costly."

He said he'd prevailed in some cases to persuade the DA not to seek death even before trial, had won some hung juries, and managed to beat back the death sentence for one client in the penalty phase. But this case was not going to be anywhere near that easy. He now had the seemingly impossible task of trying to win sympathy and mercy from a jury by explaining how Skylar Deleon had come to be such a complicated being.

"This is a very sad case," he said. "His life is as sad a life as you can imagine, but unfortunately, he took his sadness and inflicted it on the Hawkses and the Jarvis."

30

Jennifer brought her newborn son to Skylar's pretrial hearing in March 2005, where the judge let Skylar hold the infant for a minute as the Hendersons and their friends cried in the otherwise quiet courtroom.

Afterward, Jennifer wrote Skylar to say it was good to see him, regardless of the circumstances, although she couldn't believe he'd gotten so thin and his hair was so short. She said she really missed seeing and talking to him; she'd been crying as she re-read his letters, reliving the beautiful memories they shared and hoping for the day their family could be together again.

I just love you and my heart is broken for you, for us, and our family. All of this just feels so wrong and surreal, she wrote. *We have been permanently bonded together through so many things, in so many ways—there is nothing that could tear that apart.*

For months now, the detectives had been chomping at the bit to arrest Jennifer and put her behind bars, but Murphy encouraged them to be patient so she could continue visiting and writing Skylar.

"Big picture, big picture," Murphy kept saying. "We're going to get gold. Let's let her keep going."

The prosecutor was right. The recorded visits and endless love letters would only help at trial. Also keeping in mind that taxpayers would have to pay for the delivery of her baby behind bars, they waited seven weeks after Skylar's arrest, until after Kaleb was born, when Murphy couldn't offer any more reasons to keep her out of jail.

Murphy asked Dave Byington to do him a favor and let Michael Molfetta know that police were ready to arrest his client.

"I'm not doing that," Byington said stubbornly. "She's going to jail."

On Friday afternoon, April 8, when he figured Jennifer would pay her usual visit to Skylar, Byington brought his team to the men's central jail. To ensure she wasn't armed, they waited until Jennifer had gone through the metal detector with her father and her two children, and asked the deputies to let them know when her visit was over. The police were pleased that Steve Henderson had come, too, so he could take the kids home.

While Byington was sitting outside, waiting, he grudgingly called Molfetta.

"I'm doing this because Murphy told me to," he said. "We're going to arrest your girl."

"Where are you?" asked Molfetta, whose office in Newport Beach was twenty or thirty minutes away, depending on traffic.

"We're up at central jail."

"Well, can you wait?"

"I'll give you a few minutes, but as soon as she comes out, we're going to take her."

So Molfetta sped over there, arriving just in time. "Can I go in and tell her that you're out here?" he asked.

Through the glass partition between the jail waiting room and the area where visitors got off the elevator, Byington and Sailor watched Molfetta approach Jennifer and let her know what was about to happen. Murphy had warned him the arrest was coming soon, so Molfetta had already prepared Jennifer for the moment when Sailor put the handcuffs on her.

"We have a warrant for your arrest for murder," Sailor said.

"Am I going to jail, too?" Steve asked, worried.

Byington figured he could have charged Steve as an accessory after the fact, but he and Murphy had decided that Steve would make a good witness, especially if he would say unflattering things about Skylar—and maybe even Jennifer—on the stand. Byington didn't blast Steve for failing to recognize that he'd been harboring two murderers and subsidizing their activities. He simply took Steve aside and told him he wasn't going to be arrested, but he needed to pull himself together.

"You need to be a man right now," Byington said. "These kids, I don't want to freak them out."

He and Sailor let Jennifer say good-bye to her children so they didn't have to watch Sailor put her in the back of the police car. They took her to the Huntington Beach city jail for a couple of days so she could pump the milk from her swollen breasts, but then she was taken to the women's jail in Santa Ana, right next door to her husband, where they wrote to each other every day.

* * *

A week later, all five defendants in the case pleaded not guilty at their arraignment, which the Hendersons' church friends attended. Skylar refused to waive his rights to a preliminary hearing within ten days and a trial within sixty days, a move his attorney hoped would force the prosecution to throw together a half-baked case. But Murphy showed no concern.

"It doesn't bother us a bit," he told reporters outside the courtroom. "We'll be ready to go."

Skylar made quite an impression by showing up in a T-shirt marked *OCWJ,* short for Orange County Women's Jail, underneath his orange-gold jumpsuit. This became a running joke with the prosecution team, especially when he added an OCWJ jumpsuit to the ensemble and began wearing lipstick and eyeliner made out of pencil shavings and ChapStick. He'd asked friends and relatives to mail him Wet 'n' Wild, an inexpensive brand of lipstick, claiming his mouth was chapped, but he told Jennifer he had to wear it for the jail deputies, who made him act out the song "I'm a little teapot, short and stout, here is my handle, here is my spout," or they wouldn't give him a new adult diaper.

Armed with Alonso's statement and a truckload of cell phone records, Murphy was able to persuade Myron's attorney, George Bird, that his client should come forward with information he'd been withholding about his part in the conspiracy. Myron's series of calls to Orlando, Skylar, and JFK clearly showed that he was the key to Skylar hooking up with JFK.

On April 22, Murphy, Larry Montgomery, and the

detectives met with Myron and Bird at the Newport station, where more puzzle pieces fell into place. Myron laid out how he brought the Long Beach players to Skylar, but he vehemently insisted that he'd thought it was for a drug deal in Mexico, not murder. Because they couldn't prove otherwise, this was the version they went with.

That same afternoon, Alonso identified John Jacobson from a photo lineup as the belly-man Skylar had tried to recruit as their partner. Served with a subpoena, John testified before the grand jury a couple weeks later.

On April 29, Lana and Steve Henderson filed a petition to become guardians of Haylie and Kaleb, which was still pending four years later. Lana quit her job as soon as Jennifer was arrested, so she could take care of the little ones. Compounded with fears of losing her son, Michael, who was doing his second tour in Iraq, Lana had a lot to deal with.

31

On July 29, 2005, which would have been Tom and Jackie Hawks's sixteenth wedding anniversary, three memorial ceremonies were held concurrently in San Diego, California, Prescott, Arizona, and Concord Township, Ohio. More than one hundred people attended each service.

As the sun began to set on that breezy evening in San Diego, the crowd gathered in Mission Bay Park, including some strangers who had been following the case in *The San Diego Union-Tribune*. The folded program featured a smiling young Tom in a bolo tie, his dark hair slicked back; Jackie wore long, dangly earrings, her brown curly hair cut short and sun-bleached. Inside was a quote from poet Henry Van Dyke: *Time is too slow for those who wait, too swift for those who fear, too long for those who grieve, too short for those who rejoice, but for those who love, time is eternity.*

A Newport Beach police chaplain started off the service by saying that death was not a dead end, but a valley one passes through before being embraced by the arms of God.

Jim Hawks recalled the last time he saw the couple,

during their minicruise to Catalina: "I've never seen them so happy together, and so much in love. . . . I do believe they are in a better place."

Ryan Hawks's voice cracked with emotion as he struggled to get through his poignant remarks. And it was heartbreaking to hear his grief. "I will forever carry the tension in my shoulders for the individuals who murdered my parents," he said, "and a pain in my stomach for the manner in which it was done."

In Prescott, Jackie's friend Tricia Schutz organized a service overlooking Watson Lake, with a big awning over candlelit tables and two giant bouquets of white and hunter green balloons, the colors of the *Well Deserved*.

It was a beautiful, clear night as Tricia, Tom's friend Hal Slaughter, and Tom's son, Matt, said a few words before they played the song "I Hope You Dance," and released the balloons into the clearing. As everyone watched them float away, two hawks flew overhead and a lightning bolt flashed in the distance.

"We knew they were there with us," Tricia said. "It was the weirdest thing."

At the same hour in Ohio, Jackie's family held a gathering at Concord Woods Nature Park. Jack O'Neill's monsignor cousin Kevin flew in from New York to conduct the service, to which relatives came from Alabama, Tennessee, Michigan, and Pennsylvania.

"Let us for a few moments tonight, instead of focusing on the loss, focus on those things you have not lost," the monsignor said, encouraging everyone to hang on to their fond memories of Jackie.

Gayle, Jack, and their four children walked the pathway beside the fishpond, carrying a wreath of red roses and white carnations. They stood, youngest child to oldest, leaving a space where Jackie would have been, and passed the wreath from one to the next. The ritual ended with Jack, who silently tossed the flowers into the water.

But the memories and the mourning of Tom and Jackie continued long after the services were over.

Tom's first wife, Dixie, had sent the O'Neills a scrapbook full of pictures of Jackie she had collected during visits over the years, and a big blowup photo of Tom and Jackie, kissing, for the memorial. Gayle used the photos to create a permanent memorial to her daughter.

"Our house is like a shrine," she said. "We have pictures of her everywhere."

In the dining room, she hung a flying dove and a plaque lined with the broken links of a chain, laid over a backdrop of leaves, with this message: *Our family chain is broken and nothing seems the same, but as God calls us one by one, the chain will link again.*

Gayle couldn't help but think of Jackie every time she talked to one of her daughters, because their voices all sounded so similar.

"It was a waste," she said. "That's where Skylar made his big mistake, thinking that they had this beautiful boat, so they must be millionaires. He promised those guys millions of dollars. They [Tom and Jackie] didn't have millions of dollars. . . . Nothing was gained by anyone from this. And it's just a shame that two beautiful people had to be taken. For nothing."

32

Tom Charles Hawks came from a law-abiding family with deep roots in public service. His maternal grandparents ran a Baptist Italian church in Alhambra, California, and taught his mother, Eleanor Mable Ré, about the importance of helping others. She, in turn, taught basic family values, strength of character, and a strong work ethic to Tom and his brother, Jim.

Tom was born to Eleanor and Charles "Chuck" Hawks Jr., a U.S. Army Air Corps commander, on December 24, 1946. The boys grew up on a farm in Arcadia and a chicken ranch in Chino, where their family kept cattle for beef and sold sweet corn, eggs, peaches, and watermelons at a roadside stand. Because farming was seasonal, Chuck worked part-time at the betting windows of Santa Anita Park, Hollywood Park, and the Del Mar race track.

Chuck's parents lived in a farmhouse next door to the Hawkses' eight-hundred-square-foot house, with Tom and Jim in an attached bunkhouse.

"They were a strong influence on our lives. They were a genuine, caring, loving people who gave Tom and me a whole lot of support," Jim said.

Of the two brothers, Tom was the more outgoing and gregarious. Jim took care of the big animals and drove the tractor, while Tom kept a menagerie of critters, often leaving a snake in Jim's bed as a practical joke.

During the late 1950s, the family spent weekends at a trailer in Oceanside, where the boys were introduced to beach life. In 1963, after Jim graduated from Chino High School, the Hawkses sold the ranch and moved south to Cardiff-by-the-Sea.

When the family wasn't tooling around in a twenty-one-foot Chris-Craft speedboat, the *Charleo,* the teenage brothers were busy making their own surfboards, using the same fiberglass technology to refurbish a fourteen-foot dory they bought in Newport Beach. Later, they saved up for an outboard motor and sailed the dory on thirteen-hour voyages to Catalina, where Tom worked as a sailing instructor and lifeguard.

"Someday I'd like to live on a boat," Tom often said.

Like Jim before him, Tom was voted "Best-Looking" during his senior year at San Dieguito Union High School in 1965. He was also one of two varsity wrestlers to make it to the state finals.

The Vietnam War was raging, and Tom and Jim soon followed in their father's footsteps to fulfill their patriotic duty. In 1966, Jim enlisted in the U.S. Army and got accepted into the flight-training program, while Tom entered the U.S. Air Force, where he served for nearly two years as a security guard and policeman at Clark Air Base in the Philippines, a logistics hub during the war. He flew security on B-52s over Vietnam, but never landed there, and finished out his service as a missile security guard at Minot Air Force Base in North Dakota. After training to be an air police supervisor, he left as a staff sergeant in August 1970.

After returning home, Tom took classes at Mira-Costa College, where he was on the wrestling team. Through a fellow athlete, Tom met Dixie Dee Hendry, a striking woman with long dark hair who was two years younger. At the time, Jim was dating his future wife, Sandy, to whom Tom kept posing questions about appropriate dating behavior.

"This guy looks like a movie star, and he's asking advice from me," Sandy recalled thinking with amusement.

Dixie, whose stepfather was a judge, worked as a court reporter. Tom was smitten, and two months after being hired as a Carlsbad firefighter in 1972, he married her. Jim married Sandy several months later.

Jim had done two tours in Vietnam, flying helicopters through Agent Orange and getting shot down twice. After failing to find a civilian job as a helicopter pilot, Jim decided to join Tom in Carlsbad, as a police officer, and worked his way up to chief before retiring in 2003.

"If it weren't for Tom, I don't think I would have become a cop," Jim said.

Taking risks to help people, Tom had his helmet melt on his face inside fiery buildings and was written up in the newspaper for heroically pulling a boy from a burning car.

But he also loved to play. He and Don Trefren often went surfing, locally or in Baja California, and while the community of La Costa was being built, its newly paved roads became their skateboard park. Tying a rope to a car bumper, they pulled each other around—with "no helmet, no elbow pads, and probably barefoot," Don recalled.

When it came to athletics, Tom was very competitive. "He was always trying to race everybody," Don said. "He was much stronger than me. Physically, his upper body was just amazing."

Tom enrolled in night classes to finish his bachelor's degree in social sciences at Chapman College, while also working at the fire department.

Dixie and Tom bought property in Rancho Santa Fe, and with friends' help, he started building a house for his growing family. Tom was twenty-nine when Ryan was born, and thirty-one when Matt came along.

Meanwhile, Tom and a partner opened an upscale restaurant and bar on 1st Street in Encinitas called Easy Street, serving fish and steak dishes on white tablecloths, but the restaurant was only open for about a year.

"He and his partner had a falling-out," Don recalled. "Things just kind of flew apart when he . . . started the restaurant."

And, as his new business began to fail, so did his marriage.

"That was a tough time for him," Jim said, explaining that Tom would do construction all day, starting at 6:00 A.M., work at the restaurant until the bar closed at 2:00 A.M., then wake up and do it again. "Tom worked two jobs all his life."

Tom formed O'Hawk Industries Inc. on April 30, 1979, and quit his firefighter's job a week later. Dixie filed for divorce the following month.

It would be seven years before their divorce was final. Dixie, who got engaged three times but never remarried, always seemed to have a soft spot in her heart for Tom. But clearly, their goals and dreams diverged somewhere along the way.

Tom used to say he'd have a million dollars by the

time he was forty, but that attitude soon faded. "That was Dixie. She wanted all that," Sandy said, alluding to their lifestyle in Rancho Santa Fe, now a wealthy enclave.

Tom liked roughing it outdoors; Dixie was more of a city girl, and over time, she apparently couldn't—or didn't want to—keep up with his love for adventure. She also didn't share his go-go-go mentality or his longing to live on a boat.

So Tom moved to five acres he owned in rural Prescott, where he refurbished a modest cabin into a nice home, and shared legal custody of the boys with Dixie. But he wasn't done being an entrepreneur. He and another partner bought a bar, known as Matt's Saloon, on Prescott's historic Whiskey Row. It was a long, narrow establishment, with a balcony and walls lined with patrons' photos. The bar became even more popular after Tom fixed it up and brought in live acts, including an Elvis impersonator. Missing the physical challenge of one-on-one competition, Tom bought arm-wrestling tables and competed in contests there.

Todd DeMasseo, who held the world champion middleweight title for several years, remembered going up against Tom. Although Tom was twice his age, De-Masseo said, "he was a tough guy. Physically imposing," enough to win the state title for his weight class.

Great with his hands, Tom refurbished the bar himself, fixed up two more homes, built a boathouse on his property, and renovated a Victorian apartment complex for rental income.

"He had a way of putting things together," Don said, recalling that Tom would craft door handles out of found wood, turned an old leather boot into a birdhouse, and transformed a boiler he found in an abandoned building into a fireplace for Don.

After a few years of running the bar, Tom wanted the security of a full-time job with benefits, so he joined the Yavapai County Adult Probation Department in 1985. He loved owning Matt's, but with its crazy hours and two young boys to raise, he—and the county's presiding judge—thought it best that he focus just on being a probation officer.

The bar did very well in the summers, when LAPD officers flocked to Prescott for the July 4 weekend, but it made little money during the snowy winter months, when "all you have is a few drunks to sustain you," Jim said. Tom sold Matt's several times over the next few years, because he carried the loans, and got it back when buyers were unable to make payments.

Tom did probation work for the next sixteen years, trying to rehabilitate the mostly male criminals who wanted to turn their lives around. He earned a reputation for being fair but firm, and was promoted to supervisor around 1990.

"He would hold people accountable, but he would also try to help them. You could call it more of a fatherly thing," said coworker John Ryder, adding that their typical probationers were convicted of substance abuse, with the occasional assault or white-collar embezzlement. But they didn't deal with the more violent criminals.

"Usually, murderers don't get probation," John said.

Perhaps that's why Tom wasn't too concerned about his safety. Jim said he gave Tom a bulletproof vest to wear during searches, but "he just never seemed to worry about it. I just think it was part of his personality. He had a tremendous amount of self-confidence."

"He always looked for the good in people," Sandy added.

Dixie soon realized that Tom could do a better job of parenting, partly because Ryan missed his father so much that he wasn't eating or sleeping well. So they agreed that she would keep the boys in Cardiff during the summer, and Tom would have them the rest of the year.

Tom took his sons for visits to their grandparents' farm in nearby Chino Valley, where they liked to ride the tractors. He also worked them hard on his own minifarm, though he rewarded them with boating trips on alternating weekends. Tom usually had a boat of some kind, which he took out on Lake Havasu. Flipping through boating magazines and dragging Don to boat shows had long been a favorite pastime.

Tom had no shortage of girlfriends in those days. He was a serial monogamist, but none of his relationships lasted long. However, that all stopped in the summer of 1986, when his friends Hal and Mary Slaughter introduced him to their friend Jackie, a very pleasant woman with whom he fell deeply—and permanently—in love.

Jacqueline "Jackie" Ellen O'Neill was the second of five children, and the oldest daughter of Gayle and Jack, who got married in 1953, right after high school. Two months later, Jack went into the army, and served the next two years as a tank commander at Camp Irwin in Death Valley, California.

Gayle had their first child, Bill, in 1954, and after

Jack was discharged, they moved into a three-bedroom house in the manufacturing town of Mentor-on-the-Lake, Ohio, a couple blocks from Lake Erie.

It was snowing the day Jackie was born on April 26, 1957. Colicky at first, she soon grew into a sweet, shy little girl who liked to cook and help her mom care for her younger sisters, Kathleen and Beverly Ann.

Jack ran a service station, worked at two factories, then got a college maintenance job. Gayle went to work on the factory line to help make ends meet, but had to quit when Jennifer was born in 1966, because she had a birth defect that required her to be fed with a syringe. If it wasn't done just right, she would sneeze and cough.

"It was very difficult, so Jackie helped me a great deal with Jennie," Gayle recalled. "She kind of adopted her as her own."

A few years later, Gayle had to go back to work, so Jackie cooked dinner for her father and siblings, including her father's favorite dish, crispy fried potatoes. She shared bunk beds with her sisters, but she and her brother remained close, visiting with neighbors until bedtime.

Jackie was a slender five feet six inches tall, with brown eyes and brown curly hair. She entered a cosmetology program in high school, working afternoons in a salon and as a checker at a local grocery store, where she met Terry "Les" Newell.

Les, who had brown hair and a mustache, stood five feet ten inches and was a divorced father of two. Eleven years older than Jackie, Les worked as a lineman for the Cleveland power company. He asked her out after coming through her checkout line a few times, and soon brought Jackie out of her shell, taking her shopping for a bright orange pantsuit that plunged down to her belly. Not long after graduating from Mentor High School in 1975, she moved in with him.

Les always seemed very sure of himself. Almost too sure. He and Jackie were about to move to Texas when he and Gayle had a conversation that would come back to haunt her.

"There isn't a situation in this world I can't handle," he said.

"There's going to come a time when there *will* be a situation that you *can't* handle," Gayle replied.

After a brief stay in Texas, the couple moved to Dewey, Arizona, where Les worked for the power company. Jackie was nineteen when they eloped. In 1983, she got a checker's job at Safeway, where she met another checker, Tricia Schutz, who would become her best friend.

Deciding to build a new house, Les and Jackie bought a trailer in which they could live with their two Rottweilers during construction. They remodeled the trailer, then poured the foundation for their new home.

After installing insulation for hours one Sunday in December 1985, they went for a motorcycle ride to Kmart for supplies. They were at an intersection two miles from home when a sixty-five-year-old man, who had been drinking in bars all day, pulled his truck in front of them. Les turned the bike to try to avoid a collision and skidded across the road, but it was no use.

"When the truck hit them, the guys that were there said all they saw were bodies flying," Gayle said.

Les, his neck broken, was killed instantly. Jackie suffered a broken pelvic bone and compound fractures in both legs; bones were sticking out of her left leg. The only thing Jackie remembered was looking up before they wiped out and seeing the house they were building up on the hill. Her mind blocked out the rest.

"She had not a mark on her from her waist up that you could see, except a little raw mark on her forehead," Gayle said. "But by the time the rescue unit was called and got there, she had lost about half her blood."

They flew her by Life Flight to St. Joseph's Hospital in Phoenix, where doctors removed her spleen and inserted screws and bolts in her leg. They also took a skin graft from one of her butt cheeks to repair some of the leg damage, and the scar was visible when she wore a thong bikini. But the doctors could do nothing to repair her pelvic bone, which, after being rendered permanently tilted from the impact, made it too dangerous for her to have children. Gayle knew how much Jackie had always wanted to have kids.

A day or so later, Jackie learned that her husband was gone, and she was plainly upset that she couldn't leave her hospital bed to attend his funeral.

"She never had a real chance to say good-bye, and I think that bothered her," Tricia said.

Once Jackie was released, a friend nursed her at home until she was ready to fly to Mentor, where her parents had invited her to stay until she recovered.

Jackie ultimately sued the driver and the two bars that had served him too many drinks. She attended the trial, and, in what Gayle characterized as "a pretty darn good settlement," Jackie received an award worth several hundred thousand dollars, including both bars.

Jackie stayed with her parents for several months,

until she could get around on crutches, although she still needed a wheelchair to go long distances. By the time she flew home, her neighbors had finished the house she and Les had started, making sure to build the fireplace one stone at a time, just as she would have.

Jackie, who had no problem staying trim, put herself on a strict three-times-weekly exercise regime.

"She never missed," Tricia said. "Jackie was a real meticulous person," writing a list of goals every morning and checking them off throughout the day.

In June 1986, Jackie was all set to be Tricia's maid of honor. However, the night before the ceremony, Jackie ended up in the hospital with an intestinal blockage, the result of scar tissue from the accident. She was still healing in August, when Hal Slaughter invited her to a chili cook-off by Goldwater Lake.

After the picnic, Jackie told Gayle that she'd met a man, and she was worried in retrospect that she'd told him where she lived. She was amazed that someone like Tom would be interested in her, a woman in a wheelchair with a gimp leg.

Tom worked at Camp Verde, about forty-five minutes from Prescott, and started stopping by Jackie's house with Häagen-Dazs ice cream on his way. Some days, he'd miss her, but he'd leave a sticky wrapper on her doorstep, as if to say, "You missed out."

They hadn't been dating long when Tom took Jackie to Cardiff to meet Don Trefren. He thought she was sweet, but knowing Tom's dating habits, he didn't think she'd last long.

Surprisingly, Jackie was the one who was hesitant about getting more serious. She was excited to be involved with someone again, but she was scared.

Scared to give up her house in case things didn't work out with Tom, leaving her nowhere else to go. And scared of the responsibility of raising two young boys.

But those fears soon fell away. She'd fallen in love with Tom, but ultimately "it was the boys that stole her heart," Tricia said. "She loved children. She just absolutely loved them."

Jackie loved to cook, so the boys won a reprieve from their father's repetitive meal of homemade goulash. Tom even remodeled his kitchen for her, and stenciled her nickname Patches over the women's bathroom at Matt's Saloon. In turn, Jackie tattooed Tom's name on her butt cheek, putting the *O* over her scar to camouflage it.

"She just fit perfectly into their lives," Tricia said.

Les had never wanted more children, and now that Jackie was unable to have any of her own, this was the perfect solution.

"She got her family through Tom," Tricia said. "I think it was something she'd always wanted."

On January 29, 1989, about 150 friends and family members attended their Hawaiian-themed wedding in the backyard of Tom's rustic, Western-style home, which had a big wooden deck, a koi pond, and a hot tub, where the couple liked to go skinny-dipping.

Inside, the house was decorated with stained-glass artwork that Tom had designed himself. He'd cut a corner out of the roof in the living room for a spider crawling across a web. One narrow window featured a flock of birds in flight, and at the end of the hallway was a pane featuring a vase of flowers. Later, Jackie got into the act, creating a glass wall picturing her likeness, standing on a beach wearing a wrap, but baring her naked bottom with the *Tom* tattoo.

It had long been Tom's dream to find a boat big enough for them to live on, a dream that Jackie had also shared with Les, and they were gearing up for the adventure.

After going to considerable expense to boost his military and firefighting retirement pay, Tom was able to retire early on August 17, 2001. He and Jackie sold their house and antique furniture, and moved into a trailer next to their boathouse.

As he continued to browse through boating magazines, Tom finally found the one he wanted—a fifty-five-foot white-and-green trawler called the *Well Deserved*—down in La Paz, Mexico. The mechanically propelled boat, which weighed twenty-seven gross register tons, had been built in Kaohsiung, Taiwan, in 1980.

Tom hired a captain, and he and John Ryder went down to get the vessel. The three of them sailed it up to Wilmington, an industrial port in Los Angeles, where Tom determined he could install new navigational equipment and other amenities more cheaply.

"They sanded and varnished," Sandy said. "They reupholstered everything and put in curtains."

Knowing they'd be out of touch once they headed out to sea, Jackie spent a few days with her parents in upstate New York, where they paddleboated around Chautauqua Lake, none of them knowing this would be their last visit.

During Tom and Jackie's first year as boat owners, they went back and forth between Wilmington and the trailer, taking minicruises to Catalina to slowly familiarize themselves with the vessel. The plan was to head down to Mexico for a year or two, where they could enjoy the cruising life full-time.

"Jackie was pretty nervous about it," Don said. "It was her first time, being away from home, going on an adventure and not knowing what to expect."

So Tom taught Jackie everything she needed to know about the boat so she would feel more comfortable there.

"She was like a sponge," Tricia said. "Every piece of information, she retained it."

They set off on their voyage, and soon developed a daily routine. After wiping off the condensation that had formed on the railings, Tom made one of his famous omelets, using dinner leftovers. Chores came next, then Jackie would read her latest novel or do the intricate beadwork she loved so much, while Tom worked out. They'd head into the nearest town or take a hike, then sunbathe, laze around, swim, or go kayaking. Jackie would start dinner around 5:00 P.M. (except for Fridays, Jackie's night off, when they'd eat tacos or pizza) while they took a cocktail cruise or had happy hour with other boaters. Then they'd eat, watch videos or TV, and hit the hay by 10:00 P.M.

Tom believed that by keeping himself in shape, he could guard against injuries if they should hit rough seas. Summing up his workouts for *Latitudes & Attitudes,* he described his routine as one hundred sit-ups, fifty push-ups, and ten chin-ups, and a thirty-minute weight-lifting regimen three times a week. He said he was pleased to see quick results so he could keep consuming his favorite snack of Pacífico beer, chips, and salsa.

I'm not sure if good conditioning will extend your life, but

*I'm confident it will extend the quality of your life and your
cruising time on the water,* he wrote. *My wife and I wish
you all many happy and safe years cruising at sea. May
you have fair winds and following seas.*

Tom and Jackie made friends easily during their
two-year voyage, including Chuck and Cheryl Thomas,
whom they met at a Fourth of July celebration in
Bahía de Concepción. It was well over 100 degrees, so
the couples were standing chest deep in the bay, sip-
ping beer, when they started chatting. From that day
on, the couples got together regularly as they cruised
around Mexico, staying in touch via their single side-
band radios.

In February 2004, the Thomases were in Huatulco
when Cheryl fell ill. She was diagnosed in Acapulco
with cancer and severe pancreatitis and was advised to
return to the United States for treatment right away.
Tom offered to help, so the Thomases sailed to Zihua-
tanejo, where Tom and Jackie were anchored, picked
up Tom and a friend, and sailed to Puerto Vallarta,
where they secured the boat and flew to California.
Jackie cooked the men a bag of burritos for the trip
and gave Cheryl a special bracelet she'd made, bless-
ing each bead to keep Cheryl safe.

"When you have something like that happen, you
definitely feel isolated and alone in a strange country," Chuck said later. "For them to leave their
wives . . . to tend the boats alone, with always the
possibility of bad weather, or the winds coming up
or whatever, that's a big thing. . . . I wish I had a thousand more friends like them."

* * *

After two years of cruising around Mexico, the Hawkses decided to bring the *Well Deserved* back to California to try to sell it after having the hull painted in La Paz. Knowing it would be a rough return trip on the boat, Jackie flew back to Arizona to spend time with their new grandson. Tom took this opportunity to turn the voyage into a boy's party cruise, so Jim Hawks and Don Trefren flew down to meet him and another friend that June. They bought $300 worth of groceries, including lunch meats, beer, and chips, and figured they'd catch some fish to eat on the way.

Tom was studying for his coast guard captain's license, so Don quizzed him to help pass the time. Don tried to stump Tom with some pretty obscure questions, but Tom knew all the answers. Meanwhile, Jim traded off with his brother, operating the boat.

Along the way Tom kept a log of their travels, drawing artistic renderings of caves and places to anchor, noting kelp patterns or rocks to avoid. He also videotaped what he figured would be their farewell voyage on the *Well Deserved,* chronicling their daily discoveries and the beautiful scenery.

Don, who typically saw Tom only a couple times per year, was pleased to spend some quality time with two of his oldest friends. Jim hadn't thought he could get away, but Sandy had encouraged him to go, and later he was glad she had.

"I was expecting we'd have a lot more of those times," Jim said.

33

On August 12, 2005, nine months after the Hawkses' murder, the preliminary hearing was finally held for the five codefendants, who were seated throughout the jury box, with two empty seats between them. This would be the last time they would all be in the court-room together.

Skylar, who wore a dark sweater and goop in his carefully groomed hair, was becoming increasingly thin, pale, and effeminate with each court appear-ance. In contrast, Jennifer, who wore her hair up, with a pink blouse and a black skirt suit, seemed to be growing fuller in the face.

Warned not to communicate, the couple made a point of not looking at each other while Judge John Conley met with the attorneys in chambers. Nonethe-less, Skylar quickly mouthed "I love you" to his wife during a subsequent break.

As Myron and JFK were brought in, their legs shackled, Alonso put his head down, his short dark hair combed forward. He looked very young, slight, and scared.

Ryan Hawks seemed anxious and uncomfortable as

he sat with his uncle in the front row on the far right side of the courtroom, the same spot they would sit for almost every appearance over the next four years.

Back on the record, Judge Conley announced that Alonso and Myron were being "severed" from the proceeding and sent back to jail; they would have their prelims down the road. For his own protection, Alonso's whereabouts were kept under wraps, so no one but the authorities knew he had his own cell at the Newport Beach police station. Myron and JFK were also housed in different county jails.

Although the case had gotten widespread media play, Sergeant Dave Byington still wasn't prepared for the bevy of reporters and photographers who showed up. Conley had banned cameras from the courtroom to prevent the jury pool from being tainted, but the TV reporters hung around, anyway, gathering string for their stories.

As Alonso was led out of the courtroom, he held a Spanish-language Bible behind his back. Knowing his life was in danger for being a snitch, he likely needed all the comfort he could get, although defendants frequently "find religion" once they're behind bars.

With so many defendants and attorneys in the room, the testosterone-charged gamesmanship was in full force that day. The two counsel tables were crowded with attorneys, sandwiched, shoulder to shoulder, with the defendants and their respective stacks of binders. Skylar was the only one to have two lawyers.

Matt Murphy was ready to present the skeleton of his case, just enough evidence to persuade the judge to deem it worthy of a full-blown trial. Under California law Murphy was allowed to convey his evidence through the detectives working the case. So, after calling Byington to the stand, Murphy had him run through details of the overall investigation and his impression of the Deleons.

Like Skylar, Byington said, Jennifer "was calm" during the interview at Hope Chapel. "She was playing with her child. . . . She seemed fine, very cordial, very polite."

Byington was careful not to elaborate unnecessarily or volunteer answers to questions he wasn't asked. When Winston McKesson, JFK's Beverly Hills attorney, asked a question implying that the prosecution had no witness who could testify about what happened on the boat, Byington looked at Murphy for visual approval before replying that they most certainly did: Alonso Machain, the guy who had helped kill the Hawkses.

At the end of the day, Matt Murphy and Ryan Hawks were surrounded by a throng of television cameras on the second floor of the courthouse, the only place they were allowed. Perhaps as a legal strategy and to protect his witness's safety in jail, Murphy wouldn't disclose Myron's role in the crime, which wouldn't be released publicly for several years. Moltetta revealed only that Myron was the "facilitator."

The prelim continued the following Tuesday, when Murphy called Detectives Sailor and Wingert to fill in the later portions of the investigation, including key points from Alonso's confession about what had transpired on the boat. Byington had warned the Hawks family beforehand that the testimony would be tough to listen to, but he couldn't release certain specifics, and there was really no way to prepare them for such a horrific story.

As Murphy walked Sailor through Alonso's graphic description of events, Jim Hawks grew so upset that he got up abruptly and left the courtroom, crying. The judge called a recess.

"Jesus Christ," Ryan said as he followed his uncle out of the room. Ryan, at least, was pleased to hear that his father had fought back, kicking Skylar in the crotch.

The defense attorneys, each with his own agenda, tried to poke holes in the detectives' investigative work and impugn the notary's credibility in light of the immunity deal she'd forged with Murphy. They also tried to impeach Alonso's credibility, given that he was the prosecution's only cooperative witness of the Hawkses' murder.

McKesson—a former associate, friend, and pallbearer for the late Johnnie Cochran, the lead attorney on O.J. Simpson's "Dream Team"—was the most aggressive during cross-examination. In what would be a road map to his client's defense at trial four years later, McKesson hammered home the point that Alonso had lied during several interviews with police before he finally gave his most recent version of events. He also noted that Alonso didn't get JFK's initials right and contended that his description of JFK was squishy, unsure whether he'd been "clean shaven" when he clearly had a long braided beard.

Every time Sailor answered a question about Alonso, McKesson followed up with a loaded, inflammatory question.

"You believed Mr. Machain, even though he was lying through his teeth?" he asked.

"Yes," Sailor answered.

The detective acknowledged that police had found no trace of blood, DNA evidence, or fingerprints on the boat, a point McKesson underscored as he argued that his client had never been on the *Well*

Deserved. Contending that the whole case rested on the testimony of Alonso, "an admitted liar," he argued there was "insufficient evidence to hold my client on these charges."

"The story makes no sense," he said, noting that JFK didn't look like an accountant, nor would he have agreed to meet two complete strangers at a liquor store, change into dress slacks, and ride down to Newport with them to commit a murder without bringing a weapon. JFK wasn't even a suspect until he was identified by the Long Beach gang detectives, with whom he had a contentious history.

Murphy countered that Alonso had identified JFK in a photo six-pack, which was enough to bind someone over for trial. But more important, he said, police were able to corroborate Alonso's statements with the evidence they'd collected, and only one of Alonso's initials for "CJ" Kennedy turned out to be wrong.

Judge Conley sided with the prosecution, and sent the case to trial. "The court feels there is sufficient evidence," he said. He noted that the defense attorneys made some good points about Alonso's statement, but it was the jury's job to weigh his credibility as a witness.

"It's the worst story I've ever heard, and I've been doing this for thirteen years," Murphy said. "The truth is they preyed on these people and subjected them to an inhumane death. That's the reality, and that's what happened."

But what grabbed people's attention most in the courtroom that day was the oddly inappropriate sideshow between Skylar and Jennifer as he repeatedly tried to get his wife's attention during the breaks.

"Jenn . . . Jenn!" he kept whispering, trying to get her to look at him. "I love you."

He also made eye contact with reporters, exhibited childlike restlessness as he rocked his chair back and forth on its rear legs, silently communicated with church friends in the gallery, and smiled at the attorneys' jokes. Although Jennifer sat stone-faced during the testimony, she, too, grew more animated during breaks, mouthing messages to her mother.

At first, Murphy couldn't believe what he was seeing. Well, actually, he could. "She's laughing!" he said to a reporter. "Did you see that?"

Jennifer acknowledged Skylar's lovesick pleas with a slight nod, but mostly, she remained aloof. After all, her attorney was arguing that Skylar was the lying scum who had gotten her into this mess. She seemed more concerned that the jail deputies had failed to comply with the court order to let her dress in street clothes.

Afterward, Michael Molfetta said he could see why the Hawks family could be offended by Jennifer's demeanor, which he passed off as "nervousness." Describing his client as just "a good and simple kid," he acknowledged that theories abounded for how the murder scheme had played out, but "I do believe as we sit here today . . . we're not any closer to knowing what happened."

As for Skylar, he said, "If his lips are moving, he's lying."

Disputing Murphy's contention that Jennifer was fully involved in the scheme, Molfetta contended that she knew nothing before going to the bank in Kingman with Skylar. "The whole case is going to hinge on what Jennifer knew, and when she knew it," he said.

He, too, dismissed Alonso's "confession," saying

that defendants routinely felt out officers to tell them what they wanted to hear. "What other reason can there be for Alonso to take seven hours to come up with this tripe?"

Noting his past relationship with Murphy, Molfetta made a self-deprecating joke about their upcoming courtroom battle.

"The mentor is about to get his ass kicked by his student," he said facetiously.

But it was clear that he genuinely wanted—and intended—to win.

Jennifer, however, was making that prospect tougher by the day. Still ignoring Molfetta's advice, she wrote Skylar a letter that night, saying her tummy was upset after the day's events, but it had been nice seeing him.

Love, I want to apologize about that thing I said. I was trying not to flip out and wasn't doing a very good job. Sweet baby kisses! she wrote, drawing a smiley face.

Around midnight, after playing cards with her seven new cellmates, she picked up the letter again to tell him how wonderful he was. She was so grateful for the way he made her smile, and made sure she knew how much he loved her, just as she did him. Promising to love him forever, she said she'd be dreaming of him.

The next day, news of the preliminary hearing played on national TV and reached newspaper readers as far away as England and Australia. Ryan Hawks, Molfetta, and Murphy's boss, DA Tony Rackauckas, were interviewed on MSNBC's *The Abrams Report,* and the story was featured again on Greta Van Susteren's show on FOX.

Meanwhile, Jennifer's mother, still blind to Skylar's lies and manipulative ploys, was praying that her daughter and son-in-law would soon be found innocent so they could come home to their kids.

"They're very much in love with each other. Very much," she said. "And it breaks my heart."

34

By comparing Skylar's bank and cell phone records with JP Jarvi's, the Newport detectives were able to track what had transpired in JP's last days. He and Skylar exchanged a number of calls on December 26, 2003, one of which came seven minutes after JP cashed two $25,000 cashier's checks, and Skylar deposited $20,119 at Bank of America two hours later. Of that, $3,982 went toward a credit card and $9,000 to pay off the Deleons' car loan.

Although Jennifer and Skylar spoke to each other often by phone, the records showed that they exchanged an unusual seventeen calls on December 27 during his Mexico trip with JP. In addition, the records showed that Skylar and Jennifer both called Robbins Brothers before Jennifer picked up her new, resized ring.

Finally, the records helped detectives build a timetable and travel route for the Mexico trip by tracking the cell tower "pings," just as they had in the Hawks case. But the coup de grace was confirmation from the U.S. Customs Service that Skylar's car had been videotaped coming back from Mexico at 7:03 P.M.

"After calling Detective Bahena [with the LAPD], it definitely raised our suspicions," Byington said. "But once we discovered his license plate crossed the border northbound from Mexico into the U.S. on the night of the murder, we knew we owned him."

On July 12, 2005, Detectives Krallman and Short went to Kingman, Arizona, to interview Skylar's cousin, obtain his DNA, and search his home and vehicles.

After combing construction sites all over Kingman, the detectives located Michael Lewis driving a black Dodge truck. They interviewed him at the Mohave County Sheriff's Office.

Michael did whatever he could to minimize his involvement in the Jarvi homicide. He admitted seeing Skylar pay a stack of hundred-dollar bills to repair his Sea Ray, *Dr. Crunch,* on December 26, but he denied having gone to Mexico with Skylar recently. He claimed he was familiar with the Jarvi homicide investigation only because he'd heard about it from his mother, Colleen Francisco, and had read about it on the Hawks website. Skylar wasn't a violent person, he said, and neither was he.

Once the detectives confronted him with his cell phone records and said a witness had accused him of being involved in the murder, Michael said he would cooperate.

"Okay, I'll tell you guys everything you want to know about it," he said.

He said he wasn't trying to lie to the cops, but he didn't understand what he was involved with. Then, after releasing a few more inconsequential details, he clammed up and said he wanted an attorney, so they went to his house in Oatman and searched it. Shown

Jarvi's driver's license photo, Michael would only say he looked familiar.

Over the next few weeks, Short spoke with Lewis a half-dozen times as he changed his story, added inconsistencies, and told more lies. He said, for example, that he went with Skylar to a jewelry store to put money down on Jennifer's ring, but he couldn't remember where it was or see what Skylar was doing there, because he'd been looking at watches. Krallman subsequently learned that Skylar had, in fact, bought a wedding ring for $2,200 at Robbins Brothers, but the store didn't sell watches. Apparently, lying ran in the Jacobson family.

During the third interview on July 19, Short asked why Michael was so reluctant to speak to detectives if he wasn't there when Jarvi was killed and had no advance knowledge about the murder. Michael said he was scared.

"The thing that trips me out the most, or worries me the most, is that if he could have the audacity to, while he's in prison, try to get his dad killed, what says that he can't do that to me?" he said. "If he's got such a cold heart, that he could do something like that, who am I to be any different to him?"

But, he assured the detectives, "If I had seen someone get killed or seen something like that, you can count on me telling you."

It wasn't until the sixth interview on July 28—after Short advised Lewis's wife that he was likely to be arrested because his statement wasn't adding up—that Michael finally admitted he'd been lying and that a man who resembled Jarvi had traveled to Ensenada with him and Skylar, reportedly to go surfing.

Michael claimed to have wandered around "doing the tourist thing" for several hours in Ensenada, while Skylar was off doing "business" with Jarvi, first at a bank, then at some unknown location. Michael claimed that he'd thought it was drug related, but he didn't ask because he didn't want to know.

Later that evening, he said, he and Skylar crossed the border and had pizza before Skylar returned to jail for the night. He admitted that Jarvi didn't come back with them; Skylar said Jarvi wanted to get away from everything so he'd stayed behind.

About ten days later, Skylar told him that Jarvi had his throat cut, and if asked, Michael should tell police that he and Jennifer had gone to Tijuana for some ice cream, a story that even Michael knew wasn't believable. Skylar, he said, was mostly concerned about getting a probation violation because he wasn't supposed to leave the country.

The detectives could tell Michael was either still lying or omitting important details, so they decided to let him stew in jail for a while.

It is my opinion based upon the totality of the circumstances, evidence obtained, and the witness statements taken with this investigation, that Michael William Lewis Jr. was involved with Jon Jarvi's homicide, Krallman wrote in the arrest warrant affadavit, noting that *other unknown individual(s) may be involved with this crime either directly or indirectly.*

Short interviewed Michael one last time, on August 2, before he was arrested in Arizona, and was brought back to Orange County on August 19.

Murphy filed murder charges against Skylar, with the special circumstance allegation of killing for financial gain. Michael was charged with being an accomplice to murder, and Jennifer as an accessory to murder after the fact.

* * *

That same morning, Byington and Sailor went to the central jail complex in Santa Ana to notify the Deleons of the new charges, and to see if they would talk. Jennifer refused to meet with them, so Byington left her a note.

Half an hour later, the detectives met with Skylar, who said he wanted to speak with his attorney, but kept on talking.

"I want to do a lie detector test," he said. "I will prove that I didn't do what you guys say."

Asked which murder he was referring to, Skylar said all of them. After he was Mirandized, Skylar vehemently denied any involvement in Jarvi's murder, and said once again that he was in fear for his family's safety if he told police what he knew about it.

When Byington explained that Skylar had to identify Jarvi's killer if he wanted to exonerate himself, Skylar said flatly, "My dad did it."

"How do you know that?"

"Because he told me."

For the next ninety minutes, Skylar spinned his latest yarn. JP Jarvi, he said, had confided in him about an illegal moneymaking venture that JP and John Jacobson were going to do in Mexico on December 27, 2003, returning the same day. Skylar agreed to be JP's alibi if his probation officer should inquire.

JP, who was planning to use money from the Mexico job to buy Skylar's Sea Ray, gave him several thousand dollars on December 26 as a down payment. Skylar said he used that money to pay Mo Beck for the repairs and to reduce his credit card debt.

On December 27, he said, JP drove his van to

Skylar's house, left him the keys, and said he'd be back later. Skylar's father showed up, and Michael, who was going to act as "security" for the deal, arrived shortly thereafter. They took off after Skylar loaned his Ford pickup and cell phone to Michael, who followed John and JP in John's car.

Skylar said he spoke to Michael on the phone several times that day, but he couldn't recall what they talked about. Michael returned the truck and cell phone a few days later. When JP didn't return for his van, Skylar drove it to Greg Logan's car lot so JP wouldn't get a parking ticket on the street. He didn't learn it had been impounded until some Interpol officers told him a few weeks later that Jarvi's throat had been cut.

Several weeks after that, Skylar said, his father invited him and Jennifer for a free overnight stay at the Riverside Hotel in Laughlin, Arizona, where John privately confessed that he'd killed Jarvi. John was extremely upset with Michael, who had "screwed him over," and told Skylar not to associate with him anymore.

"'Mike went down with me to Mexico, and we were supposed to do some transaction, and Mike bailed on me,'" Skylar quoted his father as saying. "'I had to take things into my own hands because of him. Things got bad and Mike split. . . . Mike left me to hang. . . . I had to take crap into my own hands. I had to get rid of [Jarvi].'"

Skylar said he'd tried to talk to his cousin about this, but Michael was too afraid to say anything and hadn't spoken to John since Jarvi's death. Skylar said his father had also recruited an unidentified member of the Hells Angels motorcycle gang, who subsequently

had been arrested in Laughlin for an unrelated crime
to help kill Jarvi.

After Skylar, Jennifer, and Michael were arraigned
on the new charges, the three of them were placed on
the same bus back to jail. Michael later told detectives
that he'd been sitting in the back when Skylar, fully
shackled, walked over and asked Lewis to join him
and Jennifer for a strategy session up front. Michael
refused. He didn't want to sit with his cousin, partly
because the detectives had told him to stay away from
Skylar, and also because he was pissed at his cousin
for sucking him into this nightmare.

So Skylar leaned down and whispered that if they
told their lawyers the same story about John Jacobson
killing Jarvi in Mexico during a drug deal, they could
go for a speedy trial, and they could both get off.

The story: "Money was forgotten or left at home,
and . . . my uncle had to kill the guy," Michael recounted when he testified at Jennifer's trial. "My
cousin told me that . . . if I got convicted, that he
would take care of my family, pretty much. And he
also told me that I wouldn't get convicted because
everything would be my uncle's fault."

Michael soon heard from other inmates, who
didn't know he was Skylar's cousin, that Skylar was
out to get those who were narking on him, Jennifer
included. So Michael wasn't about to tell detectives
the whole truth. Besides, the Jacobsons were a family
that hung together. No matter what.

"You protect your family. You don't call the police.
You don't report things," Michael explained. "You
watch each other's back."

Knowing that his uncle John had been heavy into

doing and selling drugs, Michael figured that Skylar was hanging out with the same people. Given that Skylar had been trained in jujitsu, and that he and his friends liked to beat up people in high school, Michael saw Skylar as a wild card he didn't want to play. So Michael didn't tell the truth to police until January 5, 2006, after his attorney told him that he, too, could get the death penalty for Jarvi's murder.

Including phone interviews, this was the ninth time the detectives had interviewed Michael. But even then, the Newport detectives believed Michael knew more than he was saying.

"In our opinion he still wasn't being completely truthful with us," Byington said later. "We were sure that he was present and witnessed the actual murder, but only two other people knew for sure. One had his throat slit and the other was [Skylar]."

Nonetheless, they released Michael on his own recognizance, with the agreement that he would testify at Skylar and Jennifer's trial, thinking he'd be more helpful to their case as a witness. This would be the best the detectives were going to do, so they prepared for trial with his final version, which they fleshed out with their subsequent investigation.

No one would ever know the exact details of the get-rich-quick scheme that Skylar concocted to get JP's money, but Jeff and Jeanne Jarvi figured that Skylar had told JP they would buy drugs with his $50,000 in Mexico, then make hundreds of thousands of dollars in profit by selling them in the United States.

35

As Byington's team continued to interview witnesses, they kept hearing that Skylar had told various stories about being born a hermaphrodite—with male and female sex organs—and, depending upon who he was talking to, that he'd already had or was going to have a sex change operation.

Skylar's stepmother, Lisa, told police matter-of-factly that he'd been born a hermaphrodite, however, his birth mother, Lynette, said that wasn't true.

Skylar first broached the topic with Alonso by claiming that he was a triplet, with a twin brother and sister, after splitting off from his siblings in the womb. This caused him to develop both female and male sexual organs, he said, but the male hormones proved to be more dominant.

"Do you want to see something crazy?" Skylar asked, showing Alonso the same post-op photo he showed Adam Rohrig.

Skylar said he'd already paid a million dollars to get the best doctor to remove his penis, and as a result, he was going to start looking like a woman, and have less hair.

Alonso told police he felt very awkward hearing this, and didn't know what to think. He knew from their time at the Seal Beach jail together that Skylar had worn diapers since the motorcycle accident, but he'd never seen Skylar naked to confirm the rest of his story. When Skylar mentioned that Jennifer was pregnant, Alonso asked how that could be.

"Oh, she was pregnant before I had the operation," Skylar said.

Skylar had also made numerous references to his seizures, a lack of testosterone, and breast development. As Byington watched Skylar grow increasingly feminine in court, he recalled that Jennifer's cousin, Danielle Dunning, had referred during a jail visit to his lack of body hair, the growth of his fingernails, and the makeup he was wearing.

So after he heard that Tom Hawks had landed a solid kick into Skylar's groin, Byington obtained a search warrant to check Skylar for scars or any lasting trace of the injury. The underlying purpose, however, was to disprove Skylar's hermaphrodite claim.

On March 3, 2005, Byington and Sailor showed up at the men's jail with a warrant, along with CSI Gage and his camera. Four deputies brought Skylar to an interview room by walking him through the women's jail, which apparently was no big deal to him, because he was still wearing the women's jail jumpsuit. Skylar also had been asking for feminine maxi pads.

Skylar dropped his jumpsuit as instructed, and stood there in his diaper like a little kid, with an innocent expression.

"Is that it?" he asked.

"Take it all off," Byington ordered.

So Skylar removed his soaked diaper, looking embarrassed. Sailor immediately thought of his baby son's diapers, which got really wet—and he was only a baby. He didn't even want to imagine the contents of Skylar's, which Skylar folded up and put to the side of the room so the police could take pictures of his not-so-private parts.

"When he pulled off his diaper, I had no idea what I was going to find," Byington said. "He had normal junk, but he was hairless," except for some hair on his genitals.

Skylar claimed he'd been taking hormones, but Byington believed he more than likely had shaved off his body hair.

"What we searched for and found was that he never got hormones," Sailor said, adding that they were never able to get all of his medical records so they couldn't say for sure. "He looked shaved to me."

But as far as they could see, Skylar had no female genitalia. He was a man, at least on the outside.

"The hermaphrodite story was crap," Byington said.

After some follow-up research, Byington was able to translate the terms he'd seen Skylar and Jennifer using in letters and heard in his jail visits: SRS was short for "sexual reassignment surgery," GRS meant gender reassignment surgery, and Dr. Marci Bowers was a nationally renowned surgeon who performed these procedures in Trinidad, Colorado, after having had the procedure herself. Formerly Mark Bowers, the doctor had her own Wikipedia page and had been described in the *Denver Post* as a "transgender rock star" of the sex change operation.

In December 2005, Byington called Bower's office and explained to her office manager, Julie Savage, that he needed to get copies of Skylar's medical records to prepare for trial. Savage confirmed that Skylar hadn't been seen by the doctor yet, but he'd submitted an application for the $15,500 surgery and a $500 deposit on June 19, 2004, which, Byington noted, was five months before the Hawkses' murder, when Skylar and Jennifer were already deeply in debt.

Savage explained that transgender patients had to submit two letters of recommendation from a psychiatrist or psychologist, two psychiatric evaluations, and be on hormone replacement therapy. She said these issues had been addressed in Skylar's application, but she couldn't elaborate further without a search warrant.

A few weeks later, Byington obtained a warrant and seized documents, including Skylar's handwritten application. In his application, Skylar claimed he'd been taking hormones since 2002, but had begun his "real-life test" in 1998, a term that refers to living openly as a woman. He listed numerous relatives and friends who could vouch for this, including Jennifer and her cousin, Danielle Dunning; Skylar's mother, cousin, and aunt; and Greg Logan. Skylar listed his target date for the surgery as November 30, 2004, two weeks after the Hawkses' murder.

Bowers explained that if Skylar had been undergoing "hormone replacement therapy," he would have been experiencing physiological changes, such as the loss of body hair and breast development. The cost of taking estrogen and other related medications, she said, would be approximately $250 per month, and the only ill effects he could suffer from immediate hormone withdrawal would be the atrophy of his breasts. It was also common, she said, for pre-op transgender patients to obtain hormones on the street, which wouldn't necessarily show up on medical records.

Skylar's aunt, Colleen, told Byington that Skylar had asked her in early 2002 for a $5,000 loan, which he said he urgently needed as a down payment for a sex change operation to fix the incontinence caused by his motorcycle accident. He told her the surgery was very expensive and that he was experiencing "a huge financial hardship," so he needed "as much money" as she could afford to give him. He also warned her that he was taking medication that would cause his breasts to grow.

Byington called Danielle a few months later. She said she was unaware that he'd listed her as a reference for the surgery, but he'd told her that he intended to have it. Skylar told her that doctors discovered he had female organs while they were attempting to diagnose his bladder injury after his accident. The operation would correct the incontinence problem, he said, *and* deal with his gender issue. Initially, Danielle said, she was "pretty shocked" by this news, but once Jennifer said she was okay with it, she was, too. She was very close with Jennifer, and she didn't question her cousin's relationship with Skylar.

Byington, acknowledging that he and Matt Murphy differed on Skylar's motive for the Hawkses' murder, said he believed that Skylar needed to do something drastic to come up with the $15,000 balance for the operation, and that he also must have sincerely wanted to stop wearing diapers.

"So he had to kill these people to get the money for the surgery," he said. "He wanted it that bad. He already had the date set. He put five hundred dollars down, when they didn't even have a pot to piss in."

Michael Molfetta agreed with Byington. "Jennifer told me she was okay with it," he said of the operation, adding that she'd confided that sex with Skylar "was pretty much nonexistent."

But in Murphy's mind, it was all about money and greed. When Skylar had gotten $50,000 from Jarvi only ten months before he'd started planning this caper, he hadn't spent it on any operation.

36

By February 2006, Skylar had lost more than forty pounds, and had been moved back into the general jail population, where he was allowed only one diaper a day.

So Gary Pohlson asked the court to order the jail's medical team to evaluate Skylar for "his medical condition of incontinence and his extreme weight loss," noting that he'd been moved out of the medical unit. Pohlson also requested that Skylar "be provided with multiple undergarments" and be allowed to shower at least twice a day, "as is medically necessary." Pohlson wrote that Skylar had been told *by the medical staff that he needs double rations to get his weight stable. He reports to me now that he is not getting double rations . . . and is even being denied meals on occasion.* Judge Kazuharu Makino granted the order.

Byington said jail informants reported that Skylar had been making himself throw up after eating and was exercising frenetically. His plan, they said, was to complain of ailments enough that the jail would have to send him to a hospital, where he would try to escape.

Skylar's appearance shocked Jennifer and her family at a court hearing in March. In a letter to Jennifer afterward, Skylar said she looked "amazing as always," drawing a smiley face with a heart for lips. *You definetly* [sic] *didn't look too* [sic] *thrilled about how I looked. . . . Lana's face looked like her jaw dropped when she seen me.*

Skylar said he'd held on to the letter until he had something happier to say. Apparently, he'd been feeling Jennifer pulling away from him. Noting that the frequency of her letters was decreasing, he said it was Saturday and he hadn't received any mail since Tuesday.

When he added an update to the four-page letter on March 13, he wrote about his weekend visit with playful Kaleb. Since then, he said, he'd been transferred to another unit, where it was so cold he had to wrap himself in a blanket. His pleas for her to write became more urgent, saying he *needed* to hear from his best friend and angel.

Sleep with the angels baby. Huggs [sic] *& Kisses & Snuggles & Love.*

On April 5, Jennifer wrote to Skylar as if nothing was wrong: *I cannot imagine why you aren't getting any of my letters. . . . You should be getting all of them—one a day.*

Eight days later, Skylar wrote that he didn't understand why he hadn't received any letters from her in three days, so he would wait for one before writing again. He really missed hearing from her. *I have no clue what's going on,* he wrote. *I don't know if you are even writing me, or want me to write to you anymore.*

Skylar had called the Hendersons around nine that morning. He heard Lana pick up and the kids in the background, but she didn't say anything. When he called back, it went straight to voice mail. He sent the letter, anyway, starting a new one the next day as usual, saying he was feeling low because he'd still gotten no letters or visits, and it felt as if his only family had forgotten him. Drawing sad and happy faces where appropriate, he said he was "extremely lonely" without her mail.

In the next section, Skylar said he'd just spoken with their minister, "Pastor Dave," who broke the news to him that Jennifer had decided to stop writing him, and her family was also ceasing contact. By the second page of what would become a ten-page saga, Skylar chronicled how he was crying and vomiting over losing her. He quoted from the Bible and drew a cracked heart to illustrate his devastation over losing her and their family. Generally rolling around in the emotional muck of yesterday's memories and their pre-arrest lives together, he said he didn't understand her abrupt change of heart. He'd never felt this low or this hurt, and he felt like a fool to have had faith or believed in love.

A year you've been hear [sic] *and now you don't want to write or can't write me?* he asked. Perhaps because he knew the authorities were monitoring their correspondence, he flatly maintained their innocence. *We both know neither of us did anything, and I WILL prove it to your family and our children.*

Skylar vowed not to give up on Jennifer, to stop writing her, or to stop fighting to see his babies. He also would not let himself believe that she didn't want his letters after telling him so many times how much she appreciated hearing from him. And yet, he said, he couldn't help but wonder if she'd been lying to him all along.

Skylar spent the rest of the missive quoting Jennifer's love letters back to her, emphasizing how much it hurt to read them now. Obviously, reality still hadn't sunk in, because he expressed confusion why a happily married couple like them couldn't write each other.

Shortly thereafter, Skylar finally got Jennifer's final kiss-off letter. Unlike her previous letters, including one she'd sent only a week earlier, there were no happy little squiggles in the margins, no hearts, stars, or smiley faces. Her handwriting was very neat and controlled.

Jennifer apologized for not writing sooner, but she was having a very rough time trying to decide how to deal with her emotions. She apologized for leaving him hanging, saying she'd been trying to write, but she'd had trouble completing a letter because her message was so difficult.

Finally, she spat it out: she needed to stop their letters.

She wasn't trying to hurt him, she wrote, she was just trying to do the best thing for her and their kids, who were growing up without their parents. She hoped he would understand. This wasn't about how much they loved each other, she said, but rather the situation at hand. Her parents felt the same way, but she'd make sure he could keep seeing Haylie and Kaleb. She also said she'd see him in court the following Tuesday so they could talk in person.

I hate this, Skylar, she wrote. *This isn't where I ever saw our lives.*

This short, double-sided note, in which she said that she, too, had a broken heart, would be the last time she wrote to her husband from the county jail. And likely the last time, ever.

* * *

Skylar and Jennifer appeared together on May 5 at a comparatively brief preliminary hearing on the Jarvi case. Pohlson and Molfetta tried to argue that a murder committed in Mexico shouldn't be prosecuted in Orange County, but Murphy argued that the "preparatory acts" took place locally, so it was the proper jurisdiction to try the case.

Commissioner Thomas J. Rees said he had "a strong suspicion" that the alleged crimes had occurred, and that the special allegation of murder for financial gain was true, so he bound the charges over for trial.

In late May, Skylar was put into isolation for a week for lying to staff about an inmate who had given him a razor blade, and a week later he lost a week's privileges for possessing the blade.

Pohlson submitted another request to the judge for a medical exam and double portions, saying that Skylar had now lost sixty pounds from his original weight of 165 pounds. During a recent visit, Pohlson wrote, Skylar took off his shirt and looked like *a concentration camp victim. He reports that he feels dizzy and faint when he exerts himself at all. I am seriously concerned for his health.*

Byington believed this tactic, just like the lipstick and eyeliner, were part of an effort to look feminine and fragile so the jury wouldn't think he was capable of overpowering and killing a muscle-bound guy like Tom Hawks.

But Pohlson said Skylar just wanted to be a woman, and his weight loss was caused by depression. Skylar wasn't a homosexual, he said. A psychologist had speculated that Skylar wanted to be female because his father treated women better than him.

Later that year, in the middle of Jennifer's trial, Pohlson requested that Skylar be allowed to buy feminine care products, such as baby oil, lip gloss, women's deodorant, skin cream, and mascara from the jail commissary. Judge Makino approved the order on November 13, but the sheriff's department immediately challenged it.

For a long time, Molfetta had the same dilemma with Lana and Steve Henderson that he'd had with Jennifer. He couldn't seem to convince them to stop communicating with Skylar and bringing Haylie and Kaleb to see him in jail.

Lana had been in denial about Skylar's guilt from the beginning, and was unable to handle the emotional or intellectual reality that her daughter had married and borne two children with a bad person. Molfetta said Lana didn't know what else to do but act like a good grandma, and keep bringing his kids for visits.

Steve's denial didn't run as deep, and over time he eventually developed a new perspective. It had taken a while, Molfetta said, but Steve finally accepted that he needed to heed Molfetta's advice, and his view of Jennifer changed as well. He'd started out pleading with Molfetta to help his innocent baby, but at a certain point he began to accept that his daughter was guilty of murder, and his pleas for help morphed into a philosophy of "she deserves what she gets."

On Saturday, June 17, 2006, Lana brought the kids to see Jennifer, and dropped the bomb that Steve had unilaterally decided they would no longer be visiting Skylar.

At first, she didn't want to go into the reasons behind the decision. "Just call him, and he'll explain," Lana said.

Jennifer was furious. This wasn't her father's decision to make without consulting her, she said. She wanted her children to know their father, regardless of the circumstances.

Once Lana gave a brief and vague explanation, she suggested that Jennifer talk with Molfetta. "If you're going to be mad, be mad at me," she said.

But Jennifer refused to let her mother take the blame. She was so upset that she said Steve shouldn't visit her the next day, on Father's Day. Jennifer was bawling, which made the kids and her mother cry, too. Lana had to take the kids around the corner for a few minutes until the tears stopped.

When Jennifer called Molfetta, he said he didn't know anything about it, and told her to talk to her parents, which made her even more angry.

The next day Jennifer vented to her cousin Danielle.

"I want to know what actually happened, and what made that decision that decision. They tell me to talk to Mike, I talk to Mike. He tells me to talk to them, that he doesn't know what I'm talking about. So I told my mom yesterday, 'So either you're lying to me, or he's lying to me, which one is it?'"

Jennifer insisted that a thirty-minute visit between Skylar and their kids would not be mind-altering. "They've been seeing him for a year regular, then all of a sudden . . ."

But Danielle said she was worried that Haylie might get used to the visits as she got older, only to have them abruptly cut off when Skylar went to prison. "Not necessarily Kaleb, because he doesn't really know any better."

"She *needs* to see him," Jennifer insisted. "Yes, this involves everybody, but when it comes down to it, it's *me*. I'm the only one that seems to not know what's going on, and that's not okay. . . . I'm the one who has to sit here with nothing else to think about."

Jennifer explained that she didn't want to try to discuss the issue with Steve because it was a no-win situation. She couldn't force him to do anything from her jail cell. "No matter what I say, I'm going to lose, as far as the argument goes. He has the say."

She said she was just as angry at Molfetta for whatever he'd said to Steve.

"What else is he telling them that they're not telling me, and he's not telling me? They're not his client. *I am*. He doesn't work for me. He's come down here three times to see me, and when he hears this, he's going to be pissed, but I don't care. I've been pissed a lot longer."

"Yeah," Danielle said.

"It's not right. There's people who've got their attorneys coming down here all the time, fighting less time than me."

Jennifer said it was probably better that she didn't deal with the issue on Father's Day, anyway. "It sucks that it's got to be this weekend, but that's not my problem right now. I don't really care. He's got a Father's Day card or whatever. . . . I mean, he didn't come yesterday, he probably wouldn't have come today, anyway. . . . So he's depriving me of my dad, and so now he's going to deprive them of theirs."

"Hmmm," Danielle said.

Jennifer said Lana had clearly been trying to keep

the peace in the family. "I understand that she doesn't want to make waves, because then he'll be an asshole to her, and she doesn't need that. And I love my dad, but he's an asshole. That's just the way it's always been. You know I can be an asshole, too . . . but he's a little more of an asshole on a regular basis. He likes to control and it makes you wonder why I married someone that doesn't make any decisions, that doesn't act like he cares, at least that I know of. You know, somebody that seems to be so passive, 'cause it's like I finally get a say!"

Meghan Leathem had thought about visiting Jennifer in jail for quite some time, but she didn't come until a month or two before Jennifer's trial. She'd been so upset that Jennifer was behind bars that she hadn't wanted to make her friend feel worse by crying the entire visit.

When Meghan finally pulled herself together and bit the bullet, what she heard come out of Jennifer's mouth was very different from the last time they'd talked.

"I'm sorry for bringing Skylar into your life," Jennifer told her. "He is a psycho, he is a freak, he is a horrible person. I don't think I will ever date or marry a man again."

Jennifer called Skylar an animal, saying it would cost only a dollar to divorce him, but after learning that he'd put hits out on his own father and cousin, she was afraid of what he might do to her family.

"She feared for their lives," Meghan testified later.

Back in the medical unit, Skylar approached inmate Danny Elias to see if he could help get $200,000 out of another inmate's bank account. He told Elias that he'd "run a make on the tier," meaning he'd checked out all the inmates in their unit and had learned that Elias had a bad record—firearms and drugs—yet he was the only one without a criminal informant's file. In other words, Elias wasn't a snitch, so Skylar figured he'd be a good candidate to arrange a hit on the witnesses slated to testify in Skylar's case. Ironically, the fact that Skylar and Elias were both wearing jail-issued gowns for inmates on suicide watch didn't affect Skylar's credibility with Elias.

In a series of conversations in the dayroom and out on the yard, Skylar identified two targets, a diving instructor whose help he'd solicited in getting rid of the bodies, and a woman Skylar claimed was the diver's notary wife, drawing maps to their house and the dive shop. Skylar said there was also a guy in the Newport Beach city jail, but his attorney could toss that witness's credibility out the window, so killing the other two should be sufficient to beat his case.

But there was one more. He also wanted a hit on his cousin, Michael Lewis, because he was snitching about a separate murder they'd done together in Mexico.

Elias was interested. "I needed one million dollars, and he . . . made me believe that he had money that he could access in Mexico and that I could get out," he testified later. "He said once he was released, my friend, whoever did the job, would go down to Mexico with him and he would give them two million dollars for the murders, and a million to get me out."

Elias had connections to hard-core white supremacist groups, including PEN1, a violent racist skinhead gang known as Public Enemy Number 1, which was involved in the drug trade, had power on the streets and in prison yards, and acted as foot soldiers for more established gangs, like the Aryan Brotherhood. Surely, Elias could have found somebody to do the job for Skylar.

Skylar, talking a good game once again, portrayed himself as a drug smuggler, "tipped up in Mexico with the cartel" and the Crips, who could do the job if Elias wasn't interested.

At the time Elias had no idea that Skylar was making up stories, so he discussed the offer with inmate Kelly Henderson, a longtime jail snitch who told him he could "get out on this." Elias said he wasn't a snitch, but Henderson sent a letter for him regardless, which triggered a visit by Byington. After talking to Murphy, however, Byington told Elias, "No deal."

Elias thought about it some more, and decided to help authorities, anyway, by agreeing to talk to Skylar in a wired cell. He claimed he wanted to do the right thing—prevent Skylar from hiring anybody else—but he also hoped to win some consideration from the state Department of Corrections and Rehabilitation when he went to prison.

Murphy later said Elias was a far more dangerous inmate to solicit than Alvarado had ever been. Alvarado was jailed, essentially, for doing stupid crimes while drunk, so he was the "wrong hit man to kill the wrong witness." Elias, on the other hand, could have gotten the job done, "so we're talking about the right hit man to kill the right witnesses."

If Skylar had been successful in soliciting the murder of his father, who had been completely uncooperative with investigators, "it would have had zero impact on the case," Murphy said. Having Adam Rohrig, Kathleen Harris, or Michael Lewis killed, however, would have posed a problem.

Skylar was charged with soliciting the murder of his father and cousin, and at a July 31 hearing he pleaded not guilty and cried as Ryan Hawks gave him a death stare on behalf of his parents.

These were legitimate charges, but Murphy fully expected they would become moot in Skylar's overall death penalty case. That said, he knew Alvarado and Elias would be useful if the trial indeed went to the penalty phase, when the jury could consider Skylar's murder solicitation efforts from jail when determining how dangerous he could be in the future.

John Jacobson told reporters it was surreal that his son would put out a hit on him. Trying to gain sympathy, John said his family's hearts went out to the Hawkses, but the Jacobsons were hurting, too.

"I believe he is a sick individual," he told the *Los Angeles Times.* "I love him because he's my blood and my family. But somewhere along the line, he changed, I guess."

Several months later, on September 6, District Attorney Tony Rackauckas held a press conference, with Byington beside him, formally announcing that he was seeking the death penalty against Skylar and JFK.

Rackauckas noted that he'd sought death in thirty-three cases, his most serious responsibility as DA. So far, he said, thirteen juries had recommended death, nine had recommended life without the possibility of parole, and the remaining eleven cases were still pending.

"There are some murders, however, that are committed with such a malignant heart, such a callousness, that the only *just* penalty is death," he said.

"Deleon is accused of planning their murder for

days, coordinating with his wife and using their infant child to gain the Hawks[es]' trust, and hiring 'muscle' to murder this couple. We also found the Hawks[es] were murdered in the most cold-blooded way. . . . This couple literally watched their dreams float away as they were drowning to death. We also considered that after Deleon was charged with the Hawks and the Jarvi murders, he was charged with soliciting the murder of his own father and a cousin, both witnesses. . . . Even though Mr. Kennedy was late in joining the conspiracy, without Kennedy providing the muscle, this crime could not have been carried out. . . . These two joined in this cruel and callous murder. Deleon the brain, Kennedy the brawn. Now they will face the same penalty, and their fate will be decided by the people of Orange County."

Rackauckas didn't mention it at the news conference, but he'd also sent a letter to Molfetta, letting him know that Jennifer was *not* going to be facing death.

Molfetta wasn't surprised, because Murphy had already told him he hadn't asked his supervisors to seek a death sentence against her. It would be tough even for a top-notch prosecutor like Murphy to win such a verdict against a twenty-four-year-old woman who had no criminal record, was the mother of a young daughter and newborn son, and hadn't even been present during the murders.

When Molfetta discussed strategy with Jennifer, she said she wanted a quick trial and didn't want to wait another year until Skylar was tried. So Molfetta filed a motion to try her alone, hoping to avoid a repeat of the disastrous looks and glances between the two puppy lovers at the prelim. He also knew he could better malign Skylar if he was absent.

"I could say whatever I wanted to say about the guy, and he'd have no one there to defend him," Molfetta said.

Murphy didn't oppose the motion, and was even in favor of trying Jennifer separately from Skylar and JFK. If she was sitting alongside her evil, manipulative husband and the menacing-looking Crips member at the defendants' table, the jury might look at her with more mercy. Especially when the couple dubbed "the Bonnie and Clyde of Orange County" started pointing fingers at each other.

Murphy figured the chances were good—maybe fifty-fifty—that Molfetta would put her on the stand. Molfetta might even be able to convince the jury of her innocence, Byington said, "if the defense had gotten her up there, saying, 'I had no idea what my husband was doing, I have babies, I love them, who's going to take care of them?'"

So Murphy readied himself for her testimony, planning to hold back some choice evidence to use during cross-examination. He had a slew of letters from which to choose, as well as an incriminating statement Skylar had made during one of her jail visits: "Remember that there's no bodies, no murder."

Hoping to even the score with his former teacher, Murphy also prepared for every other potential contingency as he put together his PowerPoint presentations for the most powerful opening statement and closing argument possible.

On October 27, 2006, trial judge Frank F. Fasel granted Molfetta's motion and, despite Murphy's opposition, also threw out Jennifer's accessory charge in the Jarvi murder.

Still, Murphy, who admired Fasel, felt good about getting him for this case. So did Molfetta, who considered him one of his two favorite judges.

"He's fair. He lets the lawyer try his case," Molfetta said. "When he talks, you listen. What he says is usually right. . . . He's what a judge should be."

Fasel, a sixty-three-year-old Notre Dame graduate, spent several years in the marines, and attended law school at University of San Diego while serving as a captain in the reserves. After working briefly as a private attorney, then as a prosecutor for eight and a half years in Los Angeles and Orange Counties, he became a superior court commissioner during the 1980s. Appointed to the bench by Governor Deukmejian in May 1989, he also served as presiding judge of the appellate division and the juvenile court.

Fasel was a low-talking man of few words, yet he kept tight-fisted control over his courtroom, where he was respected for being a no-nonsense stickler for the rules.

"He's not known to show favoritism either way on capital cases," Detective Short said, explaining that police liked trying a case before a good judge—with a good defense attorney—because it reduced the chance of an appeal.

Local attorneys were scared of Fasel, sharing stories of when he "showed them the vein" on his forehead, which bulged when he got angry. Fasel rarely smiled, had no patience for tardiness, and was known to issue bench warrants with $50,000 bail for late jurors.

Unlike some judges, Fasel's approach completely discouraged theatrics. Attorneys knew he didn't want to hear objections and arguments in front of the jury.

Instead, attorneys soon learned, they were expected to ask for a sidebar, to which the defendant was allowed to listen on earphones, or wait to discuss the matter in chambers. But sometimes, the judge wouldn't even agree to a sidebar, and on some occasions he was clearly annoyed at having to do so. Afterward, the dissenting attorney would often withdraw his objection.

"Trust me, he's the last guy you want to piss off," Murphy said. But, he added, "If Fasel gets mad at you, you've really screwed something up." With some judges, he said, you're angry at him for making a bad call, but "with Fasel, you drive home and you think, 'Why was I wrong?'"

Nonetheless, Fasel was not known as a friend of the media, and he wouldn't allow this particular court file, a public record, to be reviewed until all defendants' cases had been resolved, which took five years. Fasel liked to keep his courtroom . . . sanitized.

37

Undoubtedly similar to many others across the nation, the Orange County jail system has a whole underground dating network about which most regular citizens are completely unaware. Inmates meet on buses to and from the courthouse, or in the holding cells where they wait to be called for hearings. After that, they correspond through letters or notes, known as "kites," which can be passed along, say, under the door separating the men's and women's recreation yards.

At some point after Jennifer stopped writing Skylar, she met a female inmate, they fell in love, and they sent love letters to each other after the woman was transferred to another jail. Meanwhile, Jennifer met Bret Langford, an inmate in his late thirties who was accused of robbing Jewelry Express in the Westminster Mall in April 2005. Langford reportedly approached Jennifer with the goal of making a deal for himself with authorities, but their relationship soon evolved into something quite unexpected. As Jennifer grew apart from her female lover, she became closer with Langford, who became her jailhouse attorney. According to him, they fell in love and got engaged.

For nearly two years while awaiting trial, authorities said, Langford repeatedly swallowed a two-carat diamond ring worth $25,000 (or hid it in another body cavity), regurgitating and hiding it in a new shower drain every time he transferred cells. Deputies found the bauble in March 2007 after a court order allowed them to search a specific drain.

Langford made sure to tell Skylar about his relationship with Jennifer in letters that Pohlson characterized as vicious. In June 2007, for example, Langford sent Skylar a letter filled with degrading homosexual references about Skylar shaking his "bony ass" and putting on makeup. He also taunted Skylar with images of how he'd stolen Skylar's family.

Nearly a year later, Langford wrote him a similar eight-page letter from Wasco State Prison. This time he used Skylar's half sister Stephanie to provoke him, saying that her $100 gift card for Toys "Я" Us had been received. But if she wanted to spend time with the kids, she'd have to arrange it through Langford, who would talk to Lana and *my lil* [sic] *wifey-poo*, as long as "Steph" agreed not to give Skylar any information or photos of the kids, he wrote.

Under Langford's criminal hierarchy, he, a diamond thief, was superior to Skylar, who had murdered a nice couple who weren't even *in the game.* . . . *You killed innocents like a coward, and because of that you will be executed.*

Langford also blasted Skylar for manipulating Jennifer, a girl who was "soooooo wholesome" before meeting him, rather than helping to clear her. He facetiously wished Skylar good luck, saying it was lucky that Skylar believed in Jesus, because he'd certainly be meeting him soon. *There's 14 people that will NEVER believe your bullsh**, Skylar: 1 judge, 12 jurors and Jesus Christ.* And all of them, he wrote, would "condemn" Skylar.

The Hendersons couldn't pay Molfetta enough to hire a jury consultant, so in the months before trial, he tried out various defense strategies during two mock trials.

Pulling together a jury of fifteen, he held one trial at the University of California, Irvine, a couple months before the actual proceeding. About six weeks later, he took what he'd learned and conducted a second trial at his house in Santa Ana, with a jury of forty neighbors, ranging from lawyers to construction workers. This trial, which lasted about five hours, helped him test how Jennifer would do on the stand.

"She didn't grade out too well," he said. "The jury said she appeared cold and heartless."

Molfetta knew that if Jennifer did testify, Murphy would impeach her by pulling out the hordes of sappy love letters she'd exchanged with Skylar, decimating Molfetta's attempts to argue that Jennifer was scared of her husband.

But in the end, he said, "it was her decision not to take the stand, and that's why she didn't."

Even so, Molfetta still planned to argue that she feared Skylar. But the thrust of his strategy was to prove that Skylar was a lying, manipulative freak of a con man, and that Jennifer had known nothing of the murders until it was too late. Because of her crazy love for him, she'd been taken in by his wiles more than any other victim who was still alive to talk about it.

All in all, going up against a good, respected friend

was a little disarming. He also had to accept that he couldn't "outcute" Murphy to gain personality points with the jurors; he knew they were going to like his opponent, so all he could hope for was a wash.

Molfetta posed challenges for Murphy as well. Molfetta was not only Murphy's former mentor, he was also one of three local attorneys Murphy feared facing in the courtroom. As a result, Murphy didn't sleep much in the weeks before—or during—the trial. He often woke up at 3:00 A.M., re-read reports, honed his PowerPoint presentations, went over his witness questions, and tried to anticipate what Molfetta was going to do.

"With Molfetta, every case is an uphill battle," he said. "Because Mike is a heavy hitter."

Given that Jennifer's trial was a test case for the prosecution's witnesses and evidence against Skylar, there was much at stake. If the jury didn't buy Alonso's testimony, Murphy would find that out the hard way. And if the jury didn't believe his conspiracy theory, or that Jennifer was involved, he would learn that, too.

The bottom line was that Jennifer wasn't on the boat, she had no criminal record, and she had a monster husband to blame, "so it was going to be a lot tougher with her." He was confident of his evidence, but he never knew how it would play in front of a jury or how his key witnesses would do on the stand, especially on cross-examination.

Skylar's trial would undoubtedly be easier all around. "With Skylar, I had a lot less to worry about," he said. "If she goes down for murder, then Skylar is definitely going down for murder."

* * *

The demographic makeup of Orange County, known as "the Orange Curtain" for its political conservatism and wealth, didn't really affect the way Murphy tried a case.

"You'll get a good strong middle-class jury," he said. "You might get one rich guy, one poor guy, and everyone else will be somewhere in the middle."

But the O.C. was one of the toughest places in California, if not *the* toughest, for criminal defense attorneys, who, Molfetta said, had to heed two important rules: don't try to win a civil case against Disneyland and don't challenge law enforcement in a criminal case.

PART IV

TRIALS AND TRIBULATIONS

38

A brown rim of smog hung over the city of Santa Ana on the very sunny and hot Monday morning of November 6, 2006, when opening statements were set to begin in Jennifer's trial. If the participants didn't want to look at each other, they could distract themselves with the expansive view from the wall of windows on the Harbor Justice Center's ninth floor.

Immediately to the southwest was the jail complex where Skylar was sitting in his cell, presumably wondering how his estranged wife's future—and his own—would play out in the preview of the prosecutor's case against him. And there, in the distance, was the deep blue scene of this horrific crime, where, somewhere, the anchor of the *Well Deserved* was resting on the ocean floor.

In the hallway outside the courtroom, Molfetta tried to talk with Jennifer's parents, who had gathered their church friends into a prayer circle in the hallway. But they shooed him away.

"We're praying to Jesus for help," Lana said.

Frustrated, Molfetta could feel the family turning against him for trying to interrupt. Although he was an atheist, he respected others' need for religion. He just didn't feel this was the time or place for it. Even if the Hendersons' intentions were sincere, he feared the jurors might think the ritual was for their benefit, and he wished the family would have had "enough common sense to realize it might rub some people the wrong way." He knew he wasn't going to earn any points with the family, but he was irritated enough to throw one of his trademark sarcastic jabs their way.

"I don't think he's coming to help, but if he does show up here, I think he's going to go sit over there with the Hawkses," he said, gesturing over to the victims' family.

Ryan Hawks rolled off the glacially slow elevator in a wheelchair, wearing a neck brace after breaking both femurs and suffering whiplash in a motorcycle accident while touring his parents' favorite spots in Mexico. Normally tanned and athletic-looking, Ryan seemed unusually thin, drawn, and pale. Nonetheless, he put on a positive, strong face for the trial, just as his father would have expected. His brother, Matt, their mother, Dixie, and their aunt and uncle, Jim and Sandy, were all there—not to mention the dozens of friends who had come in response to his e-mail asking them to show their support.

The time has come for justice to be served for the murder of my parents, Ryan wrote. The jury needs to see how many lives they touched, and the kind of people they really were.

As a result of this outreach, most of the curved wooden-backed seats in the left-hand section of the expansive courtroom were filled with these folks, which surely sent a strong message to the jury, indeed.

The front corner of this area was the gathering place for the Hawkses, the O'Neills, and the Jarvis, who became like one big family, eating lunch in the cafeteria each day, bound by their tragic ties.

Betty Jarvi, who would testify briefly, sat with her son, Jeff, and daughter-in-law, Jeanne. And, as usual, detectives, investigators, and DA's staff filled the back rows and lined the back wall. Dave Byington sat at the prosecution table with Murphy, who was pumped with adrenaline to win the trial of his career, and even the score with Molfetta.

Before the last-minute severing of trials, Gayle and Jack O'Neill had been told to expect the proceeding to last four to six months. With no idea that it would take less than two weeks, they were bleary-eyed that first morning after a night of tossing, turning, and talking.

Lana Henderson, who sat in the front of the middle section with a few friends, wiped away a quick tear and mouthed "I love you" to a woman across the room. Rubbing her son's back, Lana took several deep breaths and whispered with a woman next to her as Murphy and Molfetta shot the breeze in an obviously familiar way.

Jennifer, her long, dark hair pulled into a ponytail, came out of the holding tank wearing a long-sleeved pink sweater, gray pants, and handcuffs. She and her mother exchanged glances as she shuffled over to the defense table and sat down, with her ponytail hanging down the back of the chair.

Act I of a very long theatrical performance in Judge Fasel's courtroom was about to begin. And after all the media buildup, Murphy felt like everyone was watching.

* * *

The attorneys had weeded through a jury pool of about 150 people to pick a panel of seven women and five men. Despite the strong media interest Fasel refused to allow cameras in the courtroom. So, in addition to the local print and broadcast reporters who were there, the national networks' prime-time crime programs—*20/20, 48 Hours,* and *Dateline*—sent reporters and producers to take notes for shows that were supposed to wait to air until after the triathlon of trials in this case.

Murphy had lost the fight to maintain the accessory charge against Jennifer in the Jarvi murder, but he'd won the battle to present some of the case evidence. If he could show a pattern of behavior on her part, he figured he could prove intent by arguing that all three murders were cut from the same plan: "Dupe someone into thinking they are doing a financial transaction, take them to a place where they are outside of witnesses' earshot, murder them, and take their money and lie to police. Financially benefit and then get rid of the victims' vehicle."

Flashing the victims' and defendants' photos on a screen to help jurors follow his 140-minute opening, Murphy quickly but efficiently painted a glowing picture of the Hawkses, and glossed over Jarvi's flaws as he described how the three victims fell into the sights of Skylar Deleon.

"He did a good job of bamboozling people," he said.

The prosecutor outlined the high points of the two murder investigations and gave the jury a taste of the forensic evidence—the cell phone records in particular—that helped create a timeline of the crimes and tied everything together.

Murphy described how JP Jarvi had crawled for quite a way toward the road from the center of a clearing, leaving a bloody trail from his gushing neck wound. Hearing this for the first time, his family was shocked and saddened to learn that his death had not been quick, after all.

As Murphy explained how Skylar carried out the overall scheme, he noted each step where Jennifer was complicit or participatory in the planning and cover-up, including her visit with Haylie to the *Well Deserved,* Skylar's "check-in" calls to her at key points, her call and subsequent promise of more money to the notary, her help in wiping down the boat, her personal deposit of Skylar's $1,300 split, her calls to Jim Hawks, and her lies to police. He also noted that Skylar had called her repeatedly before and after he killed Jarvi, and that she, too, had reaped the benefits of Jarvi's $50,000 "investment."

The evidence would show, he said, that Jennifer was fully aware of Skylar's sex machine and other "sexual proclivities." But more important, she knew that he had committed armed burglary shortly after they were married, and that he was a suspect in the Jarvi murder. Yet, she had—not one, but two—children with him as their spending continued to ramp out of control. Finally, she had stuck by his side—even after his arrest—visiting him religiously in jail.

Murphy, complimenting Molfetta as an "excellent lawyer," proactively challenged the defense strategy by charging that this case was "not about whether Skylar's a freak and a murderer, because he is." In the coming days, he said, he would prove that the strong-willed Jennifer knew exactly who her husband was, that she helped plan his nefarious activities, and that she was primed and ready to spend the millions Skylar had promised her by killing the Hawkses.

"You folks will not be fooled by Jennifer Deleon," he told the jury. "You will not let this woman get away with what she did."

Molfetta's opening, which went only forty-two minutes, consisted of a stream of witty and biting put-downs of Skylar, which, in his convenient absence, the attorney directed at a photo on the overhead projector.

Calling him "the single most malignant, evil human being around," he said Skylar lacked "a single shred of regard for human life. . . . He literally is able to murder people on the come."

He characterized Jennifer, on the other hand, as an innocent churchgoing lamb, who blindly fell in love with the Devil, a man who lied to her, manipulated, and deceived her at every turn.

"His lies were so absurd, they were believable," Molfetta said, but sadly for Jennifer, "intelligence and love are on two different wavelengths."

Molfetta took great joy in describing Skylar's sex machine, as if it perfectly illustrated how perversely low Jennifer's husband could go, lying that the doctor said it would help strengthen his anal muscles so he could stop wearing the diaper. And Jennifer believed him.

Despite Skylar's claim that Jennifer knew everything about his "hits," Molfetta said she didn't know anything about the Hawkses' murder until afterward. There may have been nothing but bedsheets tying her to Skylar, but by then she was too scared to leave or turn him in, and her fears only worsened once she learned he'd tried to have his father and cousin killed, too.

"She's still under his thumb while he's in jail," he said, so she "kept up appearances" by bringing his kids to see him.

The Hawkses, he said, "were horrifically murdered in a way that nobody deserved," but "she had no idea, and when she had an idea, it was too late. . . . She's not guilty of murder."

Murphy started off by calling a series of witnesses who testified how Jarvi pulled together the $50,000 and how Skylar spent it on his boat and credit card bills.

As Michael Lewis described the events of his Mexico trip with Skylar and JP, Betty Jarvi didn't believe a word. The metal rod in JP's spine may have prevented him from bending, but his legs and shoulders were strong, he could break three-inch pieces of wood over his knee, and he would never have quietly acquiesced to Skylar—a "twenty-pound weakling"—by putting a T-shirt over his head. The Jarvis suspected that Michael had held JP down while Skylar cut his throat.

Molfetta worked to impeach Michael on cross, noting that he'd told police at least eight different versions of this story. Implying a dynamic parallel to Jennifer's, Molfetta got Michael to explain that Skylar could get him to do things Skylar's way—even when they didn't make sense—and that Michael had tried to protect his cousin because he was scared of him.

Despite being feminine, soft-spoken, playful, and quiet, Skylar had "always wanted to be a mercenary," Michael said. He'd been raised to be a man's man and to use women, and was obsessed with snapping people's necks.

On redirect by Murphy, Michael acknowledged that Skylar got his way—except when it came to Jennifer.

"Anything that Skylar did . . . he would say he had to talk to his wife about it. And pretty much if she didn't want to do it, according to him, [then] it wasn't going to happen," even if it was just going to lunch, Michael said.

Exposing a gaping hole in the defense, Murphy asked Michael the same questions he'd ask other witnesses, proving that Jennifer had never shown any signs that she felt threatened by Skylar.

"Did you ever see Skylar physically abuse Jennifer in any way?"

"No."

"Ever have any sort of interaction with them where Jennifer showed up with bruises, black eyes, anything of that kind of stuff?"

"Not that I recall, no."

"Did you ever see Skylar raise his voice at Jennifer?"

"No."

"Did she ever appear afraid around Skylar to you?"

"No, she never appeared afraid or frightened at all," Michael said, adding that she was all smiles.

Molfetta pointed out that many things go on behind closed doors in marriages, and that Skylar could have said anything to Jennifer without Michael's knowledge.

"You never heard Skylar talk to her about going to Mexico and killing Jon Jarvi, did you?"

"No."

Michael may have never seen Skylar be mean to Jennifer, Molfetta said, "Yet we know now he killed three people, right?"

"Yes."

"And you made it abundantly clear that knowing Skylar as long as you had, that Skylar was a person that was prone to lie, correct?"

"Yes."

"And you don't stand for the proposition that he never lied to his wife, do you?"

"No."

Steve Henderson's testimony did his daughter no favors, starting with his description of her buoyant mood as they cleaned up the boat two days after the Hawkses' murder.

"How would you describe her demeanor?"

"I would say she was happy."

"What about excited?"

"Yeah, I would say excited."

Like Michael Lewis, Steve admitted he'd never seen Jennifer with a black eye or swollen lip, nor had he heard Skylar browbeat or demean her. He was also one of several witnesses who acknowledged that Jennifer "wore the pants in the relationship."

"Skylar would . . . put on this façade of being very timid," he said.

Hoping to illustrate that Steve was not intentionally hurting his daughter's defense, Molfetta started his cross-examination by asking how Steve was doing.

"Not real well."

"Did you ever think that there would come a day when you would be testifying in your daughter's murder trial?"

"No, sir."

Steve admitted he'd made some unflattering and incriminating statements about his daughter on direct, but he was telling the truth. He also admitted that he'd initially thought Skylar had a steady job and seemed "like an upright person."

"I.e., I am a good catch for your daughter?" Molfetta asked.

"Yes, sir."

"We now know that's a complete lie, right?"

"Yes, sir."

Once he realized Skylar wasn't a good guy, Steve said, he wanted to tell his daughter to "punt" Skylar, but he didn't, because he feared she would choose Skylar over him. Jennifer could be stubborn at times, prideful, very loyal, loving, and maternal, but she wasn't stupid.

In the beginning, he said, he'd thought Skylar loved his kids. But not anymore.

"My opinion of Skylar right now is that he has no love in his heart for anybody. Not you, not me, not anybody in here. I just think he is an evil person."

Testimony by Skylar's relatives, who blamed Jennifer for his current predicament, didn't do much to help her, either.

His grandmother Marlene referred to Skylar as John to demarcate his life before Jennifer, and as Skylar for his life post-Jennifer. Growing up, she said, John was a kind, loving, and respectful boy who loved animals and people. "He became Skylar when he got involved with Jennifer," she said. "Lied about who he was, how he got there, where he was from. Said he was an orphan. He told all kinds of lies to her, and she didn't want to hear the truth."

Molfetta did his best to show that Skylar's bad acts were his own doing, prompting a string of denials by Marlene, who refuted the alleged Jacobson tradition of keeping the family's criminal acts "in-house," and away from police.

When Skylar used jujitsu to do home invasions and rob innocent people in high school, Molfetta asked, "Was that Jennifer's fault?"

"I don't know anything about that," she said.

"You know that Skylar—John—submitted the paperwork to change his name before he ever met Jennifer Deleon, don't you?"

Marlene said she was "out of the loop" on that one, too. She even had an answer for Skylar's attempt to put a hit out on his father—her son—from jail.

"That's Jennifer's fault?" Molfetta asked.

"Well, I think both of the kids are in a pretty precarious place," she said. "I think that he was afraid that my son was going to go to court against him and Jennifer, and he didn't want this to happen, because he had told his father things and Jennifer had told John Senior things."

Murphy called Adam Rohrig to the stand on day three to explain his unknowing involvement in the murder scheme by setting up the notary. On cross, Molfetta illustrated that even a college-educated guy with military intelligence training could be taken in by Skylar Deleon, and live to regret it.

"So . . . to sum up all your experience with Skylar, he lied to you, he manipulated you, and then, when you realized exactly what he was up to, using your words, you were locked in, right?"

"Yeah, I guess that's an accurate description."

"Fair to say that in your entire direct testimony, in terms of your involvement through all of this, you never mentioned the words 'Jennifer Deleon,' did you?"

"No."

"It was never, 'Hey, my wife and I want to take two people out in the boat and get rid of them.' It was always, 'me,' Skylar, wanted to, correct?"

"Correct."

Murphy pointed out, however, that Adam wasn't as intimately familiar with Skylar and all his flaws as Jennifer had been.

"You were never in love with Skylar Deleon, right?"

"No."

"Fair to say you weren't married to him for three years, either?"

"Correct."

Murphy noted that Adam also hadn't known that Skylar was a convicted felon or a prime murder suspect for a guy in Mexico. "Going out on a limb, I am going to bet that if you knew that, you probably wouldn't have had him at the shop?"

"Absolutely not," Adam said.

As she listened, Gayle O'Neill couldn't help but feel that Michael Lewis and Adam Rohrig were more involved than they admitted. But more important, if

Michael had told police about JP's murder, or if Adam had reported Skylar's queries about "disappearing" bodies at sea, her daughter would still be alive.

"If they'd talked, this would never have gone down," Gayle said. Unfortunately, she said, people "don't want to get involved."

More than sixty people packed the courtroom for Alonso Machain's two hours of testimony on November 8, 2006.

It didn't take long to recognize that Alonso was not very bright or good with names, because he kept leaving the *s* off "Hawks." But he was nothing if not sincere, and the remorse was evident on his face. His voice often dropped so low that observers sitting in the gallery could barely hear him.

Despite the families' emotional preparation, they began to weep quietly as Alonso detailed the events on the boat in chilling detail, his voice cracking repeatedly. Jack O'Neill held his wife's hand as she was crying and shaking, perhaps to soothe himself as much as to support her, while Lana Henderson wept a few rows away.

Even Alonso choked up. "I am sorry. It is just really hard," he said.

Asked how Jackie reacted while she and Tom were handcuffed on the bed, Alonso said, "She was crying. She was saying that she didn't want to die, and Mr. Hawk, he wasn't saying anything. But at one point, you know, Mrs. Hawk was actually sitting up and . . . I could see Mr. Hawk, who was actually laying on the bed . . . try to reach over and hold her hand . . . comfort her."

Byington felt a lump in his throat, but didn't want

to tear up in front of the jury. Talk about impotence, he thought. Tom must have had the male instinct to protect his wife, feeling that he'd failed her by letting these guys on the boat. But this small gesture, the stroking of her hand, was all he could manage. It just killed Byington to imagine.

Gayle O'Neill knew Tom would have done anything to protect Jackie, but she assumed that Jackie felt helpless, too. She hadn't known until then that the couple had been lying on that bed for hours, probably in a state of shock. And now that she did, it was torturous to consider what had likely gone through their minds.

"Did she say anything about her grandchild at any point?" Murphy asked.

"Yes," Alonso said. "She said that she just had a new grandchild and she wanted to see him."

When Skylar told Jackie to sign and put her fingerprint on the power-of-attorney documents, Alonso said, the duct tape was loose enough for her to see around it.

"What was her emotional condition as that was going on?" Murphy asked.

"She was—she was shaking uncontrollably," Alonso stammered.

As Alonso continued, Byington turned around periodically to see how the families were doing. Feeling for them, he saw grief turn to anger on the men's faces. During the investigation Ryan and Matt kept asking Byington whether their father had fought back. He couldn't give details then, but they were about to get them now.

Once they were all up on deck, Alonso said, Skylar retied the Hawkses individually and also to each other, then put new, tighter duct tape around their eyes and mouths.

"At any point, at this time, did you see any sort of struggle by Mr. Hawks?" Murphy asked.

"Mr. Hawk, I am guessing, he, yeah, he knew what was going on, and he pushed back. I think it was his—his right leg. I guess kicked backwards and Deleon was behind him, trying to tie him, and Deleon kind of flew back on his back and landed in one of the chairs."

"What happened next?"

"The third guy took a hard swing to his right temple, and basically . . . it was a pretty hard blow. He—he was having a hard time staying up at that point. . . . He started making these, like, snoring noises. He was staggering. If it wasn't for Mrs. Hawk, he probably would have been on the floor, so it looked like Mrs. Hawk was basically holding him up."

"What, if anything, was she doing during that time?"

"Screaming, yelling, asking what's going on. And it was just really muffled because they were—their mouths were covered."

"What happened next?"

"Once they tied them together . . . Skylar ties the rope to the anchor. . . . Skylar pushes the anchor, or lifts the anchor, and throws it overboard at the same time that the third guy pushes Mr. and Mrs. Hawk over."

"Did he push them all the way over the water?"

"No," Alonso said. "Mrs. Hawk slammed to the side, to the right side of that little area, and then . . . she was yanked into the ocean."

"So, is it the anchor that pulled them over? Is that how they went in?"

"Yes, yes."

"When you say she smashed into the side, what do you mean by that?"

"She hit her—her side of the head up against that little wall area."

Giving the jury a chance to absorb all of this, Murphy told the judge this would be a good time for a break. Judge Fasel agreed, and called a recess.

Most everyone in the courtroom was reeling from a collective feeling of horror and sadness after putting themselves in the Hawkses' position, visualizing Jackie pleading for her life, Tom stroking her hand, and the both of them hearing the anchor chain being dragged around the deck, sensing they were about to die. Some observers had held in their emotions until now, but they couldn't wait any longer to break down. As others tried to comfort them, tissue boxes were exchanged in every direction.

After the break, Murphy asked Alonso about his decision to come back from Mexico and tell the truth about what happened.

"I thought that was the best. I think it was the right thing to do," Alonso said. "If I hadn't done it, I probably would have to live the rest of my life looking over my back. I just couldn't do it."

Murphy had Alonso acknowledge that the DA was seeking the death penalty against Skylar, and asked him for his motivation in testifying. It was always better for the prosecutor to ask this first, because defense attorneys loved to accuse witnesses of saying anything necessary to get a good deal.

"Are you also hoping to get some consideration, as far as the death penalty goes?"

"I hope I get some leniency, yes."

"As you sit here now, Mr. Machain, have you been formally offered anything like that?"

"No."

"To the best of your recollection, did you tell the truth?"

"Yes."

"I have nothing further."

Molfetta showed no mercy, starting off his cross with a verbal hard right jab. "I have got to believe at some point in your life, you had a shred of decency in you. What happened?"

"I was talked to by Skylar."

"And the only reason you were on that boat is that you were manipulated by Skylar Deleon, right?"

"Yes."

On the day Alonso and Skylar had first planned to commit the murders, Molfetta asked, had Alonso heard Skylar say anything to his wife like, "'No, we didn't do it, they were too big'? or 'Hey, it didn't happen like you planned, Jenn'? You never heard anything like that, correct?"

"Correct."

"You never heard him apologizing to the pants wearer of the marriage as to why this murder that she supposedly masterminded didn't take place, did you?"

"No."

Molfetta used Alonso, just like the witnesses before him, to show that Skylar was a master at his game.

"So there was always a lie, a lie, a lie, and then, bang, a truth, right?"

"Yes."

"You began to look up to him, as insane as that may seem, didn't you?"

"Yes."

"You respected him, didn't you?"

"Yes."

"From the moment you met John Fitzgerald Kennedy, to the moment he assisted in throwing those poor people over the side of the boat, how much time lapsed?" Molfetta asked.

"Maybe five or six hours."

"In those five or six hours, Skylar got a complete stranger to murder two people for the promise of money in the future?"

"Yes."

"He is good, isn't he—Skylar?"

"Yes."

Molfetta also wouldn't let Alonso off the hook, given that he—not Jennifer—had been the one on the boat, helping to kill the Hawkses. Alonso testified that on the day of the murder, Skylar, who was usually soft-spoken and mellow, became more intense than he'd ever seen him.

"Then, suddenly, he is this murderous fiend, correct?"

"Yes."

"As are you and Mr. Kennedy, correct?"

Alonso turned to the judge. "Do I have to answer that?"

Molfetta bulldozed ahead. "Well, you helped kill those people, didn't you, Alonso?"

"Yes, I did."

"Is there any way you are ever involved in anything like this if it wasn't for Skylar Julius Deleon?"

"I would not be."

"Completely destroyed your life, didn't he?"

"Yes, he did."

"Never mind the lives of the Hawkses, the Jarvis, and most everybody in here, right?"

"Yes."

* * *

Murphy, reminding the jury that Jennifer played an important role in the murder, once again brought up Skylar's call to her after the first trip to the boat.

"You are positive you heard Skylar Deleon make that phone call and say words to the effect, 'You have got to come down here, bring the kid, and put these people at ease'?"

"Hundred percent positive, yes."

This had been the toughest portion of the trial by far for the victims' families. At the end of the day, Jim Hawks looked spent as his nephew talked to reporters.

"When someone who physically murdered my parents was twenty feet in front of my eyes and was specifically going through every detail of how they were murdered, I can't imagine anything being worse than that," Ryan said.

Gayle O'Neill had been apprehensive, knowing it would be difficult to hear these horrible details. But she felt better now that she'd finally learned the truth. "Not knowing everything is worse than not knowing it," she said. "At least I knew that their suffering had ended."

The next day Kathleen Harris described Jennifer's call and the scene in the hotel room, where Jennifer had provided the specific date for Kathleen to put on the documents.

Murphy then called Detective Dave White to connect the dots for the jury by presenting the timeline of the crime on a series of charts, noting where all the calls and other forensic evidence fit in. It was pretty hard to argue with the science of it all.

White explained that the Internet browser history on the Hendersons' home computer revealed that someone had searched for a 500,000-volt Raptor stun gun on October 22, 2004, nearly two weeks before Skylar and Alonso had purchased the weapons.

Then, on November 14, the night before the murder, someone searched for California durable power of attorneys on the same computer. They clicked on various websites, downloading a document at 7:39 P.M. Ten minutes later, phone and computer records showed that Skylar called Jennifer from their home; Jennifer called him back from Cypress, where she worked, at 8:10 P.M., and that the power-of-attorney file was modified during or immediately after Jennifer's call. The couple spoke twice within the next six minutes, then Skylar called Tom Hawks twenty minutes later, at 8:55 P.M.

Using forensic software, White said, he discovered that photos and text files on Jackie's laptop computer had been deleted after November 15, and that the Deleons' family photos and documents had been added.

White explained how he used phone records to pinpoint Skylar's location when he called his codefendants to set up the third man on November 14 and 15. The records showed that Skylar and Jennifer exchanged fifteen calls on November 15, when he phoned Tom at 12:26 P.M., and again at 1:26 from Huntington Beach, to say they were on their way. They also showed that he called Jennifer at 2:56, once he reached Newport Beach, and that Jackie left a voice mail for fellow sailor Carter Ford at 4:06, right before things started to go bad.

Murphy showed the jury a map of the route the *Well*

Deserved took that evening, created from the GPS data that Skylar had entered—two waypoints at 4:21 P.M., when he went upstairs to the bridge, right after he, JFK, and Alonso had corralled the handcuffed Hawkses in the bedroom. Waypoint 33 corresponded to a spot a mile off the Newport coast, and waypoint 34 corresponded to a spot at the southern end of San Clemente Island. Phone records showed that Skylar called Jennifer six minutes after those points were entered.

Skylar's laptop showed that he created a Word document on his laptop, containing the Hawkses' bank account and Social Security numbers, at 4:51 P.M. Although he deleted the original file, he neglected to erase the temporary file the computer had also created.

Skylar and Jennifer exchanged calls four times between 6:25 and 6:47 P.M., when Skylar's phone signal pinged off a transponder a little farther south, near Corona del Mar.

The phone records corroborated Alonso's testimony that Skylar had checked in with Jennifer after he and JFK threw the Hawkses overboard, because Skylar made three quick calls to her between 8:56 and 9:12 P.M., when the signal pinged off the Blackjack cell tower on Santa Catalina Island. He then made a four-and-a-half-minute call to her at 9:22, using Alonso's phone, which pinged off a tower in Dana Point, a coastal community in southern Orange County.

Skylar called Jennifer again at 11:48 P.M. as he and his cohorts were approaching the shore, when the signal pinged off a tower at Newport's Fashion Island mall. Finally, he and Jennifer exchanged calls around 1:30 A.M., when Skylar was back in Long Beach with Alonso, most likely after dropping off JFK.

* * *

Molfetta had his job cut out for him to dispute the cell phone evidence, so his best hope was to make it sound too complicated and technical for him—let alone the jury—to understand. So, for a start, he got White to acknowledge that none of this forensic mumbo jumbo could reveal the content of those calls.

"If I go in that other room, never mind another country, but in that other room and call you on a cell phone, you will have no idea what I am doing or anything, correct?"

"Correct."

"You just know what the other person is telling you," Molfetta said.

White went through the same exercise for the Jarvi murder in 2003, running through Skylar's calls to Jennifer and her immediate calls to Bank of America and Robbins Brothers.

Molfetta tried to downplay their number of calls on the two days of the murders, noting that Skylar and Jennifer routinely phoned each other repeatedly. However, White was able to prove that those two particular days had a far higher number, on average, and that the couple had never exchanged more than their seventeen calls on the day of Jarvi's murder.

Back on redirect, Murphy noted that Jennifer had lied, but her phone records didn't. "Was there a single phone call [from] Jennifer Deleon's cell phone, after November fifteenth, to either Thomas or Jackie Hawks's cell phones?" he asked.

"No," White said.

* * *

Jennifer did not impress the jury by staring straight ahead throughout the trial. Capitalizing on her lack of emotion, Murphy illustrated how callous she could be by asking Detective Evan Sailor to describe her reaction the day he arrested her husband.

"During the time that you are in front of the house, the entire time that we have heard on that tape, did she shed a single tear with you, Detective?"

"No."

"That included the time that her husband was led out in handcuffs and put in the back of the police car. She didn't cry at all, right?"

"Not to my knowledge."

Molfetta tried to put a different face on the same incident. "Could it be that she wasn't upset?"

"I don't know."

"Could it be that she was, in fact, relieved?"

"Again, I don't know."

After calling Jim Hawks to the stand to describe his two conversations with Jennifer, Murphy played a twenty-minute DVD that brought Tom and Jackie to life for the jury. For the Hawkses and O'Neills, watching and hearing the couple during their last few months was a bittersweet reminder of their spirit of adventure, their love for friends and family, and how much they adored each other.

Byington, who had seen the video numerous times, watched for the jurors' reaction, observing that one of the men and two of the women were weeping partway through.

The beginning scenes showed the Hawkses cruising into the scenic alcoves of Mexico as Tom and Jackie traded off the narration.

"Wow, beautiful," Jackie cooed in her soft, high voice at a school of whale sharks. "Ooh, we're going to swim with those babies. Everybody is coming to see him, all the locals in their Pangas. Look at that mouth. That's just like plankton. Ooh, it's—it's—looks like a huge catfish. Oh, neato."

"I'm going to get off the swim deck, swim with it," Tom said, jumping into the water.

"There goes Tom. . . . Oh, he's gone—too fast now. Tom is never going to catch it. Ha, ha, ha, ha, almost got you."

Tom took roving shots of the *Well Deserved* and the boatyard where it was painted. And after Jackie had flown home, he filmed highlights of the "boys'" trip back from La Paz for Jackie to watch later.

Toward the end of that trip, Tom said, "Well, Jackie's coming today. Got the boat all cleaned up, and I think I'm going to take a shower after I work out and shave my beard. Not a bad beard for fifteen days, huh? Ah, so waiting to see her. This is Captain Tom Hawks, and *Well Deserved*, out."

The DVD also included some tender moments with their new grandson, Jace.

"Now, look at how cute he is in his little khaki pants," Jackie said. "He's all cleaned up and ready to get going. . . . Say, 'Hi, Grandpa. I love you, Grandpa. I miss you, Grandpa.' There's a smile for Grandpa."

Later, during their last party cruise to Catalina, Jackie uttered some unknowingly prescient comments about what was to come.

"This is our last trip to the island, because we sold

the boat, and we're all having a really good time," she said. "Hi, everybody."

"Hi, Jackie," one of their friends responded.

"I'm so glad you could join us on our last voyage on *Well Deserved*," she said.

"What do they call your last voyage?"

"I don't know, but we got our buddy Donny here, and Jimmy is here, and we're all feasting down right now on some good ol' sushi and avocado di—or artichoke dip."

In a scene later in the evening, Jackie said, "There's our best buds, Vicky and Brian [Gray], over there. They're enjoying this cruise with us, too. . . . We're having too much fun. I'm going to miss this, guys. Love you all."

"Love you, too, Jackie," Vicky said.

"Oh, here's my old house," Jackie said. "I call it 'old' because now I'm moving on again to another thing. Here's the salad. We're going to have hot dogs in a minute. Oh, well, *Well Deserved*. What's the name of the next boat, or whatever, should come along?"

That's exactly how the Hawkses' footage ended, with no editing by Murphy or the detectives. Then, as Byington put it, came "three or four seconds of blue screen and up pops the white trash."

While the Hawks and O'Neill families were so distraught about their missing loved ones, Skylar had been using Tom and Jackie's camera to film a Thanksgiving Day close-up of his pregnant wife and the innocent little daughter who had been used as a pawn in the Hawkses' murder.

Pounding the point home, Murphy put up a still shot of the closing scene. Then he played a tape of Detective Keith Krallman's two-hour interview with

Jennifer, showing she'd had every chance to confess—
and chose not to.

As Murphy's case was winding to a close, Skylar's
aunt, Colleen Francisco, outlined the details of Jennifer and her mother's visit to the Jacobsons' right
after Skylar's arrest.

Betty Jarvi recognized her from the pretrial hearing, where she'd hugged Betty and apologized for
what Skylar had done. Betty remembered feeling
sorry for Skylar for having no one in court to support
him until she saw an elderly woman bawling, who
turned out to be his grandmother, Marlene.

Colleen glanced over at Jennifer's stone face as she
testified about Jennifer's smirk and strange answers
about whether she or Skylar had killed anyone. But
Colleen stared straight at the defendant as she recounted the chilling moment when Jennifer said, "We
needed the money."

Perturbed by this, Molfetta confronted her on
cross-examination. "Why do you keep looking at Jennifer every time you answer a question?" he barked.

"I have the same disbelief that there is no expression," she replied.

Molfetta believed Colleen had an agenda and had
been enjoying being on the witness stand a little too
much, emboldened by the knowledge that everyone
was watching her, so he pounded on the fact that her
description of Jennifer's smirk and "money" comment were completely missing from the transcripts of
her four taped interviews with Detective Sailor.

* * *

Murphy recalled Sailor, the last of nearly forty prosecution witnesses, to testify that the tape recorder wasn't running when Colleen made those statements. Still, Molfetta was able to highlight Colleen's conflicting statements that Jennifer was not only cold but increasingly scared and shaken as they talked about Skylar and the murders. He also got Colleen to confirm that Skylar came from a lying, attention-seeking, manipulative family, and that she wasn't upset over her nephew facing the death penalty.

Molfetta had found only a few of Jennifer's friends who would say what he needed on the stand—what a freak Skylar was, and how simple and naïve Jennifer could be—so he called just four character witnesses: Erin Dworzan and Meghan Leathem, tax accountant Jo Ann Zahn, and Steve Henderson's friend Mark Hulce. All told, their testimony took little more than an hour.

Erin testified that Jennifer had never been one to show emotions, and Meghan testified about Jennifer's hateful comments about Skylar on their recent jail visit. On cross-examination Murphy was able to paint Jennifer's hateful and fearful remarks to Meghan about Skylar as a trial tactic, noting they occurred just six weeks before her trial.

To point out the obvious contrast, Murphy played a recording of Danielle Dunning's jail visit a few months earlier. The implication being why, if Jennifer hated her husband so much, would she voice such outrage about Steve Henderson's decision to stop her children's visits with Skylar?

* * *

The day of the closing arguments fell, ironically, on November 15, 2006, the two-year anniversary of the Hawkses' murder.

Murphy started out in his usual calm tone, but he grew more aggressive as his closing argument rose to a crescendo. Explaining how a conspiracy worked under the law, he noted that co-conspirators didn't need to be present when a crime was committed, but all were responsible for their partners' acts.

Describing this case as more of a conspiracy to steal than to kill, he said, "The killing here is a necessary component, but the goal here is to get their stuff, so any act done to accomplish that conspiracy puts any member of the conspiracy on the hook."

Although the Hawkses' bodies were never recovered, he said, the defense couldn't deny that the couple had been murdered. "They are not in Cabo having margaritas," he said.

To be guilty of murder, he said, all Jennifer had to know when she brought Haylie on that boat was that her "thief of a husband" was going to steal from the Hawkses. "What could put any of us more at ease than someone showing up with a pregnant wife and cute little girl? That was exactly the purpose of the meeting with the Hawkses, and she knew it," Murphy said, turning to shoot a penetrating look of disdain at the defendant. "Folks, from that moment on, she might as well have pushed them off the boat herself."

Thirteen days before the Hawkses were brutally murdered, the Deleons were already making plans to spend their money at the real estate agent's office, and discussing how to invest it with their tax accountants. During the next two weeks, Jennifer had her chance to send up a red flag, Murphy said, "but she didn't say a word."

On paper, he said, "this was a brilliant plan. In the commonsense world of reality, it was incredibly stupid to believe that anybody would buy off on this."

And speaking of paper, Murphy pointed out to the jury that Jackie Hawks had sent them a message, leaving off the *s* when she signed the documents.

"She signed 'Jackie Hawk.' Somebody went in later, I submit to you, and put in that *s*. What she was doing . . . was trying to communicate to the police—ultimately to you—trying to say, 'This isn't right.'"

Murphy asked the jurors to use their common sense as they weighed Jennifer's acts before, during, and after the murder, noting that although her name wasn't on the power-of-attorney documents, it was definitely on the new boat title.

"Every single piece of evidence . . . is consistent with one thing, and one thing only. That is, she helped murder those people."

Knowing this would be a tough act to follow, Molfetta started off with a jovial "Wow," but he dismissed Murphy's interpretation of the evidence as just that.

"I say it to him, like I say it to my friends—you are out of your mind if the evidence shows anything near what he said."

Pleading with the jurors to heed their oath to follow the law, he acknowledged that Murphy had done a wonderful job of hitting them in the gut, but their job was not to get angry about the Hawkses' murder or to exact revenge for them.

Skylar Deleon would surely get what was coming

to him—the death penalty. "Nobody is going to stand up for [him]," he said. But it didn't make sense to say that Jennifer—a sweet churchgoing mother and homebody—would fall $80,000 in debt, then immediately run out and commit a double murder, or that Jennifer had gone from "sweet to very, very *not* sweet, from child of God to sister of Satan—like this," he said, snapping his fingers.

Despite what Murphy had argued, Molfetta said, no one could control Skylar, not his father and not the Seal Beach jailers, who didn't even know he'd killed JP Jarvi while under their watch. "But the schoolmarm, the churchgoer, that one—she could control this runaway pile of you know what. Are you kidding me?"

Molfetta took his shot at tainting the three prosecution witnesses from the Jacobson family. Skylar, "one hundred and twenty pounds of hermaphrodite evilness . . . went to the best graduate school for being a murderer, a scumbag and a dirtbag that anybody could go to, the Jacobson home," where he "grew up in advanced placement criminology."

He acknowledged that some of the circumstantial evidence pointed toward her guilt, but "no direct evidence whatsoever." Even the time of death for this poor couple, he said, was "complete conjecture" by the prosecution. Jennifer's signature wasn't on the power-of-attorney documents because, despite the prosecutor's mission to paint her as the financial mastermind and the pants wearer, Skylar was the one who had actually planned and carried out the murders.

After arguing an unsuccessful mistrial motion in the judge's chambers over Murphy's characterization of Jennifer as a Jarvi murder conspirator, Molfetta continued his closing the next morning.

In his view, he said, the case boiled down to this: Skylar led a double life and lied to Jennifer about being a homosexual. But no one outside such a marriage could know how he or she would react in the same situation. Skylar pulled Jennifer's heartstrings until she was so dizzy and confused by his lies that she felt locked in—this was her reality.

"So she is a murderer for being an idiot in love," he said. "You'd better start building jails, because the world is full of people that are just that. Idiots in love. Love is blind. It's a cliché . . . because it is true."

Molfetta argued there was "no proof whatsoever" that Jennifer knew Skylar had killed Jarvi before the Hawkses' murder. "This is Skylar's gig, she is along for the ride. . . . This looks bad, but it isn't," he said. "It is not what it appears to be. She didn't know. She didn't kill. She had no idea what that bag of dirt was up to, and she is not guilty."

Murphy got in the final word with his rebuttal, charging that Molfetta had taken a shotgun approach in an attempt to confuse and hang up the jury.

The bottom line, though, was that no witness saw signs that Jennifer feared Skylar until several weeks before the trial. In fact, he noted, Jennifer told police she was scared of *Skylar's father.*

Murphy said the question facing the jury was really quite simple: "Did she help? That's it. Did she knowingly help?" If Skylar had told others this was going to be a murder, why wouldn't he tell Jennifer? And how could she not overhear a single call to his recruits?

As a benefit of the murder, she would get title to a $460,000 yacht and a $2 million house on the water in Belmont Shores, to move out of the garage and to be free of their crushing debt. "And she was told absolutely nothing about the Hawkses being murdered or stolen from? It is just preposterous. Her role in the conspiracy is central. . . . She is the single most important person to Skylar getting away with this."

Displaying a still shot from the video of Skylar and Jennifer at the bank in Kingman, Arizona, he said, "Look at the expression on that woman's face. There is your smoking gun. She is about to take their [the Hawkses'] money out of a bank. . . . Father said she was happy when she was cleaning the boat. Look at that expression. Picture says a thousand words. Is she afraid?"

If she wasn't in on it, Murphy said, Skylar wouldn't have let her anywhere near the Hawkses for fear she would give him away with the story she told her real estate agent and tax accountants—that they were being *given* a boat.

As the coup de grace, Murphy read aloud two of her sappy love letters, just as Molfetta had been dreading. "You just read through these and ask yourself, 'Is this a woman whose husband duped her into killing two people? Or is this a woman that's involved in this from the get-go?'

"Jackie and Thomas Hawks were fooled by Jennifer Deleon, and you folks will not be fooled by [her]," Murphy said. "I am going to ask you, ladies and gentlemen, with everything that I have got. Don't let her get away with this."

After showing no emotion throughout the trial, Jennifer finally cried during the reading of jury

instructions. When they were out of earshot of the
jury and the judge, Molfetta joked with Murphy and
Byington that he wished he'd read them to her at the
beginning of the trial. She'd earned herself zero
sympathy from the jury by looking, as Byington put
it, like "Zombie Woman."

The jurors got the case around 4:00 P.M. on Thursday, November 16, and had little more time than to
choose a foreman. They returned the next morning
to begin deliberating the evidence presented in the
six days of testimony. It took them just four and a half
hours to reach a verdict.

Having no idea the jury would come back so
quickly, the O'Neills had returned to their hotel in
Irvine and were doing laundry when they got the call
around 2:45 P.M. They hopped in their car, only to
find that Interstate 5 was a parking lot. Normally, it
would take about twenty minutes to get to the courthouse, but it took three times that long, crawling in
traffic. The DA's office kept calling, asking, "Where
are you?" but Judge Fasel wouldn't wait any longer.

"The clerk will read the verdicts, please," he said.

"'We, the jury, in the above-entitled action, find the
defendant, Jennifer Lynn Henderson-Deleon, guilty
of the crime of murder in the first degree, a felony, in
violation of section 187 A of the penal code of the
state of California,'" the clerk read. "'Name of victim,
Thomas Charles Hawks.'"

As the court clerk read the same verdict for the
murder of Jackie Hawks and affirmed the special-
circumstance allegations, Jennifer was crying, but by
this point it was far too late to do her any good. Steve
and Lana Henderson, who missed the announcement
by only a few moments, rushed into the courtroom,

and they, too, began to cry as they watched Jennifer walking away from them, toward the holding cell. Apparently, she hadn't even seen them come in.

"They're devastated," Molfetta told the reporters who clustered around him.

Byington, who had been at home with a temperature of 103 degrees, had slapped on a suit and tried to get there in time for the verdict, but he got caught in traffic as well.

By the time the O'Neills arrived, Matt Murphy and Ryan Hawks were already talking to the news media on the second floor. Gayle wasn't surprised; she'd been confident the jury would find Jennifer guilty as soon as she saw the bank video.

"You'd have to be a complete moron not to know this woman was involved in this," she said.

Molfetta had never expected an acquittal because the prosecution had such overwhelming evidence. He also knew Murphy had been holding back the letters and possibly other evidence in case Jennifer took the stand, so a hung jury was the most he could hope for. Without the letters, he said, "I would have hung it. Those letters just killed me."

With one trial down, and one, two—or three—to go, the Hawks family was obviously pleased with the verdict, even though it did nothing to bring back Tom or Jackie. But what they felt most was relief. For the moment, anyway.

"My father used to tell me that the only thing to look forward to is the future," Ryan told the *Los Angeles Times*. "And that's what we're doing."

Betty Jarvi, on the other hand, was happy enough with the verdict that, for the moment, she wasn't thinking any further ahead. "I was glad, because I felt strongly that she was a major, major influence on Skylar," she said.

She just hoped the judge wouldn't give Jennifer a chance at parole.

39

Following her jailhouse lawyer's advice, Jennifer won a sentencing delay by complaining she'd had inadequate counsel. In a handwritten letter to Judge Fasel, she said Molfetta hadn't represented her properly and she wanted a new attorney. Jennifer admitted that her letter had been prepared at her request, so it wasn't surprising that the handwriting resembled Bret Langford's.

I understand that Mr. Molfetta has been touted as one of the best attorneys in the country, the letter stated, noting that he'd been praised by Frank Mickadeit, the *Register* columnist. *I disagree with Mr. Mikadeit,* [sic] *and while Mr. Molfetta may have acquired a reputation for court room wizardry in past cases, what concerns me is his diligence in preparing a defense in MY case.*

The letter stated that Molfetta's efforts fell "far short of diligent," and were below professional standards. Without his errors, it said, she would have gotten a better verdict.

Molfetta, who had spent hundreds of hours preparing for her trial, was pissed. He'd lost a high-profile case because she'd ignored his explicit directions to cut ties with Skylar, and she wasn't owning up to what she'd done.

"I thought I had a decent shot at acquitting Jennifer if she had listened to me, and she didn't," Molfetta said, adding that he felt somewhat vindicated after a juror wrote to him, saying their first vote was 6–6.

But, as he told the *Register,* "I know what I do for a living, and I know that eventually the lawyer is going to be blamed."

During a hearing on March 2, 2007, Molfetta declared a conflict of interest and was relieved of his duties. Fasel appointed Jeremy Goldman, a former public defender, as Jennifer's new lawyer. The judge had no choice but to postpone the sentencing until Goldman got up to speed.

A few days later, John Jacobson called the NBPD, saying he wanted to talk to Murphy. Detective Don Prouty said Murphy couldn't talk to him, so John said he'd meet with detectives next time he was in the area, despite his fear of the consequences and his attorney's disapproval.

"We're not going to arrest you," Prouty said. "We never were, and you know that."

"If I talked to the kid, he'd probably plead guilty," John said.

By this point, John had already talked to a *Los Angeles Times* reporter, saying he knew Skylar had committed the murders, and he wished his son would confess to them.

"I wanted him to be so different from me. I did everything I could to bring him up right," he told the *Times.* "And he turned out worse than me."

John told Prouty it might make a difference "if he sees that newspaper, me asking him to fess up, to pony up. He knows he's not going to beat this, so what's the point of going to trial?"

Prouty noted that Skylar had been "quoting a lot of Bible verses" lately.

"He knows I'm dying," John said, adding that he'd been in a hospital in Kingman, Arizona, for four weeks recently, and one in Flagstaff for several months before that.

Skylar had tried to get him to go out on a boat and help him with the crime, he said, but he'd refused. "I told him there's just no way, I'm not interested, especially if it has to do with hurting anybody.

"If he got out again, I think he'd kill again," John said. "You think he was mental? Or you think it was pure greed?"

That June, Byington and Sailor spent a couple hours talking to John while he was in the hospital at University of California, Irvine. John, who had AIDS and wasting syndrome, had lost more than one hundred pounds, and the doctors had given him anywhere from two months to two years to live.

Before the murder, John said, Skylar brought a laptop to his hotel in Huntington Beach, where Skylar showed him the interior boat photos and outlined his plan to pirate the *Well Deserved*.

"He was showing me how big it was and why he needed help," John said, recalling that he'd been shaking his head as he listened.

"What could go wrong?" Skylar asked.

"Famous last words," Byington quipped.

Skylar asked for John's bank account number so

he could stash a couple hundred dollars in cash in it. "I said, 'You got "stupid" written across your forehead?'" John recalled. Skylar also suggested putting the boat in John's name, then leaving the country.

"That was the only smart part, between you and I," John told the detectives.

He said Skylar pulled out a Taser and tried to zap him with it, so John grabbed a pillow for protection. It was "something out of Keystone Kops, chasing me around in a frickin' circle and the beds," he said.

The night before the murders, John said, he thought about calling the police. "I wish there was something I could've done."

Afterward, he called Skylar to see if he'd really gone ahead with it. Skylar said yes, and bragged that he'd found $10,000 on the boat. "Yeah, you could've used some of that cash," Skylar told him.

"Doesn't seem like much of a payoff for taking two lives, does it?" Byington said.

Byington asked if John thought Skylar was guilty of killing more people than the three they knew about. "I feel that he is, but I don't know," John said. "He'd kill me with his blinkin' eye."

John said he didn't want to believe it, but part of the reason he didn't go out on the boat was that he thought his own son would shoot him dead, then claim he had to do it because John was a maniac.

"I felt it in every bone in my body," he said. "He was always talking sh** behind my back, trying to make me look like some kind of animal."

Five months later, after threatening a former business partner, who finally filed a restraining order against him, John died in an Orange County hospice.

* * *

Jennifer started filling out her divorce papers in October 2006, but they didn't get filed in family court until May 1, 2007. It's unclear whether she held on to them or they got waylaid for some reason. They were simple, straight, and to the point, and Skylar was served on May 31. After all those months of silence and the returned cards and letters he'd sent to his kids, Skylar wasn't surprised.

The divorce was final on December 1.

Jennifer wore the same pink sweater to her sentencing hearing on October 5, 2007, but it hung loosely on her because she'd lost at least twenty pounds since then. Her long, dark hair, eyeliner, and blue shadow couldn't hide her lack of sleep.

Jeremy Goldman had filed the usual motion asking for a new trial, arguing that the court had misdirected the jury. He also noted that Jennifer was divorcing Skylar and was returning to her maiden name.

During a hearing that lasted a mere eight minutes, Fasel denied the motion, then Tom Hawks's cousin, Bob Gayl, read a short statement on behalf of Jackie's parents.

"'Jennifer's selfishness is beyond belief. Most people work hard for what they want, but not her. Her husband and friends, all they do is take, cheat, steal and kill. . . . My daughter Jackie and son-in-law Tom were hard-working, caring and very generous people. They would do anything for anyone, and they did. They both worked hard, very hard, to get what you took away from them.'"

Noting that they could no longer see their daughter, the O'Neills asked that Jennifer be denied visitation with her own children. "'They don't need to know people like her and her husband. I hope the defendant gets life in prison since you helped sentence my daughter to death.'"

Although Ryan Hawks was frustrated that it had taken nearly a year to sentence Jennifer, he noted that he and his parents not only believed in the American justice system, but embraced it. He said he also believed that Jennifer "could care less" about his family or how her crime had affected them. He echoed the O'Neills' sentiment, urging the Hendersons to give up Jennifer's children for adoption.

"I know the best possible future these children could ever have is them growing up in an environment of not knowing who their biological parents were, what they did, and how the children themselves were used as decoys to murder my parents for financial gain," he said.

With that, Judge Fasel showed Jennifer no mercy, sentencing her to two life terms without the possibility of parole. He still had one or more trials to come in this case, so he didn't express the piercing remarks judges often make when sentencing defendants.

"The court orders consecutive sentences, because although this was a single incident, it involved two separate acts of violence and death involving two separate people," Fasel explained.

As Jennifer got up from the defense table, she turned and gave her parents one of her familiar half smiles and wiped her wet eyes. Even after the Hawks family filed out of the courtroom, the Hendersons and their church friends stayed behind, crying in each other's arms.

Jennifer was sent to the Central California Women's Facility, one of two women's prisons in Chowchilla.

Michael Molfetta insisted he wasn't bitter. Jennifer and Skylar, he said, had "a complete disregard for human life."

"I think Skylar is probably a serial killer," he said. "If you told me there were more [victims] out there, I wouldn't be surprised."

Skylar, he added, was a "combination of stupid, ballsy, and evil," concocting a plan that "never had a chance to succeed. . . . Never a moment from when you start rubbing both of Skylar's IQ points together [was there a chance] that he'd ever get away with it." The plan was a one-in-a-million shot, he said, with the same viability as killing someone for a lottery ticket.

Did he believe that Skylar told Jennifer he was going to kill those people?

"Yeah, he probably did," Molfetta said, but once she realized it wasn't just hooey, "she did the wrong thing. She seemed to be okay with it. . . . She is exactly where she needs to be. . . . Those two are a walking *Star Wars* bar."

That said, he still managed to defend Jennifer, albeit in a backhanded way. "I really don't think she's the malignant bitch everyone says she is," he said, still holding to the premise that if she'd been "the driving force behind the crime, it would have gone down a lot differently."

40

Skylar had to give up on getting a sex change operation, but he wouldn't—or couldn't—shake the notion of ridding himself of the appendage that felt so wrong attached to his body.

"He talked about it all the time," his attorney Gary Pohlson said. "I kept saying, 'Don't do it. I'll get the jail to stop you.'"

But Skylar was determined. He just had to figure out how to do it without bleeding to death.

Orange County inmates are allowed razors for shaving, even those like Skylar who are housed in the jail's medical unit, Module L, reserved for those "needing acute medical and mental-health observation."

Jail officials said they have reasons for wanting prisoners to shave—especially if they work in the kitchen—so inmates who can afford to buy razors do so through the commissary, and those who can't are issued razors in "welfare packs." Designed for the incarcerated, the blades aren't big enough to be made into shanks or sharp enough to slit anyone's wrist.

"It'll cut the skin, but not real deep," said John

McDonald, a sheriff's spokesman. "Which is probably why he wasn't able to succeed in what he was trying to do."

But that didn't stop Skylar from trying.

As his trial date approached, Skylar decided to go for it. At 9:40 P.M. on March 13, 2008, an inmate in the dayroom pressed the black intercom button to alert deputies in the control room: Skylar was sitting on the toilet in his cell, cutting his penis with something.

While the other inmates were being locked down, Deputy Arturo Arellano went to investigate. He found Skylar, dressed in a long white T-shirt and holding a blade attached to a piece of paper in his right hand, slicing away.

"It wasn't cutting as easy as I thought it would," Skylar said later, gesturing with a sawing motion as he explained that he got hung up on some cartilage along the top of his penis. "You could see inside."

Despite the numerous nerve endings in that sensitive area, Skylar claimed he "wasn't feeling nothing."

But that's not how it looked to Arellano: *Deleon looked distressed and shaking, with blood on his hands,* Arellano's report stated.

The deputy immediately notified the medical staff and the emergency response protocol was set into action. As a team of deputies dressed in riot helmets, with safety shields and Tasers, another deputy monitored Skylar to ensure he wasn't in mortal danger.

There is no official record for how long it took deputies to get inside Skylar's one-man cell. Skylar estimated it was only a couple minutes, but Byington and Murphy heard it was more like twenty. McDonald, however, said it typically takes only five to seven minutes for the team to act.

Eight deputies and a sergeant headed over to the

cell, where Arellano had ordered Skylar to drop the blade and stop cutting. Skylar, whose hands were covered with blood, refused. He had sliced a two-inch cut across the top of his penis at the base and around his right testicle. Sergeant Frank Nin commanded Skylar to stop several more times, but Skylar kept at it, so Nin told Arellano to enter the cell with his Taser. The Taser malfunctioned, however, and did not go off, so another deputy went in and took Skylar to the floor between his bunk and toilet.

As Skylar later put it, "They popped my door, came in with shields, and squished me."

Skylar finally dropped the razor on the floor—he claimed he had two blades, a single and a double-edged, but that was not reflected in the report—as two deputies each took one of his hands while the others slapped on handcuffs and leg chains. He was then escorted to the medical area, where he was placed on a gurney without a fight.

A nurse took a closer look at his wound and determined he needed to go to the hospital, so an ambulance took him to Western Medical Center in Santa Ana, where he stayed overnight.

In his cell the guards found a note on the table, apologizing to the staff for the incident.

Murphy summed up the event as "more drama than actual will. He faced out, sitting on the toilet in his cell, so that anyone could see it, and cut a . . . slice around the base of his penis, as if he's going to take the whole package off."

But in Murphy's view, Skylar never intended to finish the job. "He managed to cut absolutely nothing," he said. "No tendons were sliced, no major blood vessels were hit. It was another classic Skylar 'look at me' ploy. They stitched it back up. And the stitching was superficial. . . . There's no bones. So if you really wanted to do it, and you had twenty minutes with a razor blade, you would friggin' do it."

On this point Pohlson agreed. "I think it was an attention-getting thing," he said.

But Skylar insisted he had his reasons for going through with it. "I just want it gone," he said. Nonetheless, he admitted, "I failed. I had bad timing."

Even before Skylar pulled the penis stunt, Murphy theorized that Skylar was acting crazy in preparation for an "addled-brain" defense. Even if Pohlson didn't use such a strategy, who wouldn't question his sanity after such an incident?

Based on the visits that Pohlson arranged between Skylar and several mental-health professionals, it appeared that he was exploring these options in the months before trial. Court records show that Pohlson got permission for forensic psychologist Linda Hopkins, forensic psychiatrist Ernest W. Klatte, and neuropsychological expert Kara Cross to visit privately with Skylar in jail.

Hopkins, who specializes in drug addiction, as well as family and relationship issues, presumably could offer expert advice to Pohlson—and the jury—about the effects of growing up in a home run by a controlling, abusive, and manipulative drug-dealing addict like John Jacobson. And Klatte had been testifying about defendants' sanity in criminal trials in Orange County courthouses for four decades.

Pohlson also got "confidential medical testing" for Skylar with Dr. Kenneth Nudleman, a neurologist specializing in brain disorders, and took him for brain scans at West Coast Radiology in Irvine.

"We were trying to find out if there was any brain damage," Pohlson said, adding that they didn't discover any.

Ultimately, however, none of these doctors testified for the defense. The description of Skylar as a "sociopath" had been thrown around in the media and by various people involved in the case. Pohlson said Skylar was found to have a borderline personality disorder with sociopathic tendencies, but Pohlson decided not to present this finding to the jury because he didn't believe it would be helpful in Skylar's defense.

The year of 2008 was a tough one for Pohlson, who had spent thirty-one weeks in trial by Christmas. Skylar's case had drawn a tremendous amount of media attention, and the reporters were still calling him repeatedly, which made Pohlson's life even busier while he was preparing for trial. Death penalty cases overwhelmed his life, and were always in his thoughts.

After devoting thousands of hours to Skylar's defense, including eighty to ninety hours a week right before trial, Pohlson didn't decide on a game plan until about a week beforehand.

He didn't like Skylar's idea for a defense, which was to present evidence that the Hawkses were drug dealers "in cahoots" with his father, and they were still alive somewhere in Baja California.

"He was never really serious about any of those things, but he didn't want me to think that he did it," said Pohlson, who joked that if he'd gone ahead with that crazy story, the jury would want to "put me to death, too."

So, Pohlson decided he had only one way to maintain his credibility with the jury. He talked over his strategy with his wife and also with his investigator, Nicole Fischer, then pressed ahead with it. If a jury was going to convict his client, he said, "I focus on basically making sure that everything is done right. . . . Giving my client the best shot possible, that way I can live with myself. I never do anything negative toward the victims."

41

In the final months approaching Skylar's trial, a series of motions resulted in the Jarvi and Hawks cases being combined, and JFK being severed out so he could be tried separately.

Jury selection began October 1, 2008, but it took a week of culling through 750 potential jurors—and reading a huge stack of twenty-page questionnaires— before Murphy and Pohlson settled on a panel of seven women and five men.

On the morning of October 7, the Hawks and Jarvi families took their usual seats for opening statements, which drew more reporters than ever before in this case. Anticipation hung in the air as they called their editors and producers from the courtroom.

This was only Murphy's second death penalty trial, so he was on high alert. His ash brown hair was slicked back neatly, and his tall, thin frame was taut with adrenaline, a marked contrast to Pohlson's shorter and stockier build and white hair. The battle was on, and both were wearing their warrior faces. Oddly enough, Murphy appeared more nervous than

Pohlson, who was only too aware of the whopping stack of evidence against his client.

All eyes were on Skylar as he waddled in from the holding cell, his legs shackled and his face shielded by the overhead projection screen until he reached the defense table, where he turned to reveal a blank expression and sat down. As frail as ever, he was dressed in a long-sleeved blue dress shirt and khaki pants, his hair meticulously gelled around his pale, drawn face and his hands deep in his pockets.

Facing a death sentence, Skylar had been likened to the Devil, and described as a twisted and perversely calculating con man throughout his wife's trial; she would spend the rest of her life in prison because of him. Still, his body language gave no indication that this day was any different from his dozens of previous court appearances.

This was not the case for Ryan Hawks, however, who had put his life on hold for four long years to make sure he could attend every day of this trial. His body electric, he was more than ready for the Main Event to begin, and hoping for the proverbial knockout—a death sentence for Skylar Deleon.

Murphy's opening statement was similar to the one from Jennifer's trial, only this time his strategy was more like Molfetta's, characterizing Skylar as a master of manipulation and charm, persuading the knowing and the unknowing to help him commit his murder for financial gain.

In this round, Murphy slowed the pace as he presented some chilling details he'd withheld before, recounting, for example, what happened on that backcountry road where Skylar had led the blindfolded JP Jarvi by the arm to his death.

"That's when Skylar Deleon cuts Jon Jarvi's throat," Murphy said, flashing several graphic crime scene close-ups onto the screen facing the jury. Even so, he said, JP managed to crawl about one hundred yards from a tree-lined gulley, up a ravine, and to the road, where American missionaries found his body and reported his death at a military checkpoint nearby.

Betty, Jeff, and Jeanne Jarvi turned away from the images of JP's body lying in a pool of blood, his shirt covered with red blotches, which they were seeing for the first time. Murphy also went even further this time in describing the single stab wound behind JP's collarbone, the most direct route to the carotid artery.

Betty tried to hold in the sadness that gripped her, but she couldn't help tearing up. Murphy was doing a great job of making the horrific scene come alive for the jury, but his purposely provocative words were very difficult for her and her family to hear.

"That really broke me up," Betty said later. From that night on, when she lost the mental battle to pull down the black shade of sleep, she would lie awake, see her son lying by the side of that road, and wonder what he'd been thinking as he dragged himself up that hill, desperately trying to stem the bleeding from his neck, and hoping to be saved.

As promised, Murphy presented a road map of the detectives' investigative journey as they pieced together the complex plot. He then introduced each player Skylar had pulled into the murder conspiracy with his myriad of phone calls, including the twenty-one he exchanged with his father on November 8, 2004, in his quest for a third man.

Still addressing the jury, Murphy pointed behind him at the defense table, as if Skylar wasn't worth more than a backhanded jab. Skylar had lost a lot of weight since 2004, he explained, but even then, he and scrawny Alonso Machain needed help to over-power the brawny Tom Hawks.

Murphy stated with confidence that the jurors were going to convict Skylar, so he told them to pay close attention because he wasn't going to reintroduce the evidence in the penalty phase. With the three victims' photos on the screen behind him, he said, "At the end of this case, when it is all said and done, I am going to ask you to come back with the death penalty against Skylar Deleon."

As Pohlson got up to give his opening statement, Murphy thought to himself, *Don't concede, don't concede, don't concede.* But that's exactly what Pohlson did.

Pohlson's concession surprised most everyone else in the courtroom, except for the media he'd briefed during the lunch break. Deeming Murphy's presenta-tion of the facts as "very accurate for the most part," he said he wanted to make one thing very clear.

"My goal is simply to save Skylar Deleon's life," he said.

Walking over to the easel with a black Magic Marker, he scrawled a few words, powerful in their brevity: *Skylar is guilty of all 3 murders and special circumstances.*

"The penalty phase is starting now," he said, "be-cause that's all this trial is, as far as we're concerned."

As the jurors listened to the evidence, he said, they should keep in mind that other players in this con-spiracy were "heavily involved"—Skylar's father, John, as well as Jennifer, who had already been convicted in the Hawkses' murder, and Michael Lewis, who had repeatedly lied to the police about the Jarvi murder. In Pohlson's view Michael was also guilty of first-degree murder with special circumstances.

Pohlson asked the jury to consider the unfairly

light penalties that Michael and Alonso were going to get for their prosecutorial testimony, noting that Alonso was "hoping for some kind of mercy from the DA's office. . . . He's just as guilty as Skylar or even JFK," and yet he wasn't even facing the death penalty.

"At the end of this, I am going to be asking you to give him [Skylar] life without the possibility of parole as the appropriate sentence."

Based on the prosecution's "overwhelming evidence," Pohlson said, he knew the jury would convict Skylar. Admitting Skylar's guilt up front was not the same as a guilty plea, but he hoped this defense would give him credibility with the jurors so they would listen more carefully to his witnesses during the second phase.

"I felt we had a really good penalty phase," he said later. "I was just hoping for a hung jury."

Pohlson had indeed maintained his credibility by announcing he wouldn't disagree with much of the evidence, but Murphy still had to present it to the jury. However, because Pohlson had few if any questions on cross-examination, Murphy was able to call twelve witnesses in quick succession that first afternoon.

Murphy started with the Ensenada coroner, who explained through a translator how Jarvi had died from the slicing of his jugular vein. He ended the day with Jose Bahena, the LAPD officer who assisted in the Mexican murder investigation.

The next day, Murphy called thirteen witnesses, including Michael Lewis, whose red face reflected his discomfort as he described his Mexico trip with Skylar and JP Jarvi.

Pohlson conducted his most active cross-examination so far on Michael, trying to impeach the prosecution's key witness in the Jarvi case by claiming Michael would say whatever the DA wanted because he'd been released from jail after only eight months by agreeing to testify against Skylar.

"What happened to your case? Did it go away?"

"I don't know. It is still—we are still working on it. . . . It still is open."

"You are not going to trial, are you?"

"No, sir."

Pohlson got Michael to acknowledge his repeated lies to police, then tried to force an admission that Michael had been a party to Skylar's scheme. Michael steadfastly maintained his innocence through ignorance.

"I didn't want to know. I know myself, I know what I do, and what I am. . . . I didn't want to be involved in it. If the police had contacted me right away, I would have told them the honest to God truth instead of lying, because I was scared," he said.

"You were involved in it every bit as much as Mr. Deleon, weren't you?" Pohlson asked.

"No."

"You know you were going to profit from the fifty thousand dollars that Mr. Jarvi had . . . gotten in the loan, right?"

"No."

On redirect, Murphy tried to recover Michael's credibility by asking him to describe himself these days. "I am a father. I am a decent human being. I try to do right by people, you know. I am a Christian," Michael said.

Murphy also had Michael address Pohlson's opening

salvo about John Jacobson's involvement in the murders. "As you sit there now, did he have anything to do with the murder of Jon Jarvi that you know of?" he asked.

"Not to my knowledge."

Day three was dominated by witnesses who expounded on the many diverse and sometimes absurd lies of Skylar Deleon.

Dr. David Speiser, Jennifer's OB/GYN, testified that during her second trimester carrying Kaleb, Skylar said he was purchasing a $750,000 boat with the proceeds of selling drugs he'd stolen from his next-door neighbor. He also said he and Jennifer were moving to Mexico and asked for recommendations on a safe place to deliver the baby.

"At some point, did he invite you to take a fishing trip?" Murphy asked.

"Well, had I gone, I probably wouldn't be here testifying," Dr. Speiser quipped.

Pohlson objected and moved to strike the comment.

"You are an avid fisherman?" Murphy asked.

"Correct."

"You turned him down?"

"Correct."

Murphy called U.S. Marine Corps Staff Sergeant Shamar Underwood to discuss Skylar's forged discharge papers, which had turned him into a sniper with counterintelligence training and thirty-five kills.

Asked about the unit Skylar had typed in—Yankee White 2FR Recon Camp Lejeune, Underwood explained, "There is no such thing as a . . . When I did a

search on that, I saw that was the unit within Xbox,
but it is not—"

"Let me stop you there," Murphy said, milking the
humor of this. "Unit in a what?"

"In Xbox," Underwood said. "Like a PlayStation."

"It's from a video game?"

"Yes, sir."

Just as he had during Jennifer's trial, Detective
White explained how Skylar's murder conspiracy had
come together, again aided by the timeline charts, cell
phone and computer records for the days before,
during, and after the murders. This time, however,
White went into far more detail.

The records, he said, showed that Skylar and
Michael exchanged thirty-three calls the day of the
Jarvi murder, December 27, 2003. Skylar and Jennifer's seventeen calls started at 8:08 A.M. and ended
at 10:05 P.M., with a break from noon to 7:00 P.M.,
when they had a six-minute conversation after he
crossed the border back into San Diego. Jennifer
called Michael at 6:18 P.M. on January 28, 2004, to
leave the ice-cream alibi message after the Mexican
detectives came to her house.

Under cross-examination, White acknowledged
that Skylar and his father spoke 366 times between
April 4 and December 4, 2004—eighty-four times in
November alone, including twelve calls on November
6, the day the Hawkses' murder was originally slated
to go down. But, countering Pohlson's claim that
John Senior was involved in the murders, White noted
that the records showed no calls between John

and Skylar from July 2003 to March 2004, or between November 11 and November 18, 2004, which left several months of silence on either side of the Jarvi murder and a week's gap around the Hawkses'.

Murphy called Sergeant Byington to introduce his ninety-minute videotaped interview with Skylar on November 30, 2004, so the jury could watch the affable con man's comfortable interaction with police.

Byington said he'd sent the power-of-attorney documents to the FBI Laboratory in Quantico, Virginia, where analysts determined the Hawkses' signatures were authentic, except for the *s* that someone had added to Jackie's last name. He also noted that neither John Jacobson's fingerprints nor DNA turned up on the paperwork or the boat.

On December 16, 2004, the day before Skylar's arrest, Byington recalled, Skylar expressed frustration with the Hawkses "for causing him all this grief."

"What exactly did he say to you?" Murphy asked.

"I am going to sue them," Byington said.

On cross-examination Byington acknowledged that police found no scratches in the wooden deck where Alonso said the heavy anchor chain was dragged, and that it was Jennifer, not Skylar, who spewed anger at Byington for failing to release the boat as promised. Byington also acknowledged that Skylar acted childlike and inappropriate at times and giggled.

But on redirect, Murphy asked, "He didn't seem retarded to you some way mentally, or somehow thinking slowly?"

"No," Byington said. "He didn't seem to have a care

in the world, other than trying to get instruction on his new boat."

Alonso's testimony was almost as emotional for the victims' families the second time around, especially when a few new details emerged.

While Skylar and JFK were in the bedroom struggling with Tom Hawks, Alonso said he looked down from the galley and saw Skylar turn around to JFK and say, "What are you doing?" feigning surprise that JFK had grabbed Tom in a neck lock.

"And then what did you see Skylar do?" Murphy asked.

"I believe he kicked Mr. Hawk."

For a couple months after the murders, Alonso said, "I became very depressed. I wouldn't talk to anybody. It just became really difficult, and I just couldn't handle it anymore."

"How do you feel as you sit there now about your participation in this murder?" Murphy asked.

"Horrible," Alonso said. "There is no excuse, no explanation. I just—my life has completely turned upside down."

Alonso noted that neither Jennifer Deleon nor John Jacobson had told him what to say to police, nor had he ever discussed the plan with Jennifer.

On cross, Pohlson jumped right on him for not trying to save the Hawkses' lives.

"You could have stopped this, couldn't you?"

"I doubt it."

"Mr. Machain . . . you sat there hours with them, all you had to do was cut them free. . . . You knew

Mr. Hawks was strong. . . . You could have saved these people. Did you ever feel terrible that you didn't do that?"

"Yes, I do."

"Mrs. Hawks was very friendly, effusive, to you, right?" Pohlson asked.

"Yes."

"But you are still willing to murder her, right?"

"Yes."

Alonso was forced to admit that he'd watched Jackie cry and beg for her life for hours as Tom stroked her hand, and still, he did nothing.

"You just let them die?"

"Yes."

After four days of testimony by forty witnesses, many of them repeats from Jennifer's trial, Murphy delivered his closing, which, because of Pohlson's concession, was far shorter than usual.

He quickly summarized the evidence, citing all the reasons why the jury should believe Alonso, why Jennifer was guilty but not the mastermind that her husband was, and why Skylar should be convicted.

As for Skylar's father, Murphy said, "The one place that the police keep getting information that his dad is involved, and the only place, is that man sitting right there."

The prosecutor said they would still be in court without the witnesses whose credibility Pohlson had questioned, because the detectives had done such a thorough investigation.

"There is just no room for the defense to move," he said.

Murphy said he would have loved to have charged

Michael Lewis with the Jarvi murder, but he couldn't prove Michael knew about it before they left Orange County.

"I agree on the surface it seems incredible [that he didn't know], until you look at who he is down there with." That said, "You don't need Mike Lewis. We don't need Kathleen Harris. We don't need Adam Rohrig for you folks to put the pieces together of what happened on that boat—no gloves, handguns, stun guns, missing anchor, and a convicted felon running around with their stuff. There isn't a person in the room that wouldn't convict him based on that evidence."

Complimenting Pohlson for being an "outstanding lawyer," Murphy cautioned the jury not to base their decision on how much they liked or respected Skylar's attorney.

"Skylar's best thing that he has got going for him is Gary Pohlson," he said. "And at the end of the day, Skylar is who you are judging, not Mr. Pohlson."

Pohlson's ten-minute closing essentially primed the jury for the defense he would put on in the next phase, promising to answer the pressing question— Why?—and to help the panel determine the appropriate penalty.

"So right now, when you go out, just do your job. Consider the evidence. . . . Make sure you get it right. Come back. And we will go to a penalty phase. Good luck."

Murphy's rebuttal was short and sweet as well, saying there was just one thing he needed to address: "Mr. Pohlson said that this was about the why. You know, before I sit down, I am going to show you the why." Murphy gestured dramatically toward a photo of Skylar and Jennifer's garage studio. "Why did this happen? *This* is why it happened.

"We are going to hear all kinds of testimony about other things," he said. "I ask you to keep that image in your mind as you go through. Of course, that is their bedroom. And that picture says a thousand words. That says pretty much everything you need to know."

The jury was excused at the end of the day Thursday, and was told to come back the following Monday, when the panel would begin deliberating after lunch.

No surprise, but it didn't take long. The jury had a verdict in just two hours, which, given Pohlson's concession, took almost longer than expected.

Forty minutes later the clerk read the jury's findings, which were somewhat anticlimactic: Skylar was guilty in the first-degree murder of all three victims. The jury also upheld the special-circumstance allegations of committing multiple murders and killing for financial gain.

The panel got only one day's break before returning for the penalty phase. Meanwhile, court observers were eager to learn what made Skylar Deleon tick. What had driven this bizarre and dangerous giggler, who had tried to cut off his own penis, to murder three innocent victims?

42

Betty Jarvi had offered the O'Neills a room in her big, empty house for the duration of Skylar's trial. But after sitting through Jennifer's, Gayle decided it would be less stressful and costly to follow the guilt phase of this one on the Internet, then come out for the penalty phase if it came to that. Jack had refused to fly again after having a run-in with security at JFK International Airport on their last trip, so this time Gayle brought Jackie's sister Beverly.

Betty and Gayle were a decade apart in age, but they shared an upbeat nature and the painful loss of their children to the same killer, so they bonded easily.

"She told me about going to Mexico, that she didn't think she was ever going to find out what had happened to her son," Gayle said. "She missed him terribly, I could tell. . . . We'd talk about it for a little while, then try not to talk about it."

When they weren't in court, the women distracted each other with jigsaw puzzles or relaxed in Betty's garden of flowers, trees, and cacti, with brick and stone paths running throughout. Despite the stress of the murder trial, Betty helped put Gayle at ease, showing her photos and artifacts from her recent trips to Africa and Egypt.

"It was nice to have someone who understands," Gayle said.

During his opening statement, Murphy explained that he was going to call witnesses to testify about Skylar's armed burglary in 2002 and the hits on his father, cousin, and other key witnesses he solicited from jail. After that, Murphy said, he would call several relatives of each victim to reveal the emotional fallout of these murders. During deliberations, the jury would assign a weight to each of these aggravating factors, and weigh them against the mitigating circumstances the defense would present.

As promised, Murphy called Ted Wangsangutr and Wade Lohn, Skylar's burglary victim and codefendant, then the two inmates Skylar recruited for the witness hits, Danny Alvarado and Danny Elias.

Alvarado testified that Skylar promised money and a reward if his father's murder went off. "He actually told me at one point in time, if I could do that for him and everything went okay, he said he didn't care about the boat. I could have the boat," he said.

On cross-examination by Pohlson, Alvarado acknowledged that he'd also dealt with Jennifer, calling her to collect the $2,500 Skylar had offered him for the alibi. "She said she was going to talk to Skylar," Alvarado said. "That never happened, either."

Pohlson set out to shred both inmates' credibility by painting them as self-serving snitches, forcing Elias to admit that after agreeing to help with this case, his sentence was reduced from life in prison to eight years and eight months. But Elias maintained that the two acts were unrelated; he'd gotten no deal for testifying.

Trying to paint Skylar's murder solicitations as absurd and unlikely proposals, Pohlson questioned Elias about Skylar's promise of millions for the hits. "You looked at Skylar Deleon and you thought he could pay three million dollars?"

Elias explained that Skylar had claimed he was a drug smuggler for the Mexican cartel and the Crips, so Pohlson asked, "Do you think Skylar Deleon was one of the biggest bullshitters you ever met?"

"Probably, now that I have been hearing [that], yeah."

Murphy tried to dispel the notion that Elias was helping himself by testifying.

"What happens to snitches in prison?" Murphy asked. "Is that a good thing or bad thing to be a snitch in prison?"

"They kill you," Elias replied.

"So . . . in making the decision to cooperate for nothing, your life is at risk for the next eight years or so that you're going to be in prison, right?"

"Yeah. He also put a contract out on me."

Despite the short time each victim's family members spent in the witness chair, it was painfully obvious that every minute was a struggle.

"Tell the jury what it is like to look at a photograph of your murdered son," Murphy said to Betty Jarvi.

"It is difficult. It is very, very difficult," she said. "Especially when you see the blood and—"

"Okay. How has this affected you, Mrs. Jarvi?"

"Well, it is lonely, for one thing. And my house is a mess for another," she said, referring to the odd jobs JP used to do for her. "He came over three or four or five times a week. We would go out to dinner two or three times a week. And I just miss him. He was great to talk to, great to be with."

Gayle O'Neill was so uncomfortable on the stand that she almost froze. If Byington hadn't been sitting there, smiling at her with encouragement, she might not have gotten any words out at all.

Murphy's calm voice helped, too. "Mrs. O'Neill, what is it like to know that your daughter was murdered?"

"It is something that never leaves you," she said. "I think of them in the morning when I wake up. I think of them at night before I go to bed. I think of the boys and—or his brother, the pain that everyone has been going through. . . . Her sister is just devastated. My son is devastated. My young daughter, the youngest Jackie helped raise, she just can't even talk about it."

"Has that gotten better over time?"

"No," she said. "I thought it would, but it still hasn't."

Ryan Hawks recalled his teenage years when he would complain about his father's discipline, saying he now understood what his father meant when he said Ryan would be grateful someday "for the man you are yet to become." But it was too late.

"I never got to thank him," Ryan said. "I miss him every day."

Murphy called Jim Hawks, then played the Hawkses' "last voyage" DVD. Skylar kept his head down until the end, jerking his head up only when he heard his own voice. As Murphy displayed a series of photos of Tom and Jackie holding their new grandson, he asked Jim to sum up his family's experience grappling with the murders.

"I have seen a lot of grief and tragedy in the military and in my experience in police work, and I never quite have been so affected personally by anything like this case," he said. "There hasn't been, and won't be, a day in my life or my family's where we don't think of Tom and Jackie and remember them, and regret that this horrific crime occurred."

The audience had thinned significantly by the following Monday morning, when the defense's case would begin, although a few looky-loos showed up "to see what evil looked like."

Pohlson had reserved his opening statement until now, explaining that he would tell Skylar's life story through family members who witnessed the abuse he'd suffered from the time he was a baby until he entered the marines at nineteen.

But Skylar's life story actually started before he was born, Pohlson said, when his mother was molested and began using drugs, which she continued to do even after she became pregnant at seventeen with Skylar.

John Jacobson started abusing their son as a baby, Pohlson said, and continued through high school, when he still had control over Skylar. "One person described Skylar as John's slave," Pohlson said.

"We have heard about this acting stuff, the *Power Rangers*. John Jacobson wanted his [sons]—both Skylar and Justin—to be actors because he thought that they could make money. You will find they did make some money. John took it all. . . . You will hear about Child Protective Services . . . being called out on many occasions because John was abusing one or all of the children. This is the life they led."

What the jury would not hear, Pohlson said, was that Skylar ever did anything violent during this time. Only that he was "always polite," and "a kind, kind kid."

Skylar's stepmother, Lisa Wildin, was the first to take the stand. Although her petite body and long, ash brown hair made her look young from afar, the years of cocaine addiction had prematurely wrinkled her face, hollowed out her eyes, and left her with a raspy tenor voice.

Asked about John's parenting methods, Lisa described John's negative influence and her efforts to counter it: "With John, everything had to be the biggest, the baddest, and the best. And I kept trying to reinforce to my kids that . . . 'bigger, badder, best' does not exist. . . . He would make it more grandiose than what it was.

"Half the reason I stayed with John as long as I did was because I knew that Skylar had no one else. He would get beat if the dog messed in the house. It would have been his fault because he didn't let him out in time. It was constantly putting him down. If everything wasn't perfect, if he didn't have this perfect child to brag about, then Johnny would get beat again."

On cross-examination, Murphy poked holes every which way in Lisa's story, noting that she'd told Pohlson's investigator, Nicole Fischer, that she hadn't seen any physical abuse of Skylar for the first two years of her relationship with John.

Murphy said he wasn't trying to trick her, but his tone wasn't benevolent anymore. "Which is it? Was he abused horribly as a kid, or was he not abused horribly?" he asked.

"Yes, he was abused horribly as a kid," Lisa said, growing tongue-tied as she tried to explain that she'd been having nightmares lately as these bad memories resurfaced.

As Murphy worked to make John into little more than "a blustery blowhard" in the jury's eyes, Lisa acknowledged that she'd also told Fischer that John was more emotionally abusive than physically abusive toward Skylar. Murphy also called Lisa on the notes she'd written during her ugly divorce and custody battle with John, one of which read: *I don't feel John would ever intentionally harm any of his kids.*

"If you witnessed that horrible physical abuse, how come you didn't write a single notation about that?" Murphy asked.

"I don't know," Lisa said.

Aiming to minimize the abuse even further, Murphy forced Lisa to admit there were months and years when Skylar was completely free of John's torment because John was in prison.

Finally, the prosecutor prompted Lisa to agree that Skylar exhibited few of the typical behaviors of an abused or molested child, and that he was, in fact, respectful to people, followed rules, knew right from wrong. He showed no paranoia, anger, or regressive behavior, and didn't abuse drugs or alcohol.

After Murphy had finished with her, Lisa left the courtroom, crying. She fled down the hall, away from the media, with her mother and daughter comforting her.

The Jarvis weren't swayed by the abuse testimony, but, Jeff said, "This is stuff I need to hear. This is important."

Stephanie Jacobson, now a phlebotomist, testified that her father was an abusive "jerk," who called her "a drunken whore" from the time she was ten.

"What sort of relationship did you have with Skylar?" Pohlson asked.

"Really close. I adored him. He is my big brother. Always had fun with him. We always goofed off. . . . My highlight of my summer was to go see my big brother."

Murphy was easier on Stephanie, who testified that she'd never done anything more criminal than violate curfew, proving that a childhood of watching and suffering John Jacobson's abuse did not a criminal make.

"You obviously never murdered anybody, right?" he asked.

"Correct."

Further narrowing the time window for the abuse, Murphy had her explain that once Skylar learned martial arts as a young teenager, he was able to protect himself from John Senior by holding him down until his rage eased. And to dispel the image of Skylar's nonthreatening appearance, Murphy emphasized his physical capabilities as "a black belt, champion surfer, and a marine."

"Of course, you don't want him to get sentenced to death?" Murphy asked.

"No, absolutely not."

Implying that her testimony was therefore biased, Murphy asked, "You want to help him in any way you can?"

"Yes."

The next day, Skylar's mother, a hard-looking woman with bottle-blond hair, walked into the courtroom with her eyes on Skylar, but he wouldn't look at her. He gazed straight ahead until Lynette O'Daniel sat in the witness chair, when he finally met her insistent stare.

"I love you," she said.

Skylar nodded to her and quietly responded, "I love you back."

Throughout her testimony, Lynette appeared to be struggling not to cry, however, Gayle O'Neill never saw any actual tears.

As Pohlson asked Lynette about the drugs she'd used in the first six weeks of her pregnancy, she looked at Skylar again, and said, "I'm so sorry."

At Murphy's urging, Judge Fasel told her not to direct any more responses to the defendant, who was wiping away tears.

Lynette testified that Skylar was about two and a half when she left, but he'd already seen John pull a gun on her four times. She also described the day she had to save Skylar from drowning when he rode his Big Wheel into the pool.

* * *

Murphy followed up on this "Mother of the Year" moment. A master at leading witnesses down roads they didn't know they were on until it was too late, he asked Lynette a series of questions about her fears of dying as John chased after her with a knife. Then, taking her back to the pool incident, he walked her through the steps she took to rescue Skylar. She said he was coughing, they were both crying, and she was scared she was going to lose him.

"Kind of a traumatic event for him?"

"Yeah."

"What's that like, ma'am, to watch somebody that you love drowning?"

Lynette explained that she was trying to help him breathe.

"You were there to save him, right?"

Lynette did not respond.

"Ma'am, he wasn't tied to an anchor, right?"

Both defense attorneys objected, but the damage was done.

Lynette acknowledged that she made no effort to get custody of Skylar while John was in prison, but what really hurt her credibility were the inconsistencies between her claims that Skylar was horribly abused and her conflicting statements, to social workers and Detective Sailor, that he wasn't.

"Do you remember telling him [Sailor] that you never personally witnessed Jacobson doing anything violent?"

"Yeah," she said.

Lynette said she'd lied to the social workers and Sailor because John's threats to have her and her husband killed never stopped.

"Well, ma'am, he is dead now," Murphy said. "This

was your opportunity to get your son out of this abusive environment."

"I just wanted to be left alone," she finally conceded.

Asked if she had any concerns about Skylar lying as he grew older, Lynette said, "Little John used to never lie. Honestly." But "every time he would tell the truth, his dad would turn around and get mad at him and say, 'That's not what happened,'" and tell an embellished version of the truth for him.

"After he was arrested for this, he told you that he didn't commit these murders, right?"

"Yes."

"I know this is difficult for you, ma'am, but we can agree that's a lie, right?"

"I don't know," she said. "I wasn't there."

After several hours on the stand, Lynette stopped on her way out to express her condolences to the Hawks family. "I'm sorry," she whispered.

Lynette also apologized, sniffling, to the Jarvi family, who were standing near the elevators. "I am so sorry, Mrs. Jarvi," she said to Betty.

But the families didn't believe her, viewing her testimony and her victim approach as an insincere acting job. "Nobody felt sorry for her," Jeanne Jarvi said.

Pohlson, on the other hand, they liked. Betty and Jeanne got into the elevator with him, and rather than avoid their eyes, the former seminary student told them how sorry he was for their loss.

"My father was murdered when I was young and

I never got over it," Pohlson said. "I hope some of this will heal the pain."

The Jarvis thanked him, impressed by his graciousness and compassion.

On the morning of October 29, Skylar emerged from the holding cell wearing a long-sleeved blue T-shirt, another sign of his disrespect for the justice system. Pohlson took one look at his client and sent him back to change.

"There's no casual Fridays here," he said, as a father would scold a son. This prompted a goofy smile from Skylar, who obediently followed Pohlson's instructions and reemerged wearing a button-down dress shirt.

Pohlson called his last key witness that morning: Mark Cunningham, a clinical and forensic psychologist, who admitted up front that he'd never interviewed Skylar or investigated his background. Instead, his testimony would be based on studies of criminal behavior, a review of several hundred pages of discovery, and a summary of testimony by Skylar's family.

By using this very general and academic approach, the defense team proactively prevented the prosecution from asking its own psychological expert—renowned psychiatrist Park Dietz—to offer his professional opinion on Skylar's psychological condition and behavior. Because neither expert witness had interviewed Skylar, neither could speak about him in more than general terms. Dietz, who had worked with the FBI's serial killer profiling unit, had started reviewing the investigative reports and a great deal of evidence in this case in September 2005—at a rate of $600 an hour. And although Dietz had requested to interview Skylar, Pohlson would not allow it.

Including a somewhat acrimonious bout of cross-examination, Cunningham was on the stand for the entire day. But, essentially, his "teaching witness" testimony boiled down to this: bad parenting and a home environment marred by "risk factors" damage a child's ability "to relate to and care about and empathize with other people," and worse, it can result in them causing violent harm to others.

Anticipating that the prosecution would invoke the frequently voiced death penalty trial argument that Skylar *chose* to be a murderer, Pohlson also had Cunningham explain that a child who grew up in a drug-abusing, sexually perverse, and violent home like the Jacobson household wouldn't be able to develop the same emotional foundation as a normal kid.

"We don't all get the same choice," Cunningham said.

But Gayle O'Neill was not impressed. She'd found it difficult to listen to Lynette talk about Skylar's hard life, seeing now that Lynette could've put a stop to it. And she didn't feel any more sympathetic toward him after Cunningham's testimony.

"A lot of people are abused, but they don't turn into murderers," she said, summing it all up as psychobabble and a waste of her time. "I didn't think he was very convincing."

As expected, Murphy did have Dietz speak about choice, explaining that even someone with a childhood like Skylar's still had options other than murder to get out of debt. He could try to earn money, sell his possessions, borrow money, declare bankruptcy, or even steal without confronting his victims. Murder for profit, he said, is "at the highest extreme."

"It is not inevitable that being abused or neglected leads to someone becoming violent," Dietz said. "So it is not inevitable that having risk factors makes one violent, much less a killer."

"And just because you have an abusive childhood . . . if you do commit crime to try to ease your financial strain, it doesn't mean you have got to kill innocent people for money, right?" Murphy asked.

"Right."

Closing arguments fell on Election Day, so Murphy took the opportunity to point out that candidate Barack Obama also had had a tough childhood and a father who abandoned him, and yet here he was running for president, "a product of his decisions."

Claiming this trial was all about individual accountability, he said, "Does Skylar Deleon get to blame his dad for the decisions that he made to murder a woman begging for her life? I submit to you, that's the decision that you need to be making."

Murphy, calling John Jacobson "a clown," downplayed his abusive behavior and underscored his positive parenting acts. "There are people I am sure in this courtroom who had a lot worse than this guy who haven't killed anybody," he said.

Murphy went through the defense witnesses, one by one, challenging their claims of devastating abuse and molestation. After all, he said, the original reports of molestation came from Skylar himself, a guy who tattooed a lie on his own shoulder blade. And if the abuse had been so bad, why did he move back in with his father at age twenty?

"Essentially, ladies and gentlemen, he wants you to give him LWOP [life without parole] because his dad didn't give him enough 'loving hugs,'" he said, mocking Lisa Wildin's testimony.

Murphy also skewered Mark Cunningham, characterizing the psychologist's opinions as "lousy work" based on a superficial review of the evidence.

The prosecutor advised jurors to consider the victims' final experiences and their families' suffering in the aftermath.

"What did that feel like for Jon Jarvi, to have a cold piece of steel shoved into his jugular vein? Because that man—who had his problems, but who had a mother who loved him, who had a brother who loved him, never hurt anybody—is left on the roadside in Mexico like a piece of trash, so *he* could get money," he said, pointing at Skylar.

Betty Jarvi, he said, had to go down to Mexico to identify "the son that she loved with the big slash on his throat. . . . And when you are weighing aggravating versus mitigating factors, folks, that is like weighing a Mack truck."

Moving on to the Hawks murder, Murphy described Skylar's plot as "incredibly sophisticated," "diabolical," and "incredibly clever," particularly the way he identified and buttered up his victims, recruited and groomed his confederates, then killed the couple with "no blood and no bodies."

Murphy said Skylar was also clever enough to hedge his bets, noting that he'd asked, "What are you doing?" when JFK got Tom in a neck lock, just in case they were unable to overpower the muscular victim, and Skylar needed JFK to be his fall guy.

As Murphy recounted how Skylar had hit Tom

Hawks while JFK had him in a bear hug, Byington looked over at the defendant.

"Apparently, he was not in agreement with the exact facts as were being presented by Matt to the jury," Byington said later. "I swear to God he looked as if he wanted to scream out, 'Hey, that's not how it happened.' He was looking at Matt, he was looking at me, and he was looking at Pohlson, and then he began to whisper to Gary that Matt had it wrong. He was actually animated and trying desperately to explain to Gary that that was not the way they overpowered Tom."

Skylar knew the Hawkses were beautiful, loving people, Murphy said, yet he killed them, anyway, with the help of his wife. However, none of this meticulous planning came from his father, a small-time crook who dealt dope in the 1980s.

But the most powerful part of Murphy's closing was his slow, deliberate description of Tom and Jackie Hawks's last moments.

"That water is dark, and it is deep, and it is freezing cold. . . . No wet suits for them. No provisions for their suffering in any way. . . . The shock of that freezing, cold water, how do you cry and hold your breath? How do you swim when you are handcuffed behind your back? A sixty-five pound anchor is going to pull them down pretty quick. . . . When does the first lungful hit her? When did she stop holding her breath? And during that time, is she feeling the man that she loves struggling for his life? . . . This is the worst possible way you can die. Down into those depths, sinking fast. And he planned it, to the last detail. He planned for them to die that way."

After listing all the people Skylar had conned along

the way to advance his plan, Murphy said, "The question is, ladies and gentlemen, is he going to con you?"

Pohlson started off his closing by disputing Murphy's accountability argument, noting that the jury had already found Skylar guilty.

"He has been held accountable," he said. "Now it just depends on which punishment. He's going to die in prison one way or the other. It is just a question of where he goes to prison, how long he lasts, and does he get a needle at the end."

Displaying a baby photo of Skylar, Pohlson said, "Babies are not born murderers, they have to be turned into one."

After hearing Pohlson repeat this refrain, Byington wrote in large print on Murphy's legal pad: *You are right. HE CHOSE TO BE ONE.* While he and Murphy stifled a chuckle, Skylar glanced over at the note, then reverted back to staring straight ahead.

Still claiming that John Jacobson was involved, Pohlson told the jury to consider his twelve calls with Skylar on November 6, the day Skylar had originally planned to carry out the murder.

"John Jacobson is in his head from the time he is a little baby, because he trained him like a killing machine to do these things. He has taken him from that sweet little kid to where we are today."

Skylar's father groomed him to be a killer by abusing and even torturing him, Pohlson said; his mother and his stepmother neglected him; and they all failed him. Then, greedy Jennifer changed him into someone he never would have been otherwise.

"She is seeking riches. She wants more out of life.

She is a very demanding person," he said. "And she makes Skylar do things."

Jennifer manipulated him and orchestrated things, too, he said, telling her father to buy Clorox Wipes, accompanying Skylar to the bank, and arranging meetings with the notary and the realtor. "Nobody had a bigger role than Jennifer Deleon."

Trying to remove the prosecution's taint on his character witnesses, Pohlson asked why Lisa and Lynette would testify to such self-incriminating activities if they hadn't occurred.

"They were crack whores, basically. They did orgies and threesomes," and abandoned their child and stepson, he said. "You think they are going to make up lies about themselves that are so horrible? . . . They are here—at least those two women—because they failed him. And they feel guilty about it."

Pohlson drove his point home by noting the absence of the family that Murphy claimed was so loving.

"The Hawks family is here for them. The Jarvi family is here for them. Who is here for Skylar? Me? Nobody is here for Skylar. I am trying as hard as I can, and my investigator, [and] you know, Richard [Schwartzberg]. We all tried as hard as we can, but we are not his family. He doesn't have one person here supporting him, showing that they care what happens to him. To me, that speaks volumes about the type of life that he lived."

The abuse went on for years, he said, and nobody did anything about it. "Maybe this is not the worst abuse, but it is as bad abuse as I've ever heard. . . . It turned him into what he is. . . . Please don't give him the death penalty."

* * *

The jurors came back for instructions the next morning, and reached a verdict in just a day and a half.

Skylar scanned their faces as they filed back into the courtroom, and even though Pohlson had warned him to expect the worst, he was hoping for the best. As the clerk announced the jury's recommendation for the death penalty, Skylar's eyes welled up with tears.

The jury was shaken up, too. It had been a difficult process for all its members, who had tried to find a reason—any reason—not to choose death. None of them had taken the decision lightly.

"I would have liked to have given him life without parole, but when I saw what he did to these people and that poor Jarvi, I couldn't get it out of my mind," Arnold Steele, a retired car salesman originally from South Africa, recalled later. "We had a photo in the jury room. His head was almost cut off."

At the end of the first day of deliberations, Steele said, they watched the Hawkses' DVD, then took a juror's suggestion to go home and sleep on it.

The next day, they took another look at the molestation and abuse testimony. But after weighing those mitigating factors against the overwhelming aggravating evidence, they still couldn't see giving Skylar a lesser sentence.

"He wasn't insane. He was a guy who made very conscious decisions," Steele said, adding that he thought it was "creepy" the way Skylar giggled during his interview with Byington. Steele also was shocked by the two inmates' matter-of-fact murder solicitation testimony.

Two of the female jurors wept after the panel took its final vote. "Until you face it, it's a hell of a big decision," said Steele, who added, however, that he would have no problem watching Skylar be executed. "What he did to that family, I mean such decent people. I don't think you'd find nicer people in the world. . . . I think Jennifer was a bad influence on him."

Not allowed to communicate with the victims' families during the trial, a number of the jurors embraced them outside the courtroom.

Afterward, Murphy said he felt "a huge, massive relief," but he still had one more trial to go, and it was a bit of a wild card. Murphy figured he'd easily win a guilty verdict against JFK, but he wasn't so sure about the penalty phase. He also suspected that this trial wouldn't be as much of a slam dunk as Skylar's, especially with a defense team that had dragged out the trial date as long as this one.

"That trial is going to be entertaining as hell," Murphy said. "It's going to be a circus."

JFK's attorney, Winston McKesson, had been retained by JFK's church through the preliminary hearing, then asked the court to appoint him on the state's dime rather than a public defender who did not know his case.

McKesson was raised in the South Central Los Angeles neighborhood where the famous race riots broke out in 1992 after the four LAPD officers accused of beating Rodney King were acquitted. McKesson, who went to school with attorney Johnnie Cochran's younger brother and lived near Cochran's first cousin, would always remember the day when two dead bodies turned up on his front lawn. But he worked his way out of the neighborhood, attending Loyola Marymount University and UCLA School of

Law, joined Cochran's firm as an associate, then went on to establish his own practice. McKesson, a tall, personable, and well-dressed man, was listed among fifteen of the nation's most influential black lawyers in *Savoy* magazine in 2003.

Like Pohlson, McKesson had picked up a second chair, working together for the first time with Charles Lindner, a Santa Monica attorney who had helped Cochran write the closing argument in O.J. Simpson's murder trial in 1995. As a cancer survivor who had lost his leg below the knee to amputation, Lindner came to court in a wheelchair. His son, Abe, whose long frizzy blond hair resembled Michael Bolton's, assisted as his paralegal.

But unlike Pohlson's co-counsel, Richard Schwartzberg, Lindner would be far more participatory in the courtroom—and incite more annoyance for Matt Murphy, trial observers, and, at times, even the judge—with his many objections and lengthy cross-examinations. Although the defense's tactic of accusing law enforcement of wrongdoing may have gone over well with jurors in Los Angeles, perhaps the two attorneys should have consulted with Michael Molfetta before trying the same approach in conservative Orange County.

43

By the time John F. Kennedy's trial started on January 26, 2009, most news reporters had moved on to other stories their editors thought would be more interesting to readers or viewers than the murder trial of an African-American gang member from Los Angeles. They figured whites wouldn't care, and neither would blacks, who have long complained about seeing themselves negatively portrayed in the media. So, regardless of the Hawkses' sympathy quotient, the media largely viewed this last chapter as a tangent, which was evident in the final coverage by the three network prime-time crime shows. JFK was barely mentioned, let alone his trial. In fact, in the rush to be the first to air, *20/20* ran its show *during* his trial, which angered the attorneys and victims' families.

That said, the defendant's skin color and gang affiliation changed nothing for Tom and Jackie's families and the few close friends who attended what proved to be the longest, and often the fieriest, proceeding of them all. These last holdouts were determined to be there till the end, even though fighting the traffic between San Diego and Orange Counties every day to listen to much of the same testimony left them physcially and emotionally drained.

Those tangentially affected by Skylar's cons hadn't been as devastated as his true victims, but the ramifications of being sucked into his web of deceit—police interrogations, embarrassing questions in court, high-profile media scrutiny, and the public humiliation of it all—had clearly taken its toll by now.

Steve Henderson had lost his daughter to a lifelong prison sentence. Kathleen Harris had relinquished her notary license. And Adam Rohrig's pale skin, raccoon eyes, and dour expression conveyed the shame, not to mention the heavy drinking, he'd described to detectives.

When Winston McKesson asked Adam if he felt fortunate that he hadn't been charged with a crime, Adam retorted, "No, I don't feel that I can describe anything that's going on today as 'fortunate.'"

Although these witnesses had escaped prosecution, the defense team discredited and held them accountable for failing to go to police or lying to protect their own interests. Now that Skylar had been convicted, he wasn't much of a prominent figure in this trial, which ended up being more about the Long Beach gang culture and the racial and ideological divides that, despite Obama's recent election, could still cause offense and outrage.

JFK's defense strategy hadn't changed much since the prelim. In pretrial motions, his attorneys argued that the only evidence against him was "the otherwise uncorroborated testimonial statements" by Alonso Machain and Myron Gardner, as if records of calls made and received by JFK's cell phone in Newport Beach the day of the murders didn't exist.

After losing the battle to toss those same phone records, McKesson tried to lessen their impact during his opening statement, contending they weren't the powerful proof of guilt the prosecution claimed. There were fewer cell towers between Long Beach and Newport Beach five years ago, he said, when the signal from JFK's phone allegedly pinged on the Newport towers.

What was new was the defense's contention that JFK was the target of a long-standing feud with Long Beach gang detectives, who had essentially framed JFK out of sheer racial bias. This was an interesting tactic, considering that Detective Armando Yearwood, who sat in the back of the courtroom throughout the trial to identify gang members who showed up, was African-American.

JFK's attorneys once again challenged Alonso's story, saying it didn't make sense that he wouldn't remember JFK's name, height, weight, braided goatee, or the dark raised scar, known as a keloid, on his cheek.

McKesson portrayed JFK as a changed man since his gangbanging days, studying to be a pastor and working to keep troubled kids out of gangs. But more than that, he said, JFK didn't associate with white folks. He had never owned a green sweater, as Alonso claimed, and as a leader in his community, he certainly wouldn't have taken orders from a skinny, scrawny punk like Skylar Deleon. Furthermore, he said, JFK had never even been to Newport Beach.

Matt Murphy rose to the occasion. His voice and body language often reflected his frustration after the defense's often inflammatory and accusatory cross-examinations and during frequent sidebars with the judge, when even Judge Fasel could no longer hide his irritation. As the trial progressed, Murphy grew increasingly aggressive, showing a side that the two previous juries had rarely, if ever, seen.

But Murphy had more than paper records in his favor. As he exposed JFK's lies about living a clean life, Murphy did what he did best—he appealed to the jury's emotions as he described JFK's coldhearted, greedy, and callous actions.

Not only had he jumped at Skylar's last-minute offer to kill two complete strangers for money, but "that man right there listened to that woman beg for her life," Murphy said, describing how JFK sucker punched Tom in the head, helped Skylar push the couple overboard, searched for money, then relaxed with a beer and fishing pole.

Listening to Alonso testify for parts of two days still upset Sandy Hawks so much that she broke down, quietly sobbing as the jury filed out during a break.

"It's good for the jury to hear," Jim told his wife gently.

"You almost feel like you're there with them [on the boat]," Tom's cousin, Bob Gayl, said.

When the questioning resumed, Murphy asked Alonso to describe JFK's demeanor as he pushed the Hawkses through the hatchway.

"He was normal," Alonso said. "It didn't seem to bother him."

Pointing at JFK, Murphy asked, "Are you sure that that man sitting right there is the one who helped you kill Tom and Jackie Hawks?"

"No doubt."

* * *

Alonso underwent a relentless grilling by Mc-Kesson, who barked at him every time he looked down at the floor, stared at the ceiling, or closed his eyes, clearly humiliated by what he was being forced to admit. Alonso acknowledged, for example, that he was "a greedy, evil individual," that he had killed the Hawkses because he was thinking only of himself, and that he was doing "whatever he [could] to benefit himself" by testifying for the prosecution.

"You're looking to get probation, aren't you?" McKesson asked.

"I haven't been promised anything."

"You don't expect to go to prison for the rest of your life, do you?"

"No."

Murphy followed up on redirect. "Has anybody told you you're getting probation for this?" he asked. "Is it your expectation that you're going to serve some serious time for this?"

"I hope for some leniency, but I will be doing time," Alonso said, noting that he was obligated to tell the truth, or "the deal was off."

"How do you feel about what you did?"

"It's something that I have to live with for the rest of my life. I can't begin to explain how embarrassed I am to come up here and say, 'Yes . . . [I am guilty for] the murder of two innocent people,'" he said, his voice cracking. "I'm sorry."

* * *

Given the shroud of secrecy cloaking the details of Myron Gardner's involvement in the case, his testimony was key, and, as anticipated, quite enlightening. His time on the stand was also roundly viewed as the case's most entertaining courtroom theater.

Murphy had Myron run through the basics of recruiting Orlando Clement and finally JFK. Assuming it was for a drug deal in Mexico, Myron said, he declined Skylar's offer to pay Myron for his help.

Responding to McKesson's claim that no one had called JFK by "CJ" or "Crazy John" since his gangster days long ago, Murphy had Myron acknowledge that JFK was in his cell phone contacts as CJ.

"What about Orlando's relationship with Mr. Kennedy?" Murphy asked, connecting the dots between players in the conspiracy.

"He used to call him his son," Myron said.

When JFK asked Myron if he should take the job with Skylar, Myron recalled saying, "If [he says] he's going to pay you, he's going to pay you." Myron told JFK that it was like playing Lotto: "You've got to be in it to win it."

Myron also recounted JFK's angry calls later that night and his visit the next morning.

"What happened, man?" Myron asked JFK.

"Oh, man," JFK told him. "There was five of us on that boat. We didn't go to Mexico. . . . There was a man and a woman. . . . Man, we got rid of them."

"You did what?" Myron asked.

To explain the lack of calls between JFK and Skylar, Myron said JFK refused to call Skylar himself, so Myron continued to act as a liaison, feeling obligated and scared of what JFK might do.

* * *

McKesson started off his cross-examination with a confrontational tone, his voice rising as he accused Myron of lying, and baited him with repetitive questions. But Myron held his ground, not even trying to hide his annoyance.

"How many times do I have to answer this question?" Myron asked at one point.

McKesson returned to Myron's earlier testimony about his criminal history, painting him as a gang member.

"I never told you I was a gang member," Myron retorted, noting that he had no gang tattoos or earrings. Contending that he was simply part of what was going on in his neighborhood, he named off all the gangs, and challenged McKesson to check his prison record for any affiliation.

"You've never been a Crip?"

"I'm Myron Gardner," he replied proudly.

Asked what name JFK knew him by, Myron said, "He called me by 'Fly,'" his nickname since childhood.

"And you call him Kennedy, don't you?" McKesson said, breaking the rule "Don't ask a question you don't know the answer to."

"I call him 'Kennedy.' I call him 'CJ.' I call him 'John,'" Myron replied in a victory for the prosecution.

Just before the lunch break, McKesson switched gears and asked Myron about JFK being his illegal Viagra connection. McKesson noted that Myron was still a "young man," saying he shouldn't need a sexual enhancement drug.

"That don't mean that I don't want no Viagra," Myron quipped as if he were a comedian on a late-night talk show.

Many of the spectators had been enjoying the courtroom banter, and now soft giggles spread throughout the gallery. Trying to avoid Judge Fasel's wrath, Murphy covered his mouth as he laughed; Byington put his head down on the table, facing away from the judge, to obscure his hysterics. Even Lindner's son was smiling.

Asked why, if Myron had a prescription, he needed to go to JFK for Viagra, Myron said, "I ran out."

Asked a third time why he didn't go back to the doctor and fill the prescription through legal means, Myron retorted, "It was an emergency!"

This time the gallery erupted into laughter that could not be squelched.

McKesson quickly moved on to more serious matters—attempting to impugn the witness's credibility by accusing him of testifying for the prosecution for his own benefit. But, again, Myron stood his ground.

"You're waiting to get a deal until after you testify in this case," McKesson asked rhetorically.

"Is that what you're telling me?" Myron responded.

McKesson tried again. "Isn't that true?"

"No, sir."

Myron's testimony had damaged JFK's defense, but it also provided some needed comic relief. For the rest of the day and into the coming weeks, Myron's Viagra "emergency" was a frequent topic of jokes between police and the prosecution team.

The defense did its best to put JFK into a positive light by calling his religious mentor, the Reverend Leon Wood, to the stand. Wood animatedly described JFK's church work, referring to a slew of snapshots featuring JFK visiting nursing homes, and helping to draw teen gang members to God's house. Although

Wood came across as a gentle, decent, articulate, and well-meaning man, it became clear under cross-examination that he wore blinders when it came to JFK and could not—or would not—see him for who he really was. Wood even told the jury he thought "OG" meant "old guy."

Perhaps it would have disappointed him too deeply to accept that the disciple he'd thought was ready to pledge his love to God loved money even more.

On the morning of February 10, 2009, Charles Lindner announced he was calling one last witness—his forty-three-year-old client.

Judge Fasel asked the jury to step outside while two bailiffs moved the 240-pound handcuffed man to the witness stand, where the bailiffs remained, guarding him for the rest of the day in case he had an outburst or tried to make a break for it.

While Lindner searched for a document on his laptop, his son patted JFK on the shoulder comfortingly as he sat stoically and patiently in his navy blue suit, powder blue shirt, and dark blue tie with thin light blue stripes, his head shaved, and his dark beard graying by the minute.

Lindner had JFK lay out his background, starting with the move at age three to Long Beach, with his single mother, from Jacksonville, Florida. He said four of his seven siblings were sisters, whom he, as the oldest son, felt he needed to watch over, prompting him to join the Insane Crips at thirteen.

"I was what they call 'the man of the house' and I had to protect my sisters," he said, adding that he earned the nickname Crazy John for antics such as dancing on a car at a red light.

He was fourteen when he met Myron, who was two years older and whose fashion style he admired.

JFK talked about the circumstances behind the violent incidents and drug dealing that sent him to a CYA facility and later—after pleading guilty to attempted murder—to adult prison. Contending his plea was for the gang's sake, JFK said he got only five years when the real culprits would've had to serve twenty-five and thirty-six years, respectively.

Asked why he started selling drugs, JFK said, "Because I was under the impression that I couldn't get no employment." He said he'd hoped to join the army, but his prison time prevented that. He did, however, earn a GED and learn carpentry in the CYA.

"Any background as an accountant?" Lindner asked.

"No, sir," he said.

JFK said he went back to selling crack cocaine because "that was the fastest way to make some money."

After his sister was murdered in 1997, he said, he fought for custody of her kids for nearly two years. He started turning his life around and found religion in 2000 after his mother developed breast cancer and they "did a lot of soul-searching and talking together."

Things went bad in August 2004, he said, when he came home to find his house surrounded by police officers and yellow crime tape, and a man shot dead in his driveway. He was just trying to see who the man was when the cops tasered and cuffed him. Charged with interfering with an officer, JFK went to jail and lost his job—only to find out that the dead man had been his nephew.

JFK said he'd never heard of Tom and Jackie Hawks until he was arrested for their murder, and the first time he saw Alonso, Skylar and Jennifer, was in this courthouse.

When he heard he'd been arrested for a homicide, he said, "I was like, 'Homicide? Ain't no way.' I haven't been doing no criminal activity, period."

He tried to tell the cops, but they wouldn't listen: "I ain't never been to Newport."

Asked if he had a daily diary where he recorded his whereabouts, JFK said, "I don't got no such thing."

"Where were you on November 15, 2004, a Monday?" Lindner asked.

"Ain't no telling," he said. "No disrespect to no one. It was not a significant date to me."

Asked if he trusted white people, he said, "People that I met during church services, I talk to them . . . [but] outside of church and work, no."

Holding up JFK's cell phone bill, Lindner said that based on the prosecution's records, JFK made a phone call in Long Beach at 1:19 P.M. the day of the murder and received a call in Newport Beach at 1:50 P.M.

"Did you board a boat, any boat, sometime around four-thirty P.M. on November 15, 2004?"

"No, sir."

"Did you ever travel in a vehicle with Mr. Deleon and Mr. Machain?"

"No, sir."

JFK almost seemed believable until Murphy got ahold of him, exposing his stream of lies, evasions, and misrepresentations. It was hard not to wonder why JFK and his attorneys had thought that putting him on the stand was a good way to convince an all-white Orange County jury of his innocence. This was no O.J. Simpson trial.

For the rest of an afternoon peppered with objections flying between the attorneys, Murphy forced JFK to acknowledge his problems with the law—including his two arrests for having marijuana and PCP, and his collecting unemployment while he was self-employed and selling black-market Viagra—long after he'd reportedly changed his ways.

Meanwhile, the defense hammered some more on Alonso's conflicting description of the third man, making a melodramatic showing for the jury by asking JFK to roll up his braided goatee and tuck it in. Challenging Alonso's recollection that JFK may have been clean shaven, JFK said he'd been growing his braided goatee continuously for eight years, since his daughter was three, noting that she would say, "Daddy, take your chin out."

When Murphy asked if his purported lack of personal interaction with white people also applied to his business dealings, JFK indicated in one of his most telling remarks that he had no problem with that. "Money is green," he said.

Asked about his call from jail about locating the brown record book he didn't want police to find, JFK claimed this was a receipt book he'd wanted to preserve to prove his whereabouts on the day of the murder. He acknowledged, however, that he'd been unable to locate such a receipt.

"Can you think of why Myron Gardner would come into court and lie, saying you made two people disappear?" Murphy asked.

Lindner objected, so Murphy asked the question another way: "Can you think of any problems you have with Mr. Gardner?"

"Not really, no."

When JFK tried to claim that he'd talked to Myron

only two or three times the day of the crime, Murphy confronted him with the phone records.

"There were sixteen calls between you and Mr. Gardner that day," Murphy said. Although twelve were attempts, with only four calls completed, JFK's credibility dissipated even further when he said, "I don't know what was going on with Myron. Only thing I can think of was Viagra."

If, by chance, JFK had loaned his phone to someone that day, Murphy said, "That person could come in and free you, right?"

After reminding JFK about the murder of his sister, Murphy got in one last jab: "When Jackie went over the side of that boat, did you hear her crying?"

Murphy then called two Long Beach gang detectives as rebuttal witnesses, one of whom reported seeing JFK regularly at Grandma's House, the Insanes' hangout. They also identified the cupping-hand gesture JFK and his friend were making in the cruise photo as a Crips gang sign.

The level of agitation in the courtroom—populated by law enforcement officers from Newport, the DA's office, and, of course, the Hawks family and friends—grew palpable as Lindner cross-examined Detective Hector Gutierrez. To his credit, the detective remained unflappable, even though Lindner kept cutting him off midanswer, forcing the judge to warn Lindner to back off. Many of the attorney's questions challenged the gang unit's fieldwork, and its contention that Crips members were still "active" as long as they associated with each other and didn't remove their tattoos.

Meanwhile, the defense team's underlying message

to the jury about the Long Beach detectives' motives came through Lindner's not-so-subtle questions— "Have you ever heard the term 'driving while black'?"

Murphy put the death knell on JFK's credibility when he called Lance Wilberg, whose testimony illustrated that he'd suffered lasting damage from a head injury he'd gotten as a teenager. He said he'd been jumped by JFK and a bunch of his friends, pummeled until he was bloody, then dumped into a bush—all because he was wearing the wrong-colored bandana. This put JFK's testimony about the incident—that JFK had been attacked by a white mob led by Lance, without provocation in a "race riot"—in a whole new light.

In rebuttal, McKesson called Lucinda Williams, the cousin of JFK's cruise companion, who said JFK had taken her place at the last minute. The *C* hand gesture was innocent, she said, noting that JFK liked to call her "CC."

"They were teasing me, like, 'You're not here with us.'"

But that, like much of the defense's case, was a stretch.

During his closing argument, Murphy called attention to the protracted and meandering nature of the trial, a strategic tactic to win points with the jury. It was the sixteenth day of trial, he noted, and "we've lost track of what we're here for."

Although Skylar Deleon's plan was clever, he couldn't use deadly force on the Hawkses because he needed them to sign forms, and he didn't want a bloody, incriminating crime scene on the boat, so he needed a physically powerful guy to help him. "The cell phone towers show us it's the defendant," Murphy said.

Mocking Lindner's extensive focus on JFK's goatee, Murphy said, "'No goatee, wasn't at sea,' I think it's coming your way," a tongue-in-cheek allusion to the famous line about the glove in Johnnie Cochran's closing in the O.J. Simpson trial—"If it doesn't fit, you must acquit."

Finally, Murphy hit on the race card, asking rhetorically if anyone thought police had gone after Skylar or Jennifer because they were white. "Race has absolutely nothing to do with this, so why are we getting dragged through it every fifteen minutes? And what does it have to do with the murder of Tom and Jackie Hawks? It's shameless," Murphy declared.

"This is the one color that matters—the color green," he said, putting up a photo of a stack of cash.

Dismissing the talk of JFK's church involvement and his claim that he wouldn't lie because he was a Christian, Murphy showed the jury a photo of JFK's codefendants in this case: Skylar and Jennifer, whom he called "Hippa Christians" for their hypocritical behavior.

"This guy right there committed the worst murder imaginable," Murphy said. "You're going to have no trouble at all holding him accountable."

McKesson covered much of the same ground in his closing, claiming that JFK had "acted in a manner consistent with an innocent man" since his latest arrest.

McKesson also claimed that Alonso's timeline was in conflict with phone records.

However, during his rebuttal argument, Murphy managed to trump him again, arguing that the phone records, not Alonso, were his key witness. If JFK was still in Long Beach when his phone pinged off a cell tower in Newport at 1:50 P.M. the day of the murder, he said, then Skylar Deleon wasn't there, either.

"Boy, the police really blew it. If that's true, I've got a lot of work to do after this trial is over. I've got to find the real killers."

Taking one last stab at the defense for bringing up the race card, Murphy blasted McKesson for claiming that Tom Hawks, a street-smart probation officer, never would have believed that JFK was an accountant.

"Black in public, black this, black that—it has nothing to do with this case," Murphy said.

The jury began deliberating at 9:15 A.M. on February 19.

At noon the head bailiff walked over to the Hawks family, who was chatting with Detective Yearwood.

"The jury is going to lunch. Verdict at one-thirty," the bailiff said, and walked away.

"Did he say verdict?" Yearwood asked, as he and the Hawkses looked at each other with surprise. But they all suspected what that meant—a quick verdict was frequently a guilty one.

When the jury walked into the deliberating room, half the panel had already made up its mind to convict and wanted to take a vote. But several jurors cautioned that they needed to slow down and follow the judge's instructions.

"I was trying to play the devil's advocate," said

Shane Valdez, a thirty-seven-year-old drummer turned long-haul truck driver, with tattooed arms, who wanted to make sure they tried to poke apart the prosecution's case.

Despite the defense's efforts to deflect testimony by the prosecution's cell phone carrier witnesses, the jury still saw the records as "damning."

When they did take the first vote, it was 11–1 guilty, Valdez said, and even then the one holdout was more of a "maybe."

Noting that Alonso was the prosecution's star witness, Valdez said he was a little concerned that Alonso didn't get JFK's name right and that his memory was fuzzy about the facial hair. But for Valdez, the defense's most damaging move was when the attorneys had JFK roll up his beard.

"That killed it for him," the juror said. "It was . . . 'How could this dude look like an accountant?' and once he did it, it was '*Bing,* there it is.'"

Back in the courtroom, three bailiffs surrounded JFK for the reading of the verdict. As the panel members walked back to their seats, their faces showed no emotion, staring straight ahead, resolute.

Guilty.

Afterward, McKesson and Lindner contended that the jury had not taken the process seriously enough, and based on their ridiculously short deliberations, jurors couldn't possibly have evaluated all the evidence.

The war of words between Murphy and Lindner escalated to new heights in the death phase of the trial as their animosity for each other seeped into their arguments over the defendant, the jury's job, and an attorney's proper conduct in court. Murphy called McKesson "a classy guy and a good lawyer," but he continued to exchange barbs over race with Lindner as their battle spilled into new territories, including God, guilt, and religious hypocrisy.

As the battle grew increasingly personal, some jury members watched as Lindner tried and failed to navigate his wheelchair between the podium and prosecution table, forcing Lindner to ask Murphy or Byington to move the podium for him. Those jurors sitting closest to the prosecution table could also hear Lindner and Murphy sparring.

After one defense witness testified, Murphy said to Lindner, "Chuck, don't you even vet your witnesses?"

To which, Lindner replied, "I don't control my witnesses like you do, Matt."

Murphy delivered one of the most powerful closings some people in that courtroom had ever seen, accusing Lindner of trying to manipulate the jury with his bag of lawyerly and insincere tactics, his public offer of condolences to the Hawks family among them. Apologizing for getting "fired up" over Lindner's opening comments that boiled down the jurors' weighty decision to choosing whether they—or God—should give JFK the death penalty, Murphy laid the fault for JFK's presence in court squarely on the defendant.

"It's not yours. It's not the Newport Beach Police Department's. It's certainly not the Hawks family's. It's *his* decision," he said. "That is not on you."

Grinding through the specifics of the crime and how Skylar couldn't have done it without him,

Murphy tore through the testimony of JFK's seven character witnesses, including their hope that he could minister to inmates as part of a life sentence.

"Mr. Pastor, Mr. Christian" decided to murder the Hawkses at the "drop of a hat. . . . He decided to do it because he wanted money," Murphy said. ". . . And they want to talk about Jesus and God and church?"

Murphy pounded the jury with his rhetoric and grueling tragic imagery of the Hawkses' last few hours, evoking tears and leaving most people in the courtroom with a great emotional heaviness by day's end.

"That is why I'm asking you to put this man to death," Murphy said.

When Lindner's turn came, he adopted a victim's stance, accusing Murphy of hitting him below the belt. Lindner told the jury he was the sole survivor of a Jewish family who lost 140 members in the Holocaust, so he genuinely meant every empathic word he'd said to the Hawks family.

During the break, Murphy complained that Lindner was essentially comparing him to the Nazis who killed his family. However, by this point, Murphy had no rebuttal powers, so he couldn't convey this to the jury.

Lindner acknowledged that he hadn't connected with the jury the way he should have. As he asked the panel to return with a recommended sentence of life without the possibility of parole, he dropped his previous aggressive stance for a humbled one. And yet, while he admitted being told that Orange County juries didn't want to hear about race, his closing was still rife with racial overtones.

"The taking of a life is a terrible thing," Lindner

said, urging the jury to forgive the execution and let the good that remained in JFK "flower, develop, and pass on in its own due course."

After the jury began deliberating on February 26, McKesson explained outside the courtroom that this trial would have gone differently in Los Angeles County. He said a jury in the city of Inglewood would have been upset by the way Murphy had belittled Pastor Wood, thinking, "Ain't no way they'd [the Hawkses] let that nigger on the boat."

Before the trial, McKesson said, he and Lindner had to decide whether to take the aggressive Los Angeles approach or the "genteel" Orange County approach. Either way, JFK was likely to get convicted, he said, but there was one thing he'd learned from Johnnie Cochran: their clients really wanted somebody to fight for them.

"This is a typical trial in Los Angeles," McKesson said. "Every trial we're calling the cops liars."

Nonetheless, this proved to be the wrong strategy for the O.C. After five hours of deliberations over the course of two days, the panel recommended a death sentence for JFK.

"I really wanted to find those mitigating circumstances that would make him somebody that would be contributing to society in a positive way," Valdez said. "But we couldn't do it in the end."

44

Myron Gardner was released so quietly on March 19, 2009, that practically no one knew about it until the hearing was over. In a deal with Matt Murphy, who had come to believe Myron's version of events, Myron agreed to plead guilty to accessory after the fact in exchange for the dismissal of the two murder charges. After spending a little more than four years in jail, he was able to walk away after serving about a year longer than the three-year sentence his plea would have otherwise required.

After testifying against a Crips leader and helping to send him to death row, some said Myron would be stupid to move back into the old neighborhood, where his life would be in danger.

Jennifer Henderson's appeal, filed with the 4th District of the California Appeals Court, claimed that Skylar Deleon had lied to her from day one, making her another one of his victims. The appeal also contended that a number of errors were made at her trial, primarily that the judge should not have allowed

Murphy to present "inflammatory" evidence about the
Jarvi murder and Jennifer's activities after it occurred.

But the appeals court did not agree: *There was overwhelming evidence of Henderson's guilt,* the three-judge
panel stated in its opinion July 17, 2009, citing the
fifteen calls between the Deleons the day of the
murders, her comments to Colleen Francisco after
Skylar's arrest, and her *significant role* in trying to take
ownership of the yacht and access the Hawkses' bank
accounts.

*Evidence Jarvi had his throat slit was certainly no more
inflammatory than the details of the Hawks[es]' chilling
deaths,* the panel wrote. *We need not recount the details
again, but one can hardly think of a more disturbing image
than the anchor being thrown overboard, slamming Jackie
into the yacht wall before pulling the couple to the bottom of
the Pacific Ocean to their deaths.*

Jennifer's appellate attorney, Mark Christiansen,
tried first for a rehearing, then for an appellate review
by the California Supreme Court, but those petitions
were rejected.

While Skylar awaited sentencing, he granted interviews to an *Orange County Register* reporter, the three
network crime shows—*20/20, 48 Hours,* and *Dateline*—
and *True Crime with Aphrodite Jones,* on the Investigation
Discovery channel.

Skylar hadn't heard from Jennifer in a couple
years, and the cards and letters he'd sent to his children had been returned. Now that his father was
dead and his stepfamily lived out of state, the only
people, not with the media, who visited him were
Gary Pohlson and his investigator.

As Dave Byington watched these TV crime shows,

he was amazed to see Skylar admit for the first time to murdering the Hawkses. According to jail officials who sat in on the interviews, he gave different answers to each reporter. He also implicated ex-wife Jennifer in the crimes, claiming that she was the instigator and that he'd never committed a crime before he met her.

"Was she tired of being in debt?" the *48 Hours* reporter asked.

Yes, Skylar said, "Tired of the bills, tired of living at the parents'. She was like, you know, 'We've got to do something.'"

"Whose idea was it to kill them, yours or hers?" the reporter asked, referring to the Hawkses.

"She threw it out there," Skylar said. "'What if they're not here?'"

"And you agreed?"

"And I agreed."

Skylar admitted calling Jennifer right after he'd thrown the anchor overboard. Her reaction? "I remember her asking if I was sure," he said.

"What did you say?"

"I'm sure."

Asked straight out if he'd killed the Hawkses, Skylar gave this measured response: "Per, according to law, yes."

He started to answer the same question about JP Jarvi, but when he looked at Pohlson, the attorney jumped out of his chair and said, "Don't answer that."

Finally, the reporter said, "The picture I have is that you're this weasely little guy, trying to make your wife happy. You devise this big scheme, and you lost control of it."

"Yeah," Skylar replied.

* * *

Alonso Machain was offered a plea bargain on May 24, 2009. But, instead of accepting the deal—a sentence of twenty years and four months in exchange for reducing his two counts of murder to two counts each of voluntary manslaughter, kidnapping, and first-degree robbery—he balked.

Even though he got four years' credit for time served, Alonso went off on Murphy in the courtroom hallway, arguing that he deserved a better deal because he, too, was one of Skylar's victims. "You can do better," he said.

This tweaked Murphy to no end. "Alonso, how many conversations do you think I've had when I've let a f***ing murderer get in my face?" Murphy asked, incredulous. "This family wants you to go down for murder, and we're doing right by you by giving you this disposition. You need to think about this and get it right in your mind."

So Murphy had Alonso sent over to the men's jail across the street so he could spend a couple weeks coming to his senses in a vastly different and more dangerous world from the quiet, protective cell at the Newport station, where he'd spent the last four years—alone.

"My guess is he's getting his dessert taken away from him and getting his ass kicked," said Byington, adding that Alonso "was treated like a king" in Newport, compared to the county jail. "He thinks he's in a card game and has cards, but he's got nothing."

Before the trials, Murphy and Byington needed to protect Alonso so he could testify, but all bets were off now. No one could guarantee his safety in state prison.

Over the past few years, Byington had taken Alonso out to the parking lot behind the station for his state-mandated exercise, where they chatted about the case and its effect on his life. When Alonso complained about being a victim, Byington had to bring him back to reality: "You're a double murderer—you could have stopped it."

But Alonso couldn't shake his own pity party. "Well, I don't have a life," he complained.

He was right. The only people he'd seen regularly besides police were his family, who had visited one day each weekend with books and a meal, bringing trays of homemade tamales for the officers around Christmastime, and his priest, who gave him Communion for his sins once or twice a month.

By Alonso's next court appearance on June 14, 2009, he had, in fact, come around. Dressed in his amber yellow jail jumpsuit, Alonso stood behind a metal grill, biting his lower lip, as Commissioner Erick Larsh went over the plea agreement with him. As Larsh asked Alonso whether he understood each point, Alonso replied, loudly and surely, "Yes, Your Honor."

But as Larsh read aloud the specific details of the murder and asked for confirmation, Alonso closed his eyes and put his head down, looking forlorn. It was unclear whether he was just listening and remembering, or simply feeling ashamed. After a pregnant pause, Alonso finally shrugged and responded quietly: "Yes."

Larsh looked over at the Hawks family, paused, and expressed his sympathies. "I'm truly sorry," he said.

Alonso would be eligible for parole after fourteen years, in 2023.

Within a month, Murphy had dismissed Michael Lewis's case as well, ultimately believing his story, too.

With Skylar Deleon, a master manipulator and liar, anything was possible.

Now that the trials were over, the stress lifted from the Hawks, O'Neill, and Jarvi families.

Betty Jarvi was able to go back to her former happy self, and Jeff and Jeanne Jarvi's lives were able to return to normal as well. It had been so difficult having to talk to so many reporters and TV crews, and to listen repeatedly in court to the details about JP's death. They felt relieved to have this all behind them.

"Skylar got what he deserved," Jeanne said. "He was a horrible, evil person. How he killed the Hawkses was unbelievably cruel."

Ryan Hawks had managed to take away a few positive things from this whole traumatic experience. He found he didn't get so upset by the little things anymore, and he'd learned that he was much stronger emotionally than he'd thought. If anyone had told him he would lose two parents to murder and his mother to cancer in such a short time, he wouldn't have thought he could get through it. But he felt he owed it to his parents to represent them through the court process, and see that justice was served. So that's what he did.

His uncle Jim was finally feeling more like himself, too, although he was still haunted by questions about Tom's death.

"I'll always wonder if there was something I could've or should've done that would have prevented it," he said, sitting in his kitchen with his wife, Sandy.

"That's because as a kid you always took care of him," she said.

In the years after the murder, Jim said, he'd wake up in the middle of the night with the bad feeling that his brother was lost and he had to find him. After Skylar was convicted, that dream stopped and a new one replaced it. Jim and Tom were in Hawaii, riding along on a zipline.

"Typical Tom had to go first," Jim said. "He goes down this thing, he's in front of me, he falls into this canyon, and he dies."

Pausing for a moment, Jim said, "Maybe I've finally accepted the fact that he's gone."

Now, he said, he knew what he needed to do next: "I've got to get my sense of humor back. Remember all the good times and stop thinking about all this mess."

What helped most was to take his thirty-two-foot sailboat out in the ocean. A boat, he joked, was like "a hole in the ocean you throw money into," but he always felt closer to Tom and Jackie when he was at sea.

"I have his [captain's] license on my boat," he said. "I take him with me every time I go."

Sandy said she'd recently had gone to a psychic, who said she could see Tom and Jackie dancing, wherever they were. Smiling, Sandy produced a color photo that showed why this was significant: Tom and Jackie Hawks were in each other's arms, doing just that.

On August 15, 2009, at 3:00 P.M., more than one hundred of Tom and Jackie's family members and friends gathered to celebrate their lives at the Elks Lodge in Newport Beach. Photos of the couple enjoying their travels around Mexico decorated the room, where the Hawks family mingled with Tom's former probation colleagues, Betty Jarvi, Matt Murphy and Dave Byington, their investigators and detectives, and a half-dozen jurors from the trials. Reminiscent of Tom and Jackie's wedding, the guests wore leis over their Hawaiian-print shirts and dresses.

Byington was curious when he saw a five-year-old boy tearing around the stage. "Who's that?" he asked Matt Hawks.

"That's Jace," Matt replied. Seeing the sergeant's dumbfounded expression, Matt added, "I know. Crazy, huh?"

Byington had been so used to seeing Jace's baby photos and video in court that in his mind the boy hadn't aged. He couldn't believe it had been nearly five years since the couple had been murdered.

Beer, wine, salads, chips, salsa, sandwiches, and sushi rolls were served as guests listened to Tom and Jackie's favorite songs. After all the media this case had attracted, the Hawkses didn't invite any reporters.

The party was organized and emceed by Kathy Warner, a lifelong friend of Tom's. He obviously had no idea how he and Jackie were going to die, but he'd left Kathy a generous sum in his will to throw a big postmortem celebration.

"Some had stories. Most of us just felt sad that we no longer had Tom and Jackie in our lives, but more than a few cocktails were consumed, and a good time was had by all," Joe Hasenauer, Jim's retired police lieutenant friend, said afterward.

One of the most emotional moments came when Kathy introduced the jurors, and the crowd gave them a standing ovation. Some of the guests broke down in tears, and one of the female jurors began to sob.

The lighter moments came in the stories recounting Tom's pranks, although many tales didn't get told because the funniest ones were "at best R-rated" and kids were present, said Michele Fitzgerald, who flew out from Texas with her husband, Bill, for the party.

So Bill told a G-rated story about the trip Tom took with some friends to Lake Havasu, where they partied hard and went to sleep, drunk, in tents on the beach. As the group slowly awakened, panic spread when people noticed that Tom's boat had disappeared. But it was another one of Tom's jokes. He'd moved the boat down the lake a mile or so, then came back to watch their reaction.

Brian Gray recounted how he'd sent an e-mail to dozens of colleagues, including judges, telling them about a website where they could access news and other details about the ongoing case. Brian got a call from one of the recipients, saying he'd hit the link and had been directed to a porn site, so Brian tried to recall the e-mails, but couldn't. Wherever he was, he said, Tom was no doubt laughing like crazy.

In fact, Tom's friends saw the party as his final joke. "If you knew Tom Hawks at all, you would know that he is just up there . . . getting the last laugh on all of us!" Michele Fitzgerald said.

EPILOGUE

After spending all that time watching Skylar Deleon in the courtroom and researching this book, I was very curious to know what he was like in person—and, more important, what made Tom and Jackie Hawks trust him enough to take him and his partners on that fateful sea trial.

I'd heard plenty about the horrors of what he'd done, but I personally had seen little or no emotion from him in court. I didn't hear him speak until I saw him on *20/20*, and I was shocked by how high and soft his voice was. Like a teenage girl.

I'd always intended to try to interview him for this book, but when I finally paid a visit to the jail, one Friday morning after his trial, he refused to see me. I was quite surprised, because Gary Pohlson had said Skylar should have no problem talking with me. In fact, Pohlson even said he'd *ask* him to talk to me. So, not one to give up that easily, I wrote Skylar a letter.

I was surprised again that he wrote back right away, apologizing for refusing my visit and explaining that he'd thought I was someone else. He said he'd be willing to meet me if I wanted to come up to the O.C.

again. His friendly letter, dated March 17, 2009, was printed in script that slanted backward and to the left, and read as though it came from a young girl, both in tone and appearance, with little circles dotting the *i*'s. Although Skylar is right-handed, handwriting experts say left-leaning script is indicative of a person who is left-handed, cold, and indifferent, and conceals his emotions.

Skylar told me he'd have no problem corresponding with me in the future, so long as I could tolerate his bad writing skills. After all, he noted—drawing a smiley face for emphasis—I must be aware that he'd flunked English. And as he predicted, his letter was riddled with spelling errors.

Due to my training as an investigative reporter, I make it a practice not to put myself in my own books. But in this case, I couldn't see any other way to convey the information I gleaned from my conversations with Skylar, a man-child who was widely considered to be a sociopath and a pathological liar.

Starting with his letter, I could feel him trying to manipulate me so I would paint him in the best light as he wove truths into his lies, and vice versa, just as he had with his victims and his codefendants. Because I wasn't able to independently verify much of what he said, I decided simply to present our dialogue and let readers interpret it for themselves.

My plan was to avoid asking confrontational questions up front to keep him talking, and it worked. Luckily for me, his sentencing was delayed, so I was able to visit him four times over two consecutive weekends right before he was sentenced in April 2009. I'd planned to write him with some tougher questions once he was bored and isolated on death row, even though I didn't really expect him to answer them, but that was not to be.

The whole experience was illuminating and, frankly, surreal. Never before had I spoken face-to-face with an admittedly charming three-time killer con man who *sang* to me.

One of my primary goals was to get to the heart of his relationship with Jennifer, so I started off the first interview by asking how they met.

Skylar characterized Jennifer as a party girl, which I'm sure would have come out in court if it were true. He said she never did drugs in front of him, so he didn't know her substances of choice, but he'd heard from her roommate that she'd been doing stimulants.

"She was more into going out to clubs. I'm kind of boring," he said, giggling.

Moving on to his high-school experiences, I told him I heard he'd been on the surf team, hoping he would admit that he wasn't. But, as I soon learned, he went along with his previous lies or exaggerations if I fed them to him, so he said yes, and even told me the name of his coach. He surfed pretty much every day, he said, mostly in Huntington Beach, but also down in San Miguel, Mexico, and Isla de Todos Santos, an island twelve miles outside of Ensenada.

He happily told me about his two weddings. When I mentioned Lana Henderson's comment to me that he'd claimed they needed a rush ceremony because he was called back into the marines, he said he and Jennifer had been talking about him going back, but that wasn't the reason. He always told Jennifer the truth about things, he said, but they'd had to craft various stories for her religious parents.

"We'd already decided we liked each other, anyway," he said.

"Loved?" I asked.

"Yes," he said, "loved each other."

Rather than address my question about the lie he'd told Lana, he gave me a long spiel about his recruiter telling him that his RA4 code (other than honorable discharge) needed to be changed so he could try to get into another branch of the military. If he got a new RA code, he said, he could get back in.

I soon realized that if I tried to help trigger a memory, he'd almost always agree with whatever I had said, so I made a mental note not to do that. I also came to realize that when I asked a question and got a blank stare, it meant that he either wasn't sure what I wanted to hear, or he had no feelings about that issue, which seemed to happen quite often. Either way, though, I could see that prompting him didn't get me any closer to the truth. It only helped him learn more about me.

What he seemed to enjoy discussing the most was his sex change operation, which he said he'd wanted for as long as he could remember. Asked if he felt like he was in the wrong body, he said, "Yeah, that's what me and Jenn talked about" when they first met.

Because she was into partying, he figured, "I ain't got nothing to lose by telling her." So he did. "There's something you want to know," he told her. "I want to get this surgery."

"Whoa, hold on a second here," she said. "You like girls, but you want this surgery?"

He recalled telling his cousin, Russell Lewis, that Jennifer looked like a lesbian, inserting that he'd always been better friends with Russell. Michael had lied on the stand, he said; they'd "never even had a good relationship."

When I asked him about the cancerous uterus he'd described to people, he said that was one of the stories they'd told Jennifer's parents. "Jenn knew from the beginning I didn't have that," he said.

When he first met Jennifer, the two of them talked about religion. "I don't really have any religion," he told her. "I don't really believe in anything."

"She's saying her dad is practically a pastor. 'So you can't tell him I party. If you ever meet my dad, you're a Christian, okay?'"

Jennifer also prepped him on what to say when they went to church together. "So I go to church and she's, like, completely different."

I asked him when they last talked, and he said it was in a letter, which he summed up as: "'I can't write no more because of what my attorney's saying.'" For a while after that, she sent messages through other people, like, "'Keep your head up. I don't want to do what he's saying.'" But those stopped eventually, as did the visits from Lana, who used to bring the kids every weekend, but quit taking his calls around Easter 2006.

Now, he said, he was writing a girl he met "at court."

"What's she in for?" I asked.

"A lot."

"Murder?"

"That was another girl."

When I came back the next morning, I tried to get him to talk more about Jennifer, but he wasn't interested. He was far more interested in telling me about the crazy inmate who had kept him up, all night, "yelling at the wall."

Trying to make me feel like his confidante, I assume, Skylar said he wasn't sure if he was supposed to talk about this, but "they have me on meds."

"Like what?" I asked.

He said he was taking Ativan, an antianxiety drug; 1,500 milligrams of Depakote for seizures; and twenty milligrams of Zyprexa, an antipsychotic used to treat schizophrenia and bipolar disorder, which, he said, "clears your head." I asked what psychological diagnoses he'd been given, and he said he'd been told he was schizoaffective, which means he has a mix of schizophrenic and mood disorder symptoms, and he also had borderline personality disorder, although some of the doctors couldn't agree. He said he preferred female doctors because he was more comfortable with them.

"My moods are all over the place," he said, explaining that some of the doctors thought he was bipolar. "They say I go up and down too much . . . but they don't want to change anything too much because they think I'll . . . ," he said, trailing off to imply he might hurt himself.

As a result, he said, they often put him naked in the safety cell.

"I'm good," he told them.

"We don't believe you," they responded, and kept him in there.

"They're all, 'The problem is you don't tell us and you do something. When you cut, you didn't give any warning—you wait until it's too late and we have to extract you from your cell,'" he said, referring to the penis incident.

One time, he said, he banged his head against the cinderblock wall.

"Why?" I asked.

"I think I was frustrated, and somebody was driving me crazy in another cell."

Before he was in jail, he said, "I could go surfing or something, or go out and do something stupid. I could always keep distracted," but now all he could do was walk in circles or watch TV. Last night they had almost put him back in the safety cell, he said, letting me know how lucky I was, because he wouldn't have been available to talk to me otherwise.

I switched the topic back to Jennifer, and got him to tell me some more about the second wedding, which he said his mother and her two kids with Eddie Fisher had attended. I asked if he knew that Eddie Fisher was the name of a singer from Dean Martin's era.

"Before my time," he said.

"Before my time, too," I told him.

"All I know about Dean Martin is . . . ," he said, and started singing "That's Amore," the song for which Martin was famous. I chuckled, and seeing that he was entertaining me, he smiled.

I asked if he was still in contact with his family. Yes, he said, with Lisa and Stephanie, whom he called "Steph," and he'd just started writing his mother.

How did he feel about losing contact with his kids?

"Bad and mad," he said. "It's messed up."

He'd sent Christmas cards and birthday cards to them, care of the Hendersons, he said, but they came back with messages written on the envelopes: *F You. Your kids are never going to know you.*

"Yet they claim to be all Christian," he said.

I asked about his last conversation with his father, which he said took place when he called his grandparents from the Newport Beach police station and asked them to have John Jacobson come down. But his father wouldn't even come to the phone, relaying this message, instead: "No, no, no, no, I don't want to talk to you now. You had your chance to talk to me before you were arrested."

"I wasn't doing what he said."

I asked how he felt when his father died. "I thought it sucked," he said. "I don't like him, but at the same time . . . I wish I could have at least said something to him."

"What?" I asked.

"I don't know."

Asked if he hated his dad, he said yes. Then I asked if he loved his dad.

"Every time he keeps on saying, 'I've changed.' You try and give him a chance, but you keep getting screwed over again."

So I asked him again. "I can't say I didn't love him," he said. "I hated him, but at the same time I loved him." Still, before Kaleb was born, he always told Jennifer, "I don't want him anywhere near my daughter. . . . I just didn't want him in my life."

I asked Skyar when he started putting on dresses.

When he was little, he said. "Dad came home once and I was with other girls . . . and they were, like, dressing me up, and my dad was, like . . . 'You want to be a girl? I'll treat you like a girl.'"

So Skylar stopped doing it, because he "was too worried about getting hurt," until he decided to have the sex change operation, for which cross-dressing was a prerequisite.

"Jenn's clothes didn't fit," he said. "They were too big."

That segued into the subject of his weight loss. He denied that he'd been throwing up to lose weight for court. "I've been on double portions for three years," he said, adding that he ate the hot breakfast and lunch, but he didn't like the cold box lunches with bologna. "Some stuff—I'd just rather not eat it."

When they'd weighed him a week earlier, he said, he was back up to 134 pounds. As if on cue, a deputy knocked on the door behind him and handed him a brown paper bag. Skylar opened it, grinning, to reveal a package of chocolate chip cookies from the commissary.

"Cookies!" he said in a singsong voice.

I asked him what he did for exercise. He giggled as he picked up his foot and showed me the worn sole of his white tennis shoe.

"Look at how much I've walked," he said. Then he started singing again: "'These shoes are made for walking . . .'"

He also played basketball. "I have a really good game. I always win," he said, admitting that he played by himself.

I asked how he felt about Jennifer now. "No comment," he said. "I have nothing nice to say about her. . . . I think what she did was wrong."

Asked to elaborate, he said, "What she's doing with her case," apparently referring to her blaming everything on him.

I said I saw him telling her that he loved her back at the prelim, and I asked if he still did. No, he said.

"I hope that she's doing okay, and I wish her no problems," he said. "There's just been too much that's happened since we've been here."

I asked if he was scared about the upcoming sentencing hearing. He looked indifferent, and said it was "just another court hearing. Let's get it over with."

Skylar tried to switch the topic back to cross-dressing, but I told him I had another question first. Was he planning to say something at the hearing? He said he didn't know. I told him he could say something to the Hawks family if he wanted, and he just looked at me blankly. So I let him go back to his preferred topic.

Skylar said he initially had mixed feelings about the sex change surgery. He wanted it, but he was also concerned it would hurt, and "I was worried if I had it, I might lose [Jennifer]."

Skylar said he was also worried about confusing Haylie by wearing dresses. "I don't want to mess her up. 'Hey, where's Daddy?'"

But Jennifer knew he wanted it, and encouraged him to follow through. "Don't just put it off because of me," she said.

Ultimately, they decided that he should get the operation, keep dressing like a man, and not tell anybody, especially her parents.

Although I remembered Michael Molfetta saying the Deleons didn't have much of a sex life, I asked Skylar how he and Jennifer had planned to have sex. "Like two girls do," he said.

He said he even showed Jennifer pictures to prove that "you can't tell the difference, at least from the outside." They move all the nerves, he said, "but it's all still there."

Apparently, Skylar was enjoying my company, because at the end of our visit, he asked, "Are you coming back tomorrow?"

No, I told him, but I would try to come back next week.

* * *

The following Friday he was all ready with a written
list of psychological diagnoses that he'd collected for
me, complete with the identification numbers from
the *Diagnostic and Statistical Manual of Mental Disorders,
Fourth Edition,* the psychiatric Bible commonly known
as the *DSM-IV.*

One of the doctors, he said, wanted Skylar to correct and elaborate on what he'd told me in our last
session: he was actually obsessive-compulsive, with
poor insight; he was schizoaffective; and he had borderline personality disorder, gender identity disorder,
and dependent personality disorder, with a flat affect.

I asked if the doctors had mentioned anything
about sociopathic tendencies, and he said no—he'd
already checked that for a TV reporter.

"They said that I was far from that," he said.

I held my tongue.

He also said that his score on the Global Assess-
ment of Functioning scale was usually around 20, with
the highest possible score being 100 and the lowest
being 10, which is suicidal.

"Would we put a razor in your hands?" the doctors
asked him rhetorically. Obviously not.

After I left, a quick Internet check showed that his
citations and scores jibed with the disorders in the
DSM-IV, and although privacy laws prevented me from
verifying the diagnoses, they seemed to fit.

Moving on, I asked him about his fascination with
boats, and he got that blank faraway look again.

"I just like to go fishing," he said, adding that he
used to fish with his grandfather and cousins.

I pointed out that he'd gotten married on a yacht,
that he'd had the Sea Ray and the Hatteras before he
finally acquired the *Well Deserved,* the whole reason
he was here in jail. He looked at me curiously, as if

he were having an epiphany—or pretending to, I couldn't quite tell—and said, "Everything is around boats."

He was fine with just getting married on the beach the first time, he said, but Jennifer had wanted a more formal wedding.

We talked some more about God and his claims that he'd been reading the Bible, which somehow segued into his attempt to kill his father.

"I tried to kill him?" he asked with feigned wonder, as if he weren't sure how much I knew about it.

"Yes," I said, "you were charged with that."

"Oh, that," he said. "That was BS."

When I reminded him that inmates Danny Elias and Danny Alvarado had testified about that at his trial, he said Alvarado had gotten all kinds of details wrong.

"So you never tried to put out a hit on your dad?"

"No," he said.

I attempted once more to get him to talk about the dynamic between him and Jennifer.

"She's stubborn, so I'd just do what she says or she'd get mad," he said. "She had a temper. I just like to go with the flow with stuff."

I mentioned that everyone kept saying she wore the pants in the relationship, and he agreed. I said I'd also heard he thought their roles were reversed, and he conceded that, too.

But Jennifer complained that he didn't make enough money, right?

Yes, he said, but "she went back and forth on the job thing, because after I had Haylie . . . I'd work and then she'd say, 'Hold off.' She'd say, 'This job doesn't pay enough. I have to miss work and stay home and take care of Haylie,' so she'd say, 'You stay home because I make more money.' She made good money. I just wanted to make her happy. . . . I don't want to say she's, like, a show-off, but she's like . . . she wants to look good. She has expectations."

I asked him about JP Jarvi and he said he wasn't supposed to talk about the case, but "the whole Mexico thing isn't what it seemed."

I told him I was more interested in whether he'd talked to Jennifer about his plans.

"Me and Jenn talk about everything," he said. "We got that cleared up a long time ago. Always everything . . . she's all, 'I don't care, just keep things up front.' Even if she had half a doubt, she'd be, like"—Skylar stopped, leaned toward me and said, *"Skylar?"* in a questioning voice, like a mother suspicious that her child might be lying.

"I never wanted to take no chance of losing her, so I was, like, okay."

As for the Mexico trip with Jarvi, he said, "She knew we were going down to do something that day to make some money. But it was nothing to do with Jarvi getting murdered. . . . Mike straight lied on the stand.

"We purposely took two trucks down there for a reason," he said, adding that Jarvi was into making money—"he *literally made* fake money"—so they all went down there to bring back some "illegal stuff."

"Drugs?" I asked.

"Yeah. We got scared and we bailed and left him with somebody else. Another car pulled up."

At that point a voice over the loudspeaker ended our visit.

* * *

During our last interview Skylar continued to play up the possibility that he might hurt himself again, as if he thought that would gain my sympathy.

After I remarked on his several days' growth of beard, he quoted the nurse as saying, "'We're worried that if we give you a razor, you just may go for it.'"

This past week, he said, "My head's all over the place."

Switching gears, I asked if he had access to the newspaper, because I was wondering if he had followed JFK's trial. He said he got the newspaper, but only after the deputies cut articles out of it, so all he knew was that JFK got convicted.

"They pick and choose what they want me to see," he said.

"He's saying he wasn't on the boat," I said, waiting for him to answer. He said nothing, so I pressed him. "And?"

"I have nothing to say," he replied.

I said I'd heard that he'd been willing to testify against JFK.

"Yeah, I heard that" was his strange response. "Where did you hear that?"

"Reliable sources," I said.

Skylar gestured at my notebook, indicating, I assumed, that he didn't want me to write anything about JFK. I asked if he didn't want to talk about this because he was scared JFK was going to do something to him, but Skylar remained mum.

"I have no comments on that guy," he said.

Another subject he didn't want to discuss was his acting career, sloughing me off every time I tried to bring it up.

When I asked about the last time he'd seen his father, he mentioned a date a couple days before the

Hawkses were murdered, then said, "I don't think Gary wants me going into all that."

"How do you feel about what you did?" I asked, trying to make the question as nonconfrontational as possible.

"Bad," he said, his voice dropping so low it was hard to hear him over the squawking and laughing of the woman at the other end of the visiting room. I nodded, trying to encourage him to keep going.

"Feel bad, but, I mean, but I can't take—take—take it back, you know," he said, stuttering. "But at the same time, it's not—what Alonso said isn't what happened. There's still a lot of things that need to be cleared up. . . . I should have taken the stand, but Gary said no. . . . Gary said . . . the prosecution wouldn't have been very nice to me."

(I should note here that Gary Pohlson had said Skylar couldn't have testified "because he's told so many lies.")

"Are you sorry?" I asked.

"Yeah. I think that goes along with the other one [answer]," he said, as if this were obvious. I told him I didn't think so—and people wouldn't know how he felt unless he said so.

But Skylar didn't want to talk about this, either, so he started off on another track, saying he wasn't able to write anything down when he was naked in a safety cell with nothing but a wraparound blanket.

"I still can't get it out of my head whether they'll send me to the female or the male side," he said. I was starting to understand how Pohlson must have felt, but I wanted to keep him talking.

The guards delivered another little brown bag from the commissary while we were talking. This time it was cookies, a brownie, and a jalapeno cheese snack.

He explained that he wanted to be a woman and live on their side of the jail because he'd always gotten along better with them. "I don't want to be on this side," he said. Skylar claimed that he'd even questioned the deputies about this, and they said their operations manual required any man who had his genitals removed "to go to the girl side."

I asked him to elaborate on why he wanted his penis gone so much, and what thoughts ran through his head about it.

"Get it away," he said, gesturing. "It's like it's not me. I feel like it's not supposed to be there. I *know* it's not supposed to be there."

I noted that he purposely avoided the use of the word "penis," as if it were too unpleasant—or indelicate—to say out loud.

I asked if he was scared about going to San Quentin. "No, because, like, I think it'll be better than here, because everyone I've talked to [says] . . . death row is actually better than [a] life [sentence] without [parole]. There's no politics. . . . You get more privileges than you do in other places."

Knowing our time was running out, I told him I wanted to clear up a discrepancy. Why, if he'd admitted in court to killing Jarvi and the Hawkses, had he denied yesterday that he had killed Jarvi?

"I didn't," he said, explaining that Pohlson was the one who had conceded Skylar's guilt in court, which, technically, was true.

"I think Gary is really, really, really awesome, but I don't know if he and I were on the same page on that one," he said. "I didn't kill him."

Skylar alluded to Matt Murphy's explanation in court for why a person was guilty of murder, even if he

was committing a lesser crime when a victim was killed by someone else.

"I'm guilty because even if I didn't kill him, I was going down there and doing something else illegal. That still makes me guilty, and that's what made me guilty in his [Gary's] eyes. I still don't get that, but he said I was, but I didn't—I just think I'm not sure if I'm not understanding that or what. . . . I think he probably said it because it's easier to say that than to try to fight it, because it would be too hard to try and prove."

I asked if there was anything he would go back and do differently.

"I've thought about that tons," he said. "Sometimes I've thought I'll go back to when I first met Jenn, and I'm like, 'No, no, no, I still want Haylie.' So I have to go further up in time—I don't want to do any different and not have her, and sometimes I'm, like, 'I want to do other things.'" I realized then that he'd rarely, if ever, mentioned his son.

Other times, he said, he thought about going back to when he was thirteen, when he was still with his dad, "or just run away."

"What about the stuff that got you here?" I asked delicately.

"That, too," he said.

He said he'd thought about having a sex change operation in 2000 or 2001, but he kept putting it off. "I was too afraid it would hurt—and go figure. Now I'm, like, 'I'll just try to cut it off myself.' Heck, maybe it'll help you sell more books," he said, laughing.

"I don't even want to go there," I told him, avoiding his eyes, sickened by the notion.

I asked whether he read books, and he said no. "Can't get past the first page."

"Not even when it's about you?"

"No," he said.

Skylar jumped back to our conversations about the psychological diagnoses, saying that one of the doctors wanted him to clarify that these were observations based on what he was saying, not official diagnoses.

But he acknowledged that, yes, he had been officially psychologically evaluated and tested. "I'm bad at math," he said. "I know how to plus and minus. I know how to times, but that's as far as I get. Divide, I'm lost. I'm gone. Jenn tried showing me."

That wasn't the answer I was seeking, but since he'd brought her up, I asked whether he was surprised when he was served with divorce papers.

No, he said, "I already knew what was going on."

The guard came, signaling the end of our interview, so just before Skylar put his receiver down on the table, I thanked him for talking to me and told him I'd write him at San Quentin as we'd discussed.

To no surprise, Skylar Deleon was sentenced to death on April 10, 2009. The judge made no substantive comments, but the deputy probation officer stated her opinion in her presentence report: *The defendant's actions in this case are shocking, vicious and callous. It is incomprehensible how anyone could behave with such lack of concern for their fellow man.*

Six days later, Skylar was released from the county jail at 4:25 A.M. and driven to San Quentin in Northern California by two sheriff's deputies.

Skylar chatted away on the trip up as if he didn't have a care in the world. But his mood changed as soon as they entered the prison walls, where he was welcomed by two African-American correctional officers.

"Now, you the yellow Power Ranger or the red Power Ranger?" one of them asked.

Skylar immediately lost control of his bowels, so they took him to the medical unit.

"He was probably hoping he was going to go under the radar," said Dave Byington, who received this news flash from a lieutenant at the prison. "That made my day."

Four days later, Skylar had a breakdown characterized as "mental distress" and was sent to a "crisis bed" at a state mental facility in Vacaville, an hour away.

A few months later, I asked prison Lieutenant Rudy Luna what had happened, and when Skylar was expected back.

"He had a mental download," he said. "I was just told he went kind of nutty."

Luna said this can happen when a new death row prisoner comes in without a support system or a gang to welcome him. In this case Skylar had neither—and even worse, the crime he'd masterminded had gotten a Crips member sent to death row *with* him. Given that Skylar wouldn't say a word to me about JFK, he had to be scared of what his codefendant—and fellow Crips brothers—might do to him on the yard, where as many as eighty death row prisoners gathered each week for their state-mandated exercise.

When a death row prisoner first arrives, Luna said, he is taken to the "adjustment center" by four correctional officers wearing helmets and carrying batons. He is placed in a single cell, three feet by four feet, with a steel door, a concrete slab, and a mattress, and he is issued two pairs of underwear, two T-shirts, two regular shirts, two pairs of jeans, two pairs of socks, a baby toothbrush, some tooth powder, a comb, and a bar of soap, but no razor. There is no TV, so all he can do is write letters.

"That kind of sets the tone for it," Luna said.

Some of these newbies "get cuckoo for Cocoa Puffs," Luna said, so "we send them over there [to Vacaville] for six or seven months. They come back, and they're like, 'Hey, what's up?'"

Years later, Luna said, some prisoners, including wife killer Scott Peterson, sunbathe and work out so they still look as good or better than they did the day they arrived. Others let themselves go and end up looking far worse.

Even though Skylar was a master manipulator, Luna said, the prison staff was so used to these guys that pretense didn't fly with them. "They can tell when they're faking it," he said. "Most of those guys go nutty at night. Grown men, these toughies, boo-hooing. . . . [They] are like little kids. They're all like that."

John F. Kennedy was sentenced to death with little fanfare on May 1, 2009.

It does not appear that anything imposed by the court, the Probation Department or the Department of Corrections and Rehabilitation has sufficiently impressed the defendant to stay out of trouble with the law, the deputy probation officer wrote in her presentence report. *Instead, he appears to do as he pleases, regardless of the consequences to himself or others.*

JFK left the jail in Santa Ana on May 6 at 5:08 A.M., and by the time he arrived at San Quentin, Skylar was safely at Vacaville.

I waited five months to write Skylar, hoping he would have returned by then, but he was still at Vacaville and my deadline was approaching, so I sent him a letter. He never responded. Instead, an investigator working for his new attorney at the California Appellate Project wrote me a letter, ordering me to cease all contact with Skylar. So that was that.

Now that his father was dead, his children didn't know he existed, and the love of his life had abandoned him, Skylar Deleon would spend the rest of his days alone, waiting to be executed or die in prison, a fate that most believed was well deserved.

AUTHOR'S NOTE AND ACKNOWLEDGMENTS

I started following this case in early 2005. As the
case developed and circumstances changed, I grew
more and more intrigued by the dynamic between
Skylar and Jennifer Deleon because I believe it was his
obsessive love for her, and his fear he could lose her,
that motivated him to kill. Given the widespread
media coverage, I worked diligently to uncover new
and exclusive information the newspapers and TV
shows had never found, delving deep into the police
investigation and the relationship between Orange
County's own Bonnie and Clyde.

To me, it seemed that Jennifer was the only person
who had truly loved Skylar, took care of him, and
nurtured her "baby" the way he'd never been before.
I'm sure his birth mother and stepmother, Lynette
and Lisa, loved him the best they could, but they
were both addicts when he was a child, which prevented them from being truly emotionally present.
I'm guessing that even his father, who was a horrible
role model, loved Skylar in his own twisted way, but
he did as much damage with his barrage of verbal
abuse, his drug dealing, and his lying as he did by

shoving toothpicks under his son's nails, throwing him downstairs, choking and punching him.

From researching this case and then talking face-to-face with Skylar, I came to believe that he is missing some crucial connections in his psyche, and that's what produces the blank expression I kept seeing. I have to wonder what, if anything, is going on in his mind when he gets that face. Perhaps it's absolutely nothing. Perhaps he had all his feelings and compassion beaten out of him. Perhaps he doesn't know the meaning of goodness, because his own family never showed it to him. Perhaps he had some congenital problem, a gap in his conscience of some sort, or lost something in the womb because of his mother's drug use. Or perhaps he was simply taught to lie, cheat, steal, and swallow his emotions from an early age. Frankly, I'm amazed he never turned to drugs or alcohol to cope with that emptiness, but maybe he was already so numb inside that he didn't need substances.

In the end, other than his daughter Haylie, Jennifer—a woman, who, I believe, needed to be needed—was the only thing that could bring love out of Skylar. It's unfortunate that the only way he knew how to please his wife was to express his childlike puppy love and buy her things. And because he didn't know how to hold a job, he apparently felt he needed to steal to do that, even if it meant he had to kill for it. I should note that Jennifer's mother changed her benevolent views of Skylar, but declined to be interviewed again when I asked in 2009.

One of the questions I most like to ask my sources is whether a murderer is born or made, and both sides usually say "made." Honestly, I don't think anyone can say for sure. "Nature-nurture" is an age-old psychological debate that isn't going to be resolved in a courtroom. All I, as an author, can do is provide whatever insight I can gather to help answer the question "Why?"

Skylar and Jennifer made for a fascinating case study, but this story really gripped me because it was such a quintessential tale of good vs. evil. The Hawkses sounded like such a good family, and what happened to them was so undeserved. JP Jarvi, despite all his problems, certainly didn't deserve to be killed, either.

Tom and Jackie sounded like such a generous, open, trusting, and fun-loving couple, I envied their relationship; I only wish I could have met them. Betty Jarvi and Gayle O'Neill are two of the nicest people I've ever interviewed, so I have to believe their children were the same way.

I want to thank them, and all the other victims' family members and friends I interviewed for this book. My heart goes out to all of them. That said, I could not have packed this book with as much insight or as many compelling details about the Deleons and the police investigation if it hadn't been for the unflagging help of Sergeant Dave Byington, who deserves all the respect and admiration I heard expressed from most everyone who has crossed his path.

Nothing in this book was created, exaggerated, or embellished. Any error of any kind is completely unintentional. I re-created scenes primarily from police interview and trial transcripts, court exhibits, official documents, and my own interviews and observations. Likewise, the dialogue came from official transcripts and audio, whenever possible; when it was re-created from memory, I always tried to cross-check it with other sources. I sat through some or all of the three trials, so I think I can safely say I saw every witness testify at least once, some three times. In the instance where I used a pseudonym to protect a subject's privacy, I designated it with an asterisk.

I only wish I had another couple hundred pages, because my research produced enough material for a book twice this long. Five years is the longest I have ever worked on a nonfiction book, which meant more interviews, more research, more documents, more time in court, and more time to think about how to tell this complex story. Let's just say this story grew so many interesting tentacles that it became a case of what *not* to include.

So I hope you readers enjoyed watching it unfold as much as I did, and I encourage you to send me your feedback through my website, http://caitlinrother.com.

Before I close, I want to formally thank the following people for their help and contributions as I researched, wrote, and compiled photos for this book:

Dave Byington; Matt Murphy; Gary Pohlson; John McCutchen; Michael Molfetta; Winston McKesson; Evan Sailor; Jay Short; Keith Krallman; Joe Cartwright; Armando Yearwood; Gayle and Jack O'Neill; Ryan, Jim and Sandy Hawks; Betty, Jeanne and Jeff Jarvi; Joe Serna; Frank Mickadeit; Larry Welborn; Greg Hardesty; Joe Hasenauer; Tricia Schutz; Bob Gayl; Don Trefren; Chuck Thomas; Charles and Ann Silvers; Bryan Brah; Picture People; Geoff Christison; Carole Levitsky; John Futch; Susan Liebowitz, and Rudy Luna.

Special thanks goes to my readers, Carole Scott, Alexa Capeloto, Susan Gembrowski, and Sharon Whitley Larsen; to my supportive and generous friends, Carlos Beha, Bob Koven, and Samuel Autman; to my agents, Peter Rubie, Gary Heidt, and Stephany Evans; to the folks at Kensington, Richard Ember, Michaela Hamilton, and Mike Shohl; to the nice people at Einstein's bagels #3048, where I have my second "office"; and to Writing Women for their continued support and encouragement.